UNWANTED GUEST

Goans v/s Du Pont

UNWANTED GUEST

Goans v/s Du Pont

Edited by Claude Alvares

The Other India Press
Mapusa 403 507 Goa, India.

Unwanted Guest: Goans v/s Du Pont is a publication of:
The Other India Press,
Above Mapusa Clinic,
Mapusa 403 507 Goa, India.

First published in 1991.

Sole distributor in India:
The Other India Bookstore,
Above Mapusa Clinic,
Mapusa 403 507 Goa, India.

U.S.A. Distributor:
The Apex Press
Council on International and Public Affairs
777 United Nations Plaza
New York, New York 10017.

Cover designed by Arun Sawant
Original cover painting by Baiju Parthan

ISBN No.81-85569-02-9

Printed by Dominic D'Souza for the Other India Press at Maureen's Offset, Panaji, Goa, India.

CONTENTS

CONTENTS

THE UNWANTED GUEST

By Claude Alvares

On 31st August 1991, a wide ranging coalition of environment groups, cultural associations, village communities, communidades, Konkani writers and citizens, displaying rare unanimity, adopted a public document at an unusual Sabha assembled in the town of Ponda, Goa.

The document, now referred to as "the Ponda Declaration" (see page 188 of this book for the complete text), rejected a Goa government proposal to install a factory at Kerim plateau near Ponda to produce a synthetic fibre called Nylon 6,6 promoted by US chemical multinational E.I. Du Pont de Nemours, the Thapars and the Economic Development Corporation of Goa (EDC).

After setting out the reasons why it had become necessary to oppose the Nylon 6,6 plant tooth and nail, the Declaration concluded with a resolve not to allow its erection in any other part of India as well and to take steps, whenever necessary, to transfer on request the extensive documentation on Nylon 6,6 and on Du Pont collected by Goan environment groups, to other organizations elsewhere if required.

The anti-Du Pont Declaration was the culmination of a series of developments spanning more than a decade during which the American multinational tried every means at its disposal, fair and foul (mostly foul) to impose its corporate designs on one of the smallest states of the Indian Union. Barely six months prior to the issue of the Declaration, a Committee set up by the Goa State Assembly had submitted a fairly damaging report after completing a fairly exhaustive investigation into the project and its sponsors.

The House Committee Report (whose entire text forms the bulk of this book) examined evidence of irregularities in land deals requisitioned for the project, discussed the economic benefits (particularly jobs created) and compared these with the social and environmental costs and finally concluded that Nylon 6,6 was incompatible with Goan ecology and public interest. Accordingly, it recommended the project be permanently shelved.

The Nylon 6,6 story actually begins in the mid-seventies. In 1973, Du Pont introduced new tyre technologies into the US and European markets, involving basically radials based on steel and stronger synthetic fibres. The days of nylon as a basic ingredient in tyre manufacture were gradually coming to an end.

As the radials began gaining ground Du Pont decided it was time to send the older nylon technology out someplace else to milk a fresh generation of profits. India is one country that does not produce all the nylon 6 it uses, and imports all the nylon 6,6 it needs. (Although there are numerous nylon polymers, only nylon 6 and 6,6 are in commercial use). Du Pont could therefore claim it was introducing new technology. However, use of radials is growing in India too. Passenger radials are expected to achieve a commanding position by 2000AD and truck radials a significant proportion by 2005AD.

Despite being one of the world's largest multinationals, Du Pont accepted it could not simply walk into India and dump antiquated technology on the population there unawares. India has an extremely well qualified class of technicians and scientists who can readily identify an old horse when required. The machines Du Pont wished to send to India were first installed in Richmond, USA, in 1938!

Du Pont however claimed the machinery had been "overhauled, upgraded and modified from time to time" so much that the company found it "impossible to quantify the age of this equipment since so many replacements and ungradations have been continuously taking place...and it is established and certified that the remaining life of this second hand equipment is greater than 20 years." The Chartered Engineers Report, however, merely stated: "The present condition of machinery is good and expected residual life is around 20 years."

Du Pont decided it needed a dalal (middleman), and an unsuspecting public sector company which would provide a realistic enough cover for implementing its corporate strategy. This country again is generously endowed with both.

Associating an Indian public sector organization with the proposed project would not only help Du Pont get its licenses speedily, it would also compel Indian authorities to commit water, land, power and other facilities more readily than if Du Pont attempted to get these on its own,

To function as dalal, Du Pont chose the Thapar-owned Ballarpur Industries Ltd (BILT). The Thapars have a reputation (according to an internal Goa Government note at least), for helping MNCs import second-hand machines and passing them of as state-of-the-art technology. BILT was given the responsibility of setting up the project. Du Pont were aware, in addition, that the Thapars were fairly close to the Gandhi family.

The sucker the Thapars identified to cover Du Pont's backdoor entry was the EDC, one of those amoeba-like development institutions set up with good public money but ever willing to stretch in whichever direction it is pulled. In fact, the kind of organization that almost volunteers to be abused.

When the Thapars approached the EDC in 1979 with the Nylon 6,6 proposal, its officials should have spontaneously and without a second thought rejected it. Ever since the disastrous experience the small state has had with giant polluting companies like the Zuari Agro Chemicals in 1974, there has been a consensus among leaders in Goa that large scale industrialization is inappropriate to the state's natural environment and cultural ecology.

Thapar's persuasive skills, however, coupled with the glamour of the proposed mega project and the fantastic returns it promised all seem to have blinded the EDC's top brass temporarily. Any person with normal intelligence would readily have seen that the EDC was being invited to associate with the project merely to lend it a semblance of public interest, a feature the project desperately required and which it did not have at the time.

Despite this, the EDC decided to accept the Thapar suggestion that it seek the Letter of Intent from the Government of India. In November 1983 it made a routine application for a Letter of Intent to produce 6000 tonnes per annum (tpa) of Nylon 6,6 tyre cord. It also applied for a LOI to produce 5,100 tpa of nylon tyre cord fabric. It stated in its application it would set up the plant at Kerim plateau. (In its application it also lied that the site was not near any national monuments. The proposed site is actually within a few kilometres of the Mangueshi temple complex, while the Old Goa church complex is within a 15 km radius. Within a couple of kilometres distance in another direction is Goa's major source of drinking water: the Opa water works).

The EDC's application proposed the following equity participation for the new project - EDC: 26%, private promoter (Thapar): 25%, with the balance 49% going to the public (total public participation therefore being 75%). Project cost was quoted at Rs.55 crores. As for Nylon 6,6 technology, the application stated the EDC had "carried out extensive negotiations with various entrepreneurs". When probed by the House Committee as to whom these various entrepreneurs were, the EDC could only mention BILT.

In fact, the House Committee was stunned to discover that BILT and a New York based company called Chemtex Fibres Inc. had already signed a memorandum which anticipated plant start-up in Goa in the last quarter of 1985!

How this was to happen is not known for the Government of India finally issued a LOI to the EDC on its 1983 application only in 1985. (The Government also issued a LOI for 5,100 tpa of nylon fabric.) But once the letter was securely in, the Thapars now instigated the EDC to get back to the Central Government for approval to increase the capacity of the proposed unit from 6000 tpa to 14000 tpa.

This new suggestion the EDC meekly and blindly followed. So it decidedly seems. For as soon as the proposed capacity rose, the cost of the project went up from Rs.55 to Rs.200 crores, and so did equity demands. Instead of Rs.5 crores, the EDC would have to put in Rs.16 crores which was absurd because the EDC simply did not have that kind of money. (The most that the EDC lends to projects is about Rs.1 crore. In fact, the annual industrial plan budget for Goa is not more than Rs.6 crores.)

The application for enhancing capacity was also approved by the Government of India in 1986 but before that happened, the Chief Town Planner placed objections to the plant coming up at Kerim plateau. "The proposed site", he wrote in a letter dated 20.11.1985 to the Director of Industries, "cannot be agreed to from the planning point of view."

He also raised environmental objections: "The location of the industry on the Kerim plateau at a height of more than 150 metres will have some seriously ecological consequences on the surrounding orchard lands. The area is rich in ground water resources and a few sweet water channels, which should not be disturbed by any organized industrial development on the plateau. The exploitation of sweet water springs will adversely affect the thriving arecanut plantations at the lower slopes."

On the 2nd of April 1986, the Goa Government's High Powered Coordination Committee (HPCC) rejected the Nylon 6,6 proposal. The principal reasons given were that the Thapars wanted more than 500 acres of land when they could do with 30; that the Chief Town Planner had noted the location was contrary to the Regional Plan for Goa and that it was also environmentally dangerous.

However, on 27th June, 1986, Government of India hiked the capacity of the nylon fabric unit from 5,100 tpa to 11,900 tpa. Despite a rejection from the HPCC, BILT and EDC went ahead and signed an agreement on the project.

On 9th March, 1987, BILT was writing aggressive letters to the Goa government asking for the Kerim land to be acquired on its behalf. It demanded the land be handed over to it on perpetual lease or be paid by the project in installments with no interest. BILT also demanded an investment subsidy of 15% (upto a maximum of Rs.25 lakhs). It also sought exemption from electricity duty for 10 years and an interest free sales tax loan (upto 8%). It asked the government to put up a road from the site to the main road and a water pipeline at public expense.

On 2 April, 1987, the Director of Industries (Goa government) denounced the Nylon 6,6 proposal. He said the company's demand for 20 lakh sq.mts (500 acres) could be used to set up ten industrial estates, housing more than 500 small scale industries employing more than 4,500 people. He also recorded that large industries routinely seek large land allotments as a measure of boosting future prospects of making large profits out of excess land.

The EDC, however, remained undisturbed by all this. It continued to play its cards as monotonously as any puppet could. On 19th June, 1987, the Goan company made a fresh application to the Central government to permit it to reduce its equity participation in the project. Its new shareholding proposal was now: EDC 11%; Public 9%; Thapar 40%; and Du Pont 40% (public participation now 20% instead of 75% earlier). Here was as good a case of backdoor entry as any.

A few days later, the Industries Secretary, Goa Government, also attacked the Nylon 6,6 project, saying the proposed or promised benefits in terms of ancillarization, employment and taxes were "hypothetical and grossly inflated."

The following month, on 8th July 1987, the Thapars, Du Pont and the EDC formed a new company called Thapar Du Pont Ltd (TDL). Its address: the EDC office in Panaji.

The same month the EDC made one final application to the Union Government, this time to transfer the original LOI to Thapar-Du Pont.

A few months later, in June 1988, Chief Minister Rane called a special meeting on the project, forthwith overruled the objections of the Chief Town Planner and passed orders for the acquisition of 500 acres of land for the project. He also got the Communidade of Kerim to agree to hand over 88 hectares to the company prior to the formalities concerning land acquisition.

On 18th August, 1988, after checking that indeed steps were being taken to change the site's land use from green cover to industry, TDL went ahead and signed an agreement for transfer of technology with Du Pont. The most interesting aspect of the agreement was that it was signed without the presence of the EDC Director.

But there were also other rather disturbing features in the agreement. Conscious of the litigation against multinational Union Carbide in the wake of the Bhopal gas disaster, and wary of the Supreme Court judgement in the Sriram Fertilizers gas leak case, Du Pont succeeded in inserting a series of clauses that indemnified it absolutely from any liability that may arise from the plant.

The first of these clauses stated that TDL "shall hold Du Pont and its representatives or assignees harmless from any claims made in the Republic of India....alleging bodily harm or death." In addition, another clause stated that "Du Pont shall not be liable in any manner whatsoever to TDL or to any third parties for any loss or damage caused to person or property including the members of the public..."

A further clause stated that "Du Pont shall not be liable under any circumstances whatever to any third parties including members of the public or any account whatsoever due to any accident at the plant site..." The agreement placed arbitration of disputes not in USA but in England; and finally, it empowered Du Pont to quit the set-up "should Du Pont at any time, conclude that because of future legislative or judicial developments (in India) the public liability risks do not justify its continued participation as a shareholder in TDL..."

All these clauses were at direct variance with Du Pont's repeated assurances that its Nylon 6,6 technology was not only non-polluting but safe!

A week later, TDL filed applications for approval of technical and financial collaboration and capital goods import with the Central government.

The Government of India may not have known much about these machinations, but it found separate and adequate grounds for anyhow declining approval to the Nylon 6,6 plant which it did on 23 March, 1989. The Industry Ministry also signed another order in August 1989 stating the proposal did not merit favourable consideration "in view of the perpetual import of the raw materials for the plant, apart from import of secondhand machinery and no visible benefit in technology".

Thus, not only was the plant worth only 20 years, it would import its two basic raw materials - Adipic Acid and Hexamythelene Diamine (HMD) from Du Pont plants elsewhere in the world for those twenty years. Even in 1989, when the oil crisis was still not upon us the way it is now, the Central government had felt that importing raw materials permanently for the plant in this way would result in unjustified outgo of precious foreign exchange.

Thapar Du Pont filed a fresh application seeking to answer that challenge, this time promising they would export 25% of the finished Nylon 6,6. Later, when the proposal was found to be unrealistic, Thapar Du Pont promised to ensure that 42% of the production at all Du Pont plants within the country would be exported.

After three rejections, the proposal was finally accorded approval by Ajit Singh, Industries Minister in V.P. Singh's regime. Shortly thereafter it was again put up for review by the successor Chandrasekhar regime, and approved again during the final days of the caretaker government despite a general Presidential advice against such decisions.

The Rao government has once again brought the project for review. The task of approval, however, has become more difficult in view of the introduction of the new industrial licensing policy. Following the new rules, Du Pont, according to a report in the Economic Times, will have to enhance its equity to 61 per cent if it is to meet the foreign exchange requirements of the project.

Thus, for the moment the Thapars seem stuck with their project in Delhi.

In Goa, in the meanwhile, the project's fortunes fluctuated violently in the same period. In March 1990, the project's active promoter (and godfather) Chief Minister Rane was toppled through major defections. The post-Rane (defector-based) government comprising the breakaway Congress and the Maharashtrawadi Gomantak party made their peace with the project's sponsors and the new State Industries Minister was soon singing praises in favour of Nylon 6,6.

The new government, however, was precluded from taking a decision in the matter since a new and unpredictable element gate-crashed into the scenario. On 23 July 1990, during a discussion on the Nylon 6,6 project, the Goa Assembly decided to set up a House Committee to examine the project once and for all.

The terms of reference of the House Committee were to inquire into allegations that Thapar-Du Pont had indulged in several irregularities in the takeover of vast common lands in Kerim with the active collusion of government officials and had commenced work on the Nylon 6,6 project without approvals, and also to investigate the plant's pollution potential. The five member Committee was headed by A.N. Naik, a veteran politician from Margao.

The Naik Committee's deliberations set a wholly new precedent for industrial approvals in post-independent India. It instituted a series of public hearings on the project, a crucial instrument available to people in advanced countries and unsuccessfully demanded by environment groups in India for several years now.

Thapar-Du Pont were also called in to testify and explain. This was the first time in the country that a US multinational was being called to disclose everything of its operations to a public committee. For the hearings, Du Pont imported a woman scientist, Ms Rita Heckrotte, from their plant in the US and attempted to pass off her off as an "environmentalist". Ms. Rita Heckrotte attempted heroically to reassure the Committee that the process of Nylon 6,6 was as harmless and as similar to the making of omlettes. She endorsed her company's plant saying if she part of an environmental group, this was one plant she would wholly opt for. Flown in by Du Pont and on Du Pont's payroll, she could say nothing else.

In addition to Thapar-Du Pont, the Committee also invited the public to submit statements and documents and volunteer to be heard on the subject. More than 60 persons and institutions responded. The Committee then set up a special technical subcommittee comprising scientists from the National Institute of Oceanography and the University of Goa to give it guidance and assistance.

Du Pont eventually failed to carry the House Committee. On November 19, 1991, Naik submitted the Committee Report to the Speaker, recommending the project be shelved. The report rejected company arguments that the project would provide a thousand jobs and established that with current shareholding (Du Pont 40% and BILT 80%) the two companies stood to gain most from the project with the public getting crumbs.

The House Committee Report's revelations had repercussions on the population of the area in which the plant is proposed.

They fuelled a major anti-Du Pont agitation. Three village panchayats surrounding the plant area met in gram sabha and passed resolutions rejecting the unit. The Bagayatdar Society, a cooperative of 800 farmers, also passed a formal resolution demanding the project be scrapped (see page 190).

An anti-Nylon 6,6 Citizens Action Committee was set up in Ponda and the villages surrounding the plant area. It was convened by Dr. Dattaram Desai, a young doctor, who had studied the issues and had come to his own conclusion that the plant was hazardous for his people and therefore to be opposed on grounds of public health.

A request from the Action Committee to Ecoforum, Goa's network of envuironment groups, led to the formation of an all-Goa anti-Nylon 6,6 front. The Forum organised the Ponda Declaration Sabha of August 31 in cooperation with the Action Committee and gave the Goa government time till October 2, 1991, to cancel all permissions for the plant or face an agitation.

By this time, however, another defector-based government had seized power in Goa and TDL once again commenced the process of neutralizing Ministerial opposition. This was probably not very difficult to achieve as the new state industries minister was also ready to sing the praises of Nylon 6,6 and proclaim the plant was "safe". The industries minister even launched a tirade against Ecoforum while the Chief Minister dismissed all opposition to the project as "anti-national".

In October 1991, the Union Government unexpectedly granted approval for a Spandex fibre unit being sponsored by Thapar Du Pont (without EDC participation) and also to be located in Goa.

The approval for the Spandex unit ought to have come after the approvals for the Nylon 6,6 unit, since according to the original plan, it was to be located at the same site (to be acquired for Nylon 6,6 through the Land Acquisition Act).

However, within a week of the Spandex approval, Du Pont issued an announcement from its American headquarters that it was shifting the proposed Spandex unit to Singapore. The multinational was now applying stiff pressure on the Indian government to take a final decision on Nylon 6,6 or to face the transfer of that unit too to a place outside India.

Whether the Union Government finally succumbs to such blackmail and approves the project or not, the fact is that a corporate strategy that was first decided mid-seventies still remains unimplemented in 1991. And that indeed is the sum and substance of the hitherto successful rebellion put up by the Goan population.

Neither the Thapars nor Du Pont are yet willing to accept the message that they are undesirable and therefore unwelcome. The Thapars one can understand: they stand to benefit grossly once, and if, the plant is started up.

But what about Du Pont? Is the American multinational really incapable of understanding, after encountering so many years of popular hostility to its design, that it is an unwanted guest? Why does it continue to impose itself on an environment and society that has firmly rejected its overtures? What does one do with an unwanted guest?

Answers to those questions are available within the wise pages of the House Committee Report. Since the Goa State Assembly does not yet show any inclination to discuss them, it is best that the ordinary (and more responsible) Goan citizen and gaonkar - the ultimate repository of political power in the democratic state - is called upon instead to give them the attention they deserve.

DU PONT IN *GOA TODAY*

By Devika Sequeira

THE NYLON 6,6 INVASION

(*Goa Today*, September 1988)

Behind its veneer of palm fringed serenity, Goa is no innocent exception to the system, the cynicism and the arrogance of money power. Its smallness of size and political insignificance make it all the more susceptible to bullying and browbeating by corporate conglomerates who support and sustain governments.

The state's tourism policy is but one example of the long-distance puppeteering of its fate. Local considerations usually get short shrift for political or corporate expedience in the guise of 'foreign exchange' or 'employment benefits' or even 'industrial growth'. No local politician or political group has ever been able to resist the pressures - the Zuari Agro Chemicals Ltd, the tentacled growth of the five-star lobby are but two cases in point.

Unfortunately too for Goa, the dearth of professional expertise makes it an easy prey to contrived statistics in support of projects which in reality contribute little in comparison to what they reap in the state, that too, at the cost of impairing the ecology and the state's social fabric.

The Nylon 6,6 plant for which the Goa government is obsequiously set to gift away 500 acres of land is one such project whose negative implications largely eclipse its projected benefits to the state.

A vast plateau in Kerim, Ponda, surrounded by rich orchards of arecanut, cashew and bamboo plantations is being acquired by the government for Thapar Du Pont Ltd even when the project will contribute only marginally to Goa's exchequer or its unemployed numbers.

Parting with such a huge chunk of land, government subsidies and infrastructural facilities - 20 MVA (million volt amps) of power and 3 mgd (million gallons a day) of water - for a single project is in contravention of the state's industrial policy which is to encourage small, non-pollutant industry. The land could have been put to better use. The same area, 20 lakh sq. meters, could accommodate 10 industrial estates to benefit 500 small industries to provide employment to 4,500 people. And the government's investment wouldn't touch a fraction of what it will with the Nylon 6,6 plant.

Goa's Economic Development Corporation (EDC) a collaborator in the project, will block Rs. 5 crore in this one single project. This will put EDC financially in the red for the next five years. The corporation's total equity participation in other ventures has never before this exceeded Rs. 1 crore a year.

The Rs. 132 crore Nylon 6,6 project is a joint venture of the EDC, the Ballarpur Industries Ltd (BILT) of the Thapar group, and the American multinational M/s. E.I.Du Pont de Nemours.

Next door to Goa, the Thapar caustic soda factory in Karwar was compelled to close down because of uncontrolled pollution that caused fish mortality. The Karnataka government was also unable to meet the plant's power requirements.

Four of the seven main Thapar companies have shown steep declines in profits, reports *The*

Sunday Observer'. Ballarpur Industries, Crompton Greaves, Jagajit Cotton Textile Mills and Bharat Starch Chemicals have all run into rough weather. Despite this, Lalit Mohan Thapar, the group's unofficial head - also the key figure in the Nylon 6,6 project - has managed to stash away crores of rupees abroad. Mid-August, the Delhi High Court admitted a public interest litigation against the Indian government for not compelling Thapar to repatriate even the Rs. 11 crore he himself admitted to having kept abroad, reports *The Sunday Observer.*

This should be an indicator to the Goa Government of what to expect. According to an EDC spokesman, the machinery for the Nylon plant, all of it to be imported from Du Pont, will cost an astronomical Rs. 100 crore in foreign exchange. Another collaboration between Thapars and Du Pont for the manufacture of acrylic fibre in Himachal Pradesh was stalled when the central government learnt that the company was going to import second-hand machinery at the cost of new. That pattern - where the major chunk of the foreign exchange allowed to leave the country against inflated costs of imported machinery is deviated into Swiss accounts - is all too familiar with big industry in India today.

The petrochemicals ministry did at one stage warn the Goa Government that a similar attempt would probably be made with the Goa plant. But a visit by a petrochemicals official to a Du Pont plant in the US somehow steered the project clear of further objections.

Thapar Du Pont Ltd will manufacture Nylon 6,6 tyre cord and fabric for the first time in the country.

Tyre manufacturers in India today use Nylon 6 tyre cord. Thapar Du Pont Ltd will be the country's eighth nylon cord and fabric manufacturer. The company's claim that Nylon 6,6 is technologically superior to Nylon 6 is met with skepticism by leading tyre manufacturers. Nylon 6 is a Japanese invention and Nylon 6,6 is American. Tyre tycoons say they would first have to test Nylon 6,6 to prove its advantages or otherwise. Tyre plants would also have to be modified to reprocess Nylon 6,6. They are so far equipped to reprocess only Nylon 6. Nylon 6,6 is, however, the preferred material for aero tyres because of its high temperature tolerance.

Drastic ecological repercussions from the Nylon 6,6 plant are not to be ruled out, despite Du Pont's claim to being world leaders in pollution and safety controls. The Bhopal experience has made underdeveloped countries wary of the double standards adopted by multinationals in pollution and safety controls in Third World countries. Du Pont was denied permission to set up a joint sector plant in Taiwan because of the implications of heavy pollution.

The Nylon 6,6 plant got its much awaited NOC from the Central Board for the Prevention and Control of Water Pollution. But such NOCs being what they are, they only define the permissible limits of pollution. And where is the local expertise to maintain constant checks?

Six kilometres from the Kerim plateau is the Mangueshi Temple complex, one of Goa's biggest tourist attractions. The Town and Country Planning Department (T&CP) warned the government that not only was the proposed Kerim site notified as 'natural cover' in Goa's Regional Plan, but that "the possibility of seepage affecting the water courses at lower altitudes could not be ruled out". The Khandepar river which is barely 3 km away in the valley below, is Goa's main source of water.

Not 4 km away is the Ponda electricity sub-station. From the industrial point of view, the location is ideal in all respects. Though alternative sites were suggested, expectedly, the Thapar clout won the day. Kerim it is to be, with all the government machinery being geared for land acquisition.

Financially, Goa will be no richer or poorer from the Nylon 6,6 plant. It would in fact make no difference to the state if the plant were here or in Ahmedabad, a government official points out.

According to EDC, Thapar Du Pont will contribute Rs. 18 crore in excise duty and Rs. 14 crore in corporate tax yearly. Both these go to the Central coffers.

When the EDC first got the letters of intent from the Industries Ministry for the plant on February 25, 1985 and September 30, 1985 it roused the suspicion in business circles that the corporation had acted at the behest of higher powers to facilitate the backdoor entry of Thapars.

Investigations not only confirm the truth of that suspicion, they also expose the complicity of authorities far beyond the pale of the local government.

More scandalously, it appears EDC's application for the letter of intent was changed elsewhere. Permission granted by the Ministry of Industry states: 'for the manufacture of Nylon 6,6 - or Nylon 6'. None in the Goa government or at EDC were even aware of this till it was brought to their notice by this paper. Not certain of Du Pont's willingness to collaborate at that stage, Thapar was obviously not foregoing the chance of setting up a tyre cord plant in Goa with some other collaborator.

EDC was approached by Thapars for the collaboration in 1983 - and not the other way around - sources there confirm. When the state corporation applied for the letter of intent under the joint sector provisions, it little dreamt the project would backfire on it financially. With the letter of intent secured, Lalit Thapar, the head of the Thapar group, moved all his highly placed contacts to enhance the capacity of the plant from 6,000 tonnes per annum (TPA) to 14000 TPA on February 3, 1986. The original cost of the project rose from Rs. 55 crore to Rs. 132 crore and the equity portion escalated to Rs. 44 crore. EDC was rudely shaken to discover its share holding of 26 per cent would now work out to Rs. 12 crore. Where was the money to be raised from when the state's annual industries plant itself does not exceed Rs. 6 crore?

Obviously, Lalit Thapar, moving shrewdly ahead of the Goa Government, had it all worked out. He had all along been wooing Du Pont for a more committed participation in the form of foreign equity share rather than mere technological collaboration. This would ensure that Du Pont kept the plant technologically upgraded rather than just functionally maintained. As he envisaged it, the ideal pattern of holding was to be: Thapars 40 per cent, Du Pont 40 per cent and EDC plus public 20 per cent.

Even with the highest political contacts in the country, there was still the bureaucratic tangle to be got through, and much of the heartburn on this count had to be borne by the Goa Government and more specifically, chief minister Pratapsingh Rane.

On October 29, 1987 Lalit Thapar wrote to Rane: "In spite of your personal intervention, the Central Government has not yet cleared the proposal of Economic Development Corporation of Goa on the revised equity share holding pattern of Thapar Du Pont Ltd. It has been recommended by EDC and Goa State Government that both BILT and Du Pont may each be allowed to invest up to 40 per cent of the equity and at the same time EDC will like to keep its investment low...May be you would consider it appropriate to depute either chief secretary or secretary, industry, to pursue the matter with Central Government to secure speedy approval for revised equity share holding pattern."

At one point, EDC believed it would get by with a token Rs. 5 lakh investment of its 20 per cent share, keeping the rest open to public. That suggestion met with the cold disapproval of the Secretariat of Industrial Approvals (SIA).

The Goa Government then agreed to an 11 per cent participation which amounts to Rs. 5 crore - and Rane was left the disagreeable task of pleading EDC's case with Industries Minister J.Vengal Rao in a series of letters, the last of which written in April this year said: "I have been informed that the Secretariat of Industrial Approvals, Ministry of Industries has rejected the proposed reduced shareholding by the EDC on grounds that it would be in the nature of a backdoor entry by a private sector industry... I would request you personally to approve our proposal as a special case by considering our nascent state's requirements for high technology industries." Needless to say, the union minister did. The amended letter of intent came in June this year.

There were other reasons why there was such stiff opposition to this project from the bureaucracy, given even, Thapar's connections with the highest in the land. The Central Government also felt that an Nylon 6,6 plant would put a great burden on the country's foreign exchange reserves. The raw materials used to make Nylon 6,6, adipic acid and hexamethylene diamine, have to be continually imported. N6 uses caprolactum, 40 per cent of which is manufactured indigenously, and this is expected to go up to 70 per cent soon.

The warning signals for the Nylon 6,6 plant are many. Its employment generation claim, say government officials, is grossly inflated. Rane announced in the legislative Assembly that the number of jobs for the local populace would be in the range of 800 directly and 4,000 indirectly. Where are the qualified chemical engineers or management level people in Goa? Experts believe the available positions would be at menial levels.

The company's demand for 500 acres of land, that too, at concessional rates is considered preposterous. The land being acquired at Kerim belongs to the communidade. The town and country planning (T & CP) department assessed the plant's maximum requirement at 100 acres. Officials suspected that this was just another case of big industry like Zuari Agro Chemicals wanting to hog a large chunk of land to take advantage of its future price escalation. But Rane, apparently under considerable pressure from New Delhi, coerced board members of the T & CP (which he heads) to sanction the 500 acres at a meeting on June 23rd. Rane's position is hardly enviable. Asking for his personal intervention in the matter of land acquisition in a letter written in February this year, the late B M Bakshi, vice president of BILT stressed that "The Government of India voiced its concern on the delay that has occurred and mentioned that this project was being monitored at the highest level." Note the tone of the letter from a corporate man, to the chief minister of a state!

The land acquisition to be done by IDC on EDC's behalf is seen in some quarters as a way out of the financial noose for EDC by writing it off as its equity contribution. The land pricing is expected to be so worked out that its inflated value would cover upto Rs. 1.5 crore of EDC's equity share. The rest will be the Government's burden to pay off in the next three or four years, at the end of which EDC will withdraw in favour of public shares.

Will the benefit of the Nylon 6,6 plant outweigh its apparent setbacks, ecological, social and otherwise? That is for the Government to agonise over, keeping in mind the fact of Zuari Agro Chemicals, its pollution of the Sancoale valley and its creation of the Dabolim chawls.

AN ENVIRONMENTAL AND ECONOMIC POWDERKEG

(*Goa Today*, December 1988)

The *New York Times*, January 23, 1987: "E.I. du Pont de Nemours & Co. has agreed to a $ 100 million joint venture with Thapar industrial conglomerate to manufacture and market industrial nylon yarn and fabric in India. It is the largest American Indian business deal in the private sector since Prime Minister Rajiv Gandhi assumed power in 1984..."

(Now, probably, second only to the Pepsi Cola deal).

Here in Goa, India, we're merely sideline spectators to this momentous industrial development that will contribute to the country's 'technological upgradation'. And, probably, our environment's degradation. We're about to sacrifice a rain forest to Lalit Mohan Thapar's corporate ideals: 'foreign investment' 'foreign exchange' 'induction of high technology'. Impressive. Meant to impress those in high places who handle such matters. But look at the fine print of the terms of technical and financial collaboration and the application for import of capital goods and the real reasons are not hard to find.

On September 18, this year, Thapar Du Pont Ltd (TDL) (the new company promoted by Goa's Economic Development Corporation, Thapar's Ballarpur Industries Ltd (BILT) and the American multinational Du Pont to manufacture Nylon 6,6 tyre cord/fabric from Kerim, Ponda) and M/s E.I. du Pont de Nemours and Co. signed a technical and financial collaboration agreement. Though EDC still holds the letter of intent for the plant (a year ago it asked for the letter to be transferred to TDL) the corporation was neither represented at the time of signing this agreement nor was it aware of its contents, even though EDC's Managing Director, Dr. P Deshpande, is already a director of TDL.

In February this year, EDC passed a resolution empowering TDL (represented in reality by BILT) to draw up the technical and financial collaboration agreement. And look how things have got out of hand already.

Some of the salient features of that agreement:

(Article 5: Warranty & Liability) "5.3 TDL shall hold Du Pont and its representatives or assignees harmless from any claims made in the Republic of India against representatives of Du Pont or its assignees alleging bodily harm or death sustained as a direct result of, or in direct connection with, the performance of this Agreement."

Interesting indeed. From the multinational's point of view, one understands the necessity to be indemnified against claims after Union Carbide and the Bhopal gas disaster. But there's more:

"5.6 Du Pont shall not be liable in any manner whatsoever to TDL or to any third party for any loss or damage caused to person or property, including to members of the public as well as to person or property of any employees of TDL directly caused by any act or omission of TDL or its servants or agents and TDL shall indemnify Du Pont against said liability.

"5.7 Du Pont shall not be liable under any circumstances whatsoever, to any third parties including members of the public on any account whatsoever due to any accident at the plant or any act or omission of TDL (etc.). Any claim (etc.) made against Du Pont by any third party shall be defended by TDL at its cost and expense and TDL shall indemnify....Du Pont and its personnel against the same at all times; provided however, if any such ...suit arises on account of proven negligence of Du Pont..."Which would be difficult to prove, say legal experts.

There's more still. Arbitration between TDL and Du Pont is to be held in London, England. "The arbitrators shall apply Law of UK and such rules of international law as may be applicable." Why not the USA, Du Pont's country of residence? Because American laws are far more stringent and compensation awards greater than in Britain?

Du Pont has allowed for itself every legal safeguard conceivable, including one to withdraw within 30 days: (Article 17) "Should Du Pont at any time, conclude that because of future legislative or judicial developments (in India) the public liability risks do not justify its continued participation as a share holder in TDL, it shall so notify BILT, and subject to the approval of the Reserve Bank of India, BILT shall, within a period of thirty days thereafter, purchase Du Pont's shares in TDL at the prevailing market price."

That would be the end of Du Pont's coveted foreign investment of 15 million US dollars' equity contribution (that would in any case be written off against cost of second hand equipment, which will be explained later).

Does the Goa Government agree to these terms? "We will raise objections," (to the Secretariat of Industrial Approvals, Government of India) an official told *Goa Today*. Now? At this stage? Isn't that absurd? The terms of agreement are drawn up by a company owned (in part) by the State corporation which has, in its wisdom, empowered BILT (in effect) to take all decisions related to TDL. And who would object? The only dissenting voice at EDC board meetings has been finance secretary Bobby Misra's. Misra is now transferred to Delhi.

According to sources in the government, Chief Minister Pratapsing Rane initially objected to the Nylon 6,6 project being located in Goa, but he subsequently changed his mind and has since been its most insistent promoter. Rane peremptorily dismisses all valid objections to the project. 'These self-styled environmentalists,' he says, but refutes none of the issues raised.

TDL was to be given 500 acres of land at Kerim, no less, Rane had insisted at a meeting at the Town and Country Planning (T & CP) board on June 23 this year. Misra, who had his doubts all along; had asked chief town planner J A D'Souza to work out TDL's actual requirements. When there was no response from the T & CP department for six months, Misra took time off from a heavy official schedule to do so himself. His conclusion: 150 acres, no more. The government would release 50 hectares immediately and 10 hectares would be reserved for future development, Misra informed *Goa Today* last month. He also felt that EDC's participation, however small, in the project was mandatory for the Goa government to exercise control over the land.

So here we are, saddled with a colossal corporate multinational venture in our backyard, and who will benefit? Take a look at the application for capital goods import approval dated September 26, 1988.

TDL will pay Du Pont Rs. 28.51 crore for machinery, Rs. 233.85 crore for raw materials, Rs. 4.13 crore for know how/engineering, Rs. 17.57 crore (2.5 per cent) royalty for the first five years (the contract is valid for 15 years) and Rs. 2.79 crore to the foreign technicians. The foreign exchange outflow altogether works out to Rs. 286.86 crore. There will be an yearly outflow of Rs. 49 crore on the Nylon 6,6 ingredients alone. Du Pont's Rs. 20 crore equity participation would be written off against cost of equipment alone. But that's not all. Part of the equipment is secondhand. TDL proposes to relocate one of Du Pont's existing lines operating in Richmond, USA, to Goa, India. And TDL goes to great lengths to argue that the second hand, refurbished, equipment 'is just like new', that it 'has been overhauled, upgraded and modified from time to time and excels in performance even over the present day new equipment made by other suppliers.' The argument is carried further to justify that 'it is impossible to quantify the age of this equipment since so many replacements and upgradations have been continuously taking place'. Government of India regulations require a life certificate of a minimum 20 years for any machinery being imported to the country.

This leads to another question: Why would Du Pont want to pack up its Richmond plant, one of its four nylon tyre cord plants in the US? According to tyre manufacturers, Nylon 6,6 tyre cord no longer has a market either in the USA or in Europe. The French company Micheline's radial tyres have captured the automotive tyre market in the developed countries. Dividends and royalty on technology that is being phased out in another part of the world. Convenient indeed.

"The balance sheet drawn for the first five years of operation will yield foreign exchange earnings equivalent of US $ 125 to 130 million," TDL director H. Luthra notes in the application to SIA.

The company's projected foreign exchange earnings - Rs. 93.76 crore on the 25 per cent export obligation - and savings - Rs. 375 crore 'anticipated as a result of import substitution' - are hypothetical. The 25 per cent export obligation would be next to impossible to meet, considering the changed technology in the tyre market, say experts. And to counter the argument that claims that the Nylon 6,6 project "will be instrumental in developing downstream industries in the small scale sector which will rear up a new set of entrepreneur in the State of Goa." I quote from a TDL observation that "90 per cent of the total consumption of Nylon tyre cord/industrial yarn is accounted for by the automotive tyre sector." So how does the small scale sector benefit?

"The Du Pont pollution control requirements are more stringent than those of the states and localities in which their plants are operated, and the technology and plant proposed in this application incorporates all of the advances made by Du Pont in their operations," TDL claims on behalf of its collaborator. This far away from the USA, would we know any better? But proof is at hand:

From the *Wall Street Journal*, Nov 2, 1977: "Last May, Earl Mc Cune, a lab chemist at Du Pont Co's chemical plant here, became alarmed at the apparently large number of cancer cases among his fellow workers. He suspected the cause was the chemicals to which they were exposed to at the plant... he decided this time to take his complaint directly to the federal government.

"Soon after the hearing, Du Pont made a complete survey of cancer incidents and deaths at the Belle plant since 1956. The study uncovered 195 cancer incidences using statistics on active employees alone. Using statistics on both active and pensioned workers, 206 cancer deaths were found."

The Washington Post, July 15, 1979: "According to company records, there were 339 known cases for urinary bladder cancer ascribed to benzidine and beta among Du Pont workmen during the years 1956-1974. Even accounting for the 20-25 year lapsed period between onset of exposure and development of cancer, it is obvious that this continuing epidemic of cancer was both foreseen and preventable."

The Atlanta Journal, October 25, 1984: "A controversial 1976 study by the E.I. du Pont de Nemours & Co. reported higher than expected rates of leukemia and lung cancer among workers at the Savannah River Plant."

Occupational Safety & Health Reporter, May 1987: "A jury awarded nearly $ 1.4 million in damages on May 8 to six current and former employees who claimed that Du Pont company physicians failed to inform them of asbestos damage to their health.

"A jury had found that an employer had knowingly withheld medical information from employees on damage to their health allegedly caused by asbestos."

The next is taken from a report on the US government's Savannah River Atomic Plant, which the reporter calls 'an archaic power unto itself'. The report is barely two months old.

The Washington Post, October 17, 1988: "Built in the early 1950's by E.I. Du Pont de Nemours & Co. at the government's request, and operated by Du Pont since, Savannah River has increasingly become an island in a moving stream.

"In investigation after investigation, safety reviewers accustomed to the equipment procedures of modern commercial or military reactors have come away appalled at what they found at Savannah River: critical safety apparatus protected by fire fighting equipment that consisted of garden hoses; operating manuals that failed to anticipate erratic behaviour by the reactor; corroding coolant pipes; lackadaisical maintenance schedules, oil soaked and leaking gaskets in crucial diesel pumps.

"Investigators say that Savannah River's myriad problems taken individually may not constitute a major threat to public safety. Taken together, however, they indicate an installation that has not kept pace with industry changes intended to improve safety margins and inspire public confidence."

That is Du Pont in the USA. Would it be any better in India?

GOA GOVERNMENT PLAYS GODFATHER

(*Goa Today*, August 1989)

The controversial Nylon 6,6 project which made it to the headlines of the financial press when it was rejected i March (1989) by the Industry Ministry, is back in the news, though this time, quietly so.

The collaboration venture involving the American multinational Du Pont and the house of Thapars floated under a new company Thapars du Pont Ltd (TDL), is being reconsidered for MRTP (Monopoly and Restrictive Trade Practices) clearances. Government officials *Goa Today* spoke to are certain the project will this time be cleared without a hitch.

End June, representatives of the American multinational company Du Pont gave an undertaking to Government of India officials in New Delhi to raise the export committment from the earlier 25 per cent to 42 per cent. Since this agreement has been reached, it would only be a matter of time before the project gets its MRTP clearance for BILT's (Ballarpur Industries Ltd, a Thapar subsidiary) 40 per cent equity participation, government officials say.

Du Pont's 40 per cent equity participation was cleared by the Ministry of Industry in principal in December 1987 on condition of technology transfer.

Ever since the Nylon 6,6 project was shot down four months ago, frantic efforts have been made by both its collaborators to resurrect it. On March 16, Thapar Du Pont Ltd. (TDL), received a letter of rejection from S P Singh, deputy secretary, Industry Ministry.

Among the reasons cited for the rejection was the 'perpetual import of raw material and no visible advantage in technology'. Mr. Singh concluded that the project was not in 'public interest'.

Soon after, a series of meetings took place between Lalit Thapar and Du Pont representatives with Industry Ministry officials to clear the snags. In a letter to the Government of Goa, BILT said that Government of India officials had asked TDL to raise its export committment from 25 per cent to 42 per cent as a precondition to reconsider the project.

Subsequently, on May 2, TDL revamped its application based on the 42 per cent export committment and the project is now headed for clearance.

Back home in Goa the state government has been working assiduously at acquiring land and granting licences and doing every thing possible to push the TDL project through as if the Ministry's rejection didn't exist.

Just a week before TDL was formally informed about the rejection by the Ministry, the Goa Government notified the land acquisition under Section 4 in the official gazette of March 9. According to this notification, the total land to be acquired at Keri and Savoi Verem, Ponda, is 638 acres. Far beyond even TDL's demand for 500 acres.

But see what clever ruses the government adapts to make it appear that not all this land will go to TDL. The notification states the land is required for an industrial estate/Nylon 6,6 project. 'We've decided to give them (TDL) only 123 hectares (around 300 acres). The rest we're keeping for an industrial estate', says finance secretary R S Sethi, glibly. What sort of industrial estate? Sethi is conveniently vague in his reply. Dr. P T Deshpande, chairman of EDC, is more forthcoming. The industrial estate is for ancillary industries of Nylon 6,6, he says.

Even before the acquisition is notified under Section 6, TDL was given possession of 200 acres of land in Keri by the Industrial Development Corporation (IDC). In this respect, the obliging government corporations have been helped by an erratic communidade system.

Of the total 638 acres to be acquired, 326 belong to the respective communidades. The Government managed to get the Keri communidade to pass a resolution to make over its land to IDC. IDC was given possession of the land on March 27 and made it over to TDL who fenced it in with a compound wall.

The land was given to TDL on condition that it would revert to the government in case the project fell through, Sethi says. But he conveniently avoids the more pointed questions he ought to look into as finance secretary. The Goa Government has nothing to say about some controversial terms in the Thapar-Du-Pont technical and financial agreement, even though the EDC still holds the letter of intent for the project.

Once TDL's MRTP clearance comes, it would be chickenfeed for the company to see its NOC from the State Pollution Control Board (SPCB) through. Chief Secretary P V Jaykrishnan, who is chairman of SPCB, said the board's technical committee had laid down a number of conditions for the project's clearance and these are now under consideration. He also added that strict specifications would be imposed for its clearance. Should one believe him? The manner in which this mammoth project has been prodded and pushed through has already aroused considerable scepticism.

UNSUBTLE MANOEUVRES

(*Goa Today*, July 1990)

Does the future of the controversial Nylon 6,6 project in Goa now hinge on health minister Dr Kashinath Zhalmi or on chief minister Dr Luis Proto Barbosa? Or will it depend on public concern (there have been not a few audible protests of late)? Or, even more curiously, will its final approval by the Special Projects Approval Committee (PAB) in New Delhi before which it is now pending clearance, depend on Environment Minister of State Maneka Gandhi?

Thapar Du Pont Ltd (TDL) have maintained an anxious pace of construction of their plant in Keri (only a training institute, they claim) even in the face of mounting objections to the project. A significant part of the criticism now comes from none other than health minister Zhalmi, who has been assiduously studying the N 6,6 files because the plant comes within his constituency, Priol. Zhalmi was more than shocked to learn that the company has possession of 303 acres of land and began construction a year ago though the land hasn't actually been acquired.

The village too has begun to ask questions about the illegalities in the procedures. At a gram sabha meeting, in Arla on June 10 where Zhalmi was present, sarpanch Babal Satarkar was taken to task for giving TDL a conditional NOC for construction when the company does not hold title deeds for the land. The panchayat's NOC states the company would be required to show the title deeds before construction is complete.

On March 27, 1989, TDL took over the land from the Keri communidades based merely on a government acquisition notice under Section 6, and a resolution illegally moved making over the land from the communidades to the company. The Keri communidades have since challenged the transfer of land and the communidades' governing body's supercession by the Rane government in Court.

No award was fixed for the land by the government, and TDL has so far not paid a paise for it, which makes its possession by the company illegal, according to Zhalmi.

The Economic Development Corporation (EDC) which has unabashedly been playing handmaiden to the two conglomerates involved, Du Pont and Thapar, will eventually write off the land to TDL as part of its share capital in the joint venture. It can ill afford to put in Rs. 20 crore (the amount roughly its 11 per cent share works out to today) by way of capital. But the compensation to the communidades will have to be borne by the government Corporation. And as the cost of the project goes on spiralling (from Rs. 132 crore to Rs. 180 crore, and now probably more with the production capacity of nylon fabric being upped from 3,000 tonnes to 12,000 tonnes) EDC's contribution too increases. And along with it, its collaborative burden. This is the price it has to pay for walking into the Thapar trap when it posed as its front to acquire the letter of intent for the project.

Dr. Barbosa, on the other hand, has shown a desire to review the project from the environment angle. It isn't quite clear whether the beleagured chief minister is genuinely concerned for the environment, or whether he could be using this as a political opportunity to spike his predecessor, Pratapsing Rane, who was chiefly responsible for promoting the project in Goa. But Barbosa has been looking for relevant data to send to the Environment Ministry in Delhi, where he intends to have the project reviewed.

In the midst of all the heat and dust raised at the parochial level over the descent of the multinationals, comes a major global development for environment protection that might just have a bearing (though not directly related) on the approval of the N 6,6 project. A London based report (UNI, June 29) on the Montreal Protocol referred to the deadlock between India (represented by Maneka Gandhi) and western multinationals over the transfer of technology for chloro fluro carbons (CFCs) substitutes. "India has refused to sign the Protocol aimed at banning world wide production of CFCs within ten years in a phased manner until the developed countries agreed to provide enough funds and on conditional transfer of the ozone friendly technology to bring about the changeover," says the report.

The multinationals involved, who have so far refused to transfer the technology on grounds that they have spent billions of dollars on its research, are Du Pont and ICI. Du Pont's future relations with the Government of India may well hinge on how negotiations at the Montreal Protocol conference progress.

But the refusal to transfer technology is just one example of the western multinationals' double standards in developing countries. So too has been the case with the Nylon 6,6 venture in Goa, which will need more than American-style PR to see it through, if the hostile reception accorded its representatives on a whitewash job here last month is something to go by.

Representing Du Pont were Sam Singh, technical director, TDL, Arthur Miller, public relations, Asia-Pacific, Rita Heckrotte, engineering associate. The Thapar line-up had vice president Gautam Thapar, BILT general manager (fibre) Vijay Mallik and TDL general manager K S Pal.

Put to the test by a group of environment conscious people and *Goa Today* (on two separate occasions), the high-profile team were left an embarrassed and uncomfortable lot, groping for replies and unconvincing explanations.

It was certainly not what Du Pont's India communications man Roger Pereira had in mind when he roped in friend Mario Miranda to play host through INTACH for a 'dialogue' on Nylon 6,6 with 'environment groups' in Goa. Egged on by the success of a similar PR exercise in Bombay, Pereira had probably envisaged an exchange of pleasantries over tea and cakes in the idyllic surroundings of Miranda's Loutulim mansion. As it turned out, some of those present came well prepared (the Press was deliberately left out) to the discomfort of TDL representatives who couldn't supply most answers.

Things got so rough at one stage that a tea break was called and the proceedings conveniently aborted. INTACH and Nirmal Vishwa members later told the press they had given the company 21 days to address itself to the doubts raised and provide the replies in writing. "Instead of giving specific answers, the company's representatives wanted their case to be accepted on the basis of the claim that Du Pont was 98 times safer than other American companies and that Ballarpur Industries had been pioneers in safety factors at their Karwar plant," they added.

So too with *Goa Today*, the Du Pont Thapars PR team began pathetically on a patronising note. A puerile presentation by Heckrotte ("Making Nylon 6,6 is like baking a cake. Here is the flour and there are the eggs.") was an insult to the intelligence of even a ten-year-old. The team left behind more doubts than clarifications.

Asked why construction was begun when the project has not been approved, the TDL reply was typically unconvincing:

K.S. Pal: "We have not undertaken construction of factory buildings. We are only doing developmental work. There was a boundary and a road in existence and the area was levelled to raise the factory building as and when approval comes. This is strictly development work, that too with the express approval of the Goa Government and all its other agencies."

The 'express approval' as *Goa Today* has pointed out in the past, amounts to nothing short of arrogance and a pre-emption of every legal procedure. Which is what Zhalmi has discovered of late.

'If approval is not granted, what happens to all the construction and development work?'

Sam Singh: "We have all the faith in the system. Yes, they've asked some questions and we are answering them. But we will get their approval, (that's why) we've started to make sure our people are trained when we start."

The approval, EDC sources had disclosed, hinged on a hike in the export committment of the N 6,6 tyre cord, a committment Du Pont could not meet. With the introduction of new technologies in radial tyres, demand for N 6,6 in the West is on the ebb, by Singh's own admission.

'Why does Du Pont want to re-locate its N 6,6 plants from the US?'

Singh: "In the US, most production is shifting now to radial tyres (which use either steel or cavlon.) Our buyers are here now and their growth is increasing. The principal with which we operate is that our manufacturing facility should be closer to our customer."

Miller added quickly: "We are not re-locating a plant; we are only relocating some machinery."

Cavlon is a new Du Pont product. So these admissions only help confirm suspicions that the multinational intends to dump its phased-out technology in India, and get good returns for it in the bargain. Du Pont's 40 per cent equity participation (obviously being written off against equipment and technology transfers) would ensure it of a share in the booming Indian market.

'Does your 42 per cent export obligation include the export of nitric acid?'

Miller: "This is an incidence of total misinformation. We have never indicated to the government any intention to set up a nitric acid plant in India."

'But Thapars hold a letter of intent for a nitric acid plant?'

Miller: "In the process of looking for ways to help with the export situation, we're putting up an adipic acid plant in Singapore. The plant requires nitric acid. We're now looking, not only in India, but throughout Asia and the world for sources of supply of nitric acid. We're prepared to buy nitric acid from India. If Thapars supply to us at competitive prices, that's their choice."

Miller makes it sound as if Du Pont is setting up an adipic acid plant in Singapore purely to help the Indian 'export situation'. What he fails to disclose is that during negotiations with Industries Ministry officials Thapar and Du Pont tried to convince them to accept their import of nitric acid from India as an export substitution of N 6,6 tyre cord from India.

If things were as shipshape as these PR men would have us believe, why has their project's approval been kept pending for three years now?

Typically devious in their dealings with Third World countries, Du Pont has tried to bluff its way with the Goa Government and now with the Press and a concerned public lobby. The Goa State Pollution Control Board (GSPCB) has accepted on face value its claim that the materials used to manufacture N 6,6 are 'not hazardous'. "There are no hazardous substances involved," Ms Heckrotte declared quite firmly. "Both adipic acid and hexamethylene diamine are not considered hazardous even in the US," she added confidently. "Adipic acid is used to make candy. I love candy, don't you?".

There is documented evidence to show that the American government's health departments have both substances on their Hazardous Substances List. They also carry warnings in bold about both that state: "Produces poisonous gas in fire".

Heckrotte's presentation to GSPCB for a pollution NOC itself states that "adipic acid dust forms explosive mixture with air and can be extinguished with water, CO_2, chemical foam and dry chemical."

And in its very next para, the company says it intends to transport the substance in bags.

A spokesman for GSPCB, however, says the company has been allowed to transport adipic acid by road on condition that it would be carried in waterjacket tankers.

Du Pont has also avoided mention of the additives it proposes to use for the manufacture of the nylon polymer. It refers to "auxiliary ingredients (polymerization, catalyst, antioxidants, and other stabilizers) are added to facilitate chain extensions and increase the resistance of the polymer and subsequent fibre to thermal and oxidative degradations." But even its presentation to the Pollution Control Board avoids naming these auxiliaries.

Some of the Nylon 6,6 additives are heavy metal compounds, both dangerous to handle and polluting.

In the light of these serious doubts, the Pollution Control Board would do well to review the case before the situation is irreversible.

Note

As it is impermissible to edit, change or otherwise alter a document prepared by members of the Goa Assembly, the text of the Assembly's House Committee Report on Nylon 6,6 has been maintained as it appears in the original submitted by the Chairman of the Committee, Shri A.N. Naik, to the Speaker.

Quotes appearing in boxes within the body of the Report have been extracted from statements made by Thapar-Du Pont officials before the House Committee.

REPORT
OF THE HOUSE COMMITTEE

to investigate into the irregularities

of the possession of land of Kerim Communidade

and related aspects on pollution, issue of licences etc.

of Nylon 6,6 Project

at Kerim in Ponda Taluka

Goa Legislature Department,

Assembly Hall, Panaji

1990

COMPOSITION OF THE COMMITTEE

CHAIRMAN

SHRI. A.N. NAIK

MEMBERS

1. Shri. V.P. Usgaonkar

2. Shri. Ranu Prabhu Desai

3. Shri. Manu Fernandes

4. Shri. Simon D'Souza

LEGISLATURE DEPARTMENT

1. Shri M.M. Naik, Secretary

2. Shri. A.B. Ulman, Joint Secretary

3. Shri. S.A. Narvekar, Superintendent

FOREWORD

I, the chairman of the committee, having been authorized by the committee to submit the Report on its behalf, present this Report.

I wish to place on record my deep appreciation for the co-operation and courtesy extended to me by all the members of the committee. I am very much obliged to them for making the deliberations of the committee very effective bestowing whole-hearted attention.

I would like to thank profusely to the Members of the expert committee, Dr. V.N. Kamat Dalal, Dr. Joe D'Souza, Dr. S.Y. Singbal, Shri Nandkumar Kamat, Shri K.D. Sadhle, Shri Zeferino Fernandes, Shri Bonny Menezes and Dr. N.P.S. Varde who have put in labourious efforts to assist the committee within the stipulated time to enable the committee to finalize this Report. The committee is also thankful to Government Officers, Shri Anil Baijal, Development Commissioner and Shri M.M. Lal, Secretary, Revenue.

Last but not the least, the committee places on record its appreciation for the services of the officers and the staff of the Legislature Department, who worked hard to assist the Committee, to enable the Committee to finalize and submit this Report.

Assembly Hall,
Panaji,
16th November, 1990.

A. N. NAIK
CHAIRMAN

LIST OF CONTENTS

INTRODUCTION

REPORT

1. The issue regarding acquisition of land belonging to Querim Communidade by Nylon 6,6 factory was discussed in the House on 23rd July, 1990. It was sequel to the discussion on starred Question No.*1152 tabled by Shri. A.N. Naik, MLA. After discussion the Committee of the House was constituted under Rule 169 of the Rules of Procedure and Conduct of Business of the Goa Legislative Assembly to inquire into the irregularities as regards possession of land, pollution aspect, permission of the license and all other related matters.

The Committee consists of the following Members:

(1) Shri. A.N. Naik Chairman

(2) Shri. V.P. Usgaonkar Member

(3) Shri. Ranu Prabhu Desai Member

(4) Shri. Manu Fernandes Member

(5) Shri. Simon D'Souza Member

2. In the preliminary meeting held on 27th July, 1990, the Committee decided to issue a press note inviting suggestions/comments from persons interested in the subject before the Committee. Accordingly the Press note was issued on 3rd August, 1990. The Legislature Department has received over 60 suggestions/comments from different persons/institutions offering their comments/views on the subject.

3. The Committee thought of the following plan of action to come to the conclusion after examination of witnesses and verifying the documents.

(A) Examination of witnesses and the persons connected with the acquisition/possession of land from the Querim Communidade and the office bearers or the Committees:-

In this connection the Committee has examined the following persons.

(1) Shri. F.C. Fernandes Administrator of Communidade Tiswadi.

(2) Shri. R.S. Vaidhya As a President of Managing Committee of Querim Communidade.

(3) Shri. Uday Shriniwas Vaidhya As witness, and as substitute attorney of Querim Communidade.

(4) Shri. Waman Sinai Borkar As a witness and Ex-Scrivao of Querim Communidade.

(5) Shri. Suhas Vinayak Hudekar As a treasurer of Querim Communidade.

(6) Shri Babal Satarkar Sarpanch of Querim

(7) Dr. Deu Datta Kerkar As a witness component Gaonkar of Querim Communidade

(8) Shri Laxman Anant Parab Desai Witness

(9) Shri Ranganath Priolkar Witness

(10) Shri Madhusudan Joshi Witness

(11) Shri Francis Baretto Witness

(12) Shri P. Shikerkar Witness

(13) Dr. Sharad Vaidhya Witness

(B) The examination of issue connected with the pollution aspect and grant of permission to Thapar Du Pont Limited Project of Nylon 6,6 by the authorities. The House Committee in order to seek technical expertise decided to take the assistance of the experts from various organisations like Goa University, National Institute of Oceanography, Goa Research Institute for Development, Nirmal Vishwa, Indian Heritage Society (Goa Chapter), Goa Polytechnic, Goa Foundation, Anti Pollution Citizens Committee, and Environmentalists and others. Following the meeting held on 9th October, 1990 it was decided on 16th October, 1990 to appoint a small technical committee comprising of persons belonging to different disciplines related to environment/pollution/landscaping and other such related aspects and the following Committee was constituted to assist the House Committee.

(1)   Dr. V.N. Kamat Dalal Prof. Inorganic Chemistry Goa University, Convenor

(2)   Dr. Joe D'Souza Reader, Micro Biology Depart. Goa University

(3)   Dr. S.Y. Singbal Dy. Director, Chemical Oceanography Div. and Marine Scientist National Inst. of Oceanography, Dona Paula, Goa.

(4)   Shri Nandkumar Kamat Environmentalist & Executive Committee, Member of India Heritage Society (Goa Chap.)

(5)   Shri K.D. Sadhale Architect, Environmentalist & Executive Member of Nirmal Vishwa.

(6)   Shri Zeferino Fernandes Goa Research Inst. for Devp.

(7)   Shri Bonny Menezes Goa Research Inst. for Devp.

(8)   Dr. N.P.S. Varde Scientist.

4. The House Committee visited the site in question on 5th September, 1990.

M/s. Thapar Du Pont Limited proposed vide their letter No. TDL/LD/90-91 dated 6-9-1990 that a team from their foreign collaborator M/s. Du Pont of U.S.A. may like to make submissions and to answer the queries on pollution. Accordingly, the presentation was made to the Committee by the representatives of T.D.L. and U.S. team on 9th October, 1990 consisting of:-

(1)   Shri V.K. Malik Gen. Manager (Fibre) BILT New Delhi.

(2)   Dr. R.M. Kothari Thapar Corp. R & D Centre Patiala.

(3)   Shri K.S. Pal Thapar Du Pont Ltd.

(4)   Shri M.R. Lohr E.I. Du Pont

(5)   Dr. Rita W. Heckrotte E.I. Du Pont

(6)   Shri V. (Sam) Singh E.I. Du Pont

(7)   Lt. Col.(Rtd). A.L. Coutts Thapar Du Pont Ltd.

(8)   Shri Raj Pal Singh Thapar Du Pont Ltd.

(9)   Shri Ashwani Prashara Thapar Du Pont Ltd.

They also informed the Committee about the various aspects of their factory at Richmond by means of slides. The joint 'question-answer' session was held for almost entire day wherein the persons from N.I.O., Goa University and voluntary organisations participated, alongwith the members of the House Committee. Dr. Jhalmi, Minister for Legislative Affairs and Shri Mohan Amshekar were present.

5. The Committee had so far met on 27/7/90, 21/8/90, 5/9/90, 11/9/90, 18/9/90, 25/9/90, 5/10/90, 8/10/90, 9/10/90, 16/10/90, 24/10/90, 31/10/90, 6/11/90.

The House Committee had a meeting with the technical Committee of Pollution Board under Dr. Sengupta on 8th October, 1990.

PART A :

IRREGULARITIES RELATING TO HANDING OVER THE POSSESSION OF LAND BELONGING TO COMMUNIDADE OF QUERIM.

(i) Brief background regarding working of Communidades:

In the State of Goa there are in total 222 Communidades, spread over its ten Talukas, viz. Salcete, Goa (Tiswadi), Bardez, Mormugao, Ponda, Bicholim, Pernem, Quepem, Sanguem and Canacona. These Communidades are the old agricultural societies recognized by the Government. They possess vast lands, agricultural, non-agricultural and hilly lands. The Communidade is under the administrative tutelage of the Government for the purpose of its administration and supervision and for the regular and smooth running of its affairs vide Art. 5 of Code of Communidades, in force.

There is a Legislation called as "Codigo das Communidades" approved with modifications by the erstwhile Portuguese Government by Legislative Diploma No.2070, dated 15/4/1961, which is still in force, under which the affairs of the Communidades are governed.

Apart from the above legislation, the Communidades are having their own by-laws (Institutes), establishing their assets and liabilities as well as the manner in which the expenditure is to be carried out and how the net income is to be distributed among the interested parties (jonoeiros, shareholders, culacharins, participants, etc.) and how to make good the deficit, if caused. After Liberation of Goa, several modifications and amendments were introduced by the Government from time to time, and thus altering to certain extent some provisions of the Code of Communidades, in force. Similarly with promulgation of the Goa, Daman and Diu, Agricultural Tenancy Act 1964 and amendments made thereafter to the same Act, and with the application of the land Acquisition Act 1894, some provisions of the said Code were repealed.

As per the provisions of the Art. 39 of the said Code, the affairs of the Communidades are handled by the Administrative Board. As per Art. 40, the Managing Committee consists of three Members:- President, Treasurer and Attorney appointed by Government. And in their absence their substitutes carry on the said affairs. Besides the abovesaid three members there is one "Escrivao" who is designated now as Upper Division Clerk, by virtue of the Goa, Daman and Diu Communidades Employees (Conditions of Service) Act 1981, and rules made thereafter, vide Notification No.13/29/81-RD, dated 19/3/1982 and Notification No.13/29/81-RD, dated 20/8/1986. He is appointed by the Government and his action in the managing Committee's meeting is defined in the Art. 54 of the said Code. His special duties are specified in the Art. 88 of the said Code of Communidades.

The affairs of the Communidades are under the overall control and supervision of the Office called Administrator Office of Communidade under the control of Administration of Communidades, a Grade 'B' office which has to act according to the provisions of the Art. 125 of the said Code. The matters which fall beyond the powers of the Administrators of Communidades are submitted to the Government through the proper channel, vide Art. 153 of the said Code. Also some matters are referred to the Administrative Tribunal for approval, vide Art. 154 of the said Code. Most of the Communidades lands have been surveyed (cadastrados) during the Portuguese Regime and the respective records and plans were duly prepared, with the specification of the purposes for which the land should be utilised.

In pursuance of the provisions of the said Code of Communidades, the lands under paddy cultivation, coconut trees, arecanut trees, cashew nut trees and other fruit bearing trees, and fishing rights of ponds, lakes and sluice-gates were being leased by public auction for the respective periods, vide articles 257 and 291 of the said Code.

As regards to the uncultivated lands earmarked either for construction or cultivation, the same are being leased on "aforamento" basis, in the manner as provided in the Art. 324 and following of the said Code and fulfilling the Government instructions issued from time to time.

Whenever the matter of granting of uncultivated lands of the Communidades applied for permanent lease either for construction of cultivation, is entertained, the same is to be referred to the General Body of the respective Communidade for decision vide Art.324. In addition in all other matters specified in sub-para No.4-A to J of Art. 30 of the said Code, the decision of the General Body of the Communidade is essential.

(ii) Facts of the case:

The Government of Goa issued a Notification under section 4 of the Land Acquisition Act, 1894 to acquire the land for public purpose namely Land Acquisition for Industrial Estate/Nylon 6,6 Project at Keri Vaghurme, Savoi Verem & Khandepar Village of Ponda Taluka.

Subsequent Notification under section 6 was issued on 8th March, 1990. In the intravening period possession of 88.63 hectares of land belonging to the Communidade of Querim was given to the Goa, Daman and Diu Industrial Devp. Corp. on 27/3/89 by the Communidade of Querim. Initial proposal sent by GDDIDC had indicated Rs.2/- per sq. mts. in the check list submitted by them.

The Goa, Daman and Diu Industrial Devp. Corp. permitted M/s. Thapar Du Pont Ltd. to carry out Developmental activities for Nylon 6,6 Project at their own risk and costs, and informed them that "should the government of India not agree for setting up of the Project, the land will be resumed by the GDDIDC. Further M/s. T.D.L. may obtain necessary N.O.C.s from concerned authorities for Development Works". When it came to the notice of the Corporation that certain construction activities like buildings were taken up on the site by the Company in addition to the permitted development activities the clarification was asked by the Goa, Daman and Diu Industrial Development Corporation vide the letter number I.D.C./L.N.D. 65 (II)/25690 dated 24/10/1990 to the Thapar Du Pont Ltd.

M/s Thapar Du Pont Limited replied to Industrial Development Corporation vide their letter number TDL/IDC/90-91/25 dated 30/10/90 stating that "All development activities as carried out at our Project site at Village Kerim have the necessary backing of construction licences from Village Panchayat. All of these works are preparatory to start-up of construction of main plant Buildings and without these development works it will not be possible to carry out the project work effectively..............

"Construction of Training Institute at the Project site has been necessitated for imparting of skills to our employees to be recruited from Goa for construction and operational stages of the project. Without trained manpower, construction of Plant and Buildings cannot be carried out safely..........

"IDC applied for conversion certificate (NA) to the Deputy Collector Ponda. IDC was advised that a fresh application for conversion should be made by the Kerim Communidade whose ownership has been mentioned in the revenue records. President of the Kerim Communidade has since applied for conversion certificate and the matter is under consideration of the Deputy Collector Ponda."

IDC vide their letter No. IDC/LND/65(II)25782 dated 30/10/90 directed M/s Thapar Du Pont to stop forthwith the construction activities which were being carried out by them at the site at Kerim Ponda by Nylon 6,6 Project. The Thapar Du Pont Limited has conveyed its compliance on 31/10/90.

As regards the role played by Communidade in this case is also very relevant. The following persons were appointed as members of the Managing Committee of the Communidade of Kerim for the Triennium 1986-88 vide Government Gazette number series II number 6 dated 12th May, 1988.

President   : Shri. Ramchandra Srinivas Vaidya

Substitute : Shri. Durgaran Narayan Hudecar

Treasurer : Shri. Suhassa Vinayak Hudecar

Substitute : Shri. Madhukar Dattatraye Vaidya

Attorney   : Shri. Narsinva Govinda Dessai

Substitute : Shri. Uday Srinivassa Vaidya

The Administrator of the Communidade Shri F.C. Fernandes administered the oath to Shri Ramchandra Srinivas Vaidya on 11/8/88 and he was in turn supposed to give the oath to other members. There is no evidence on record that such oath was given since there are no such entries in the relevant books of records. It is also noticed by the Committee that Shri Uday Srinivassa Vaidya who has been appointed as substitute Attorney is a brother of Shri Ramchandra Srinivas Vaidya (the President appointed by the Government of the said Communidades) in contravention of art. 53 (2) of the Code of Communidades.

On 24/10/88 at 4.30 P.M. a meeting was held at the residence of Ex-Chief Minister (Shri Pratapsingh R. Rane), where the concerned high Government officers and the Managing Director of the Industrial Development Corporation and office bearers of the new Committee under Shri Ramchandra Srinivas Vaidya, including Shri Uday S. Vaidya Administrator of Communidades and Escrivao, Shri Borkar were present. In the meeting, Hon. Ex-Chief Minister explained to the members that Government wanted to acquire the land of Communidade of Kerim pending formalities of acquisition and as such the Communidade of Kerim should issue necessary N.O.C to start the work by Nylon 6,6 factory immediately.

Sequel to the above meeting a copy of the resolution passed by the Managing Committee under Shri Ramchandra Srinivas Vaidya on 28/10/1988 was forwarded to the Administrator of Tiswadi by the Escrivao, Shri Borkar informing that there is no objection on its part to issue necessary N.O.C. to the Managing Director of I.D.C. in order to start the work in the land of this Communidade by Nylon 6,6 factory pending formalities of land acquisition. However the Escrivao Shri Borkar said that he sent this Communication to the Administrator under duress as desired by the Administrator of Communidades. The Administrator has denied the statement of Shri Borkar. (The matter is under investigation of the disciplinary authority and the Committee does not want to comment on the same.) On 12/8/89 Shri Ramchandra Srinivas Vaidya wrote a letter to Escrivao of Kerim Communidades that even though he has taken the oath of office of the President the instruments of handing and taking over of old Managing Committee has not been completed and he desired to fix the date to complete the instruments within 8 days. It appears that this was never done. As the records available to the Committee show that the new Committee appointed by the Government under Shri Ramchandra Srinivas Vaidya as the President handed over the 88.63 hectares of land belonging to Kerim Communidade to the Goa, Daman and Diu Industrial Development Corporation on 27th March, 1989 by means of an agreement.

The Committee during its examination of witnesses was informed and also a document was presented to indicate that the notice was published in the Gazette series III, No.39 dated 28/12/89 where an extra-ordinary meeting was convened at Ponda at the office of the Administrator of Communidade on 3rd Sunday after publication of the notice. As per the said document it appears that a meeting took place on 14th January, 1990 at 10.30 a.m. of the old Committee under the Presidentship of Shri Madhukar Dattatraya Vaidya. As per document submitted, 29 components were present during this meeting besides old Managing Committee members. The then clerk in charge of the Communidades, Shri Laxman Desai informed that "the key of the building of the Communidades and the relevant books were with the Administrator. Therefore the meeting was held in the verandah of the Communidade building and without relevant books. During this meeting the President explained that the land of Kerim Communidade had been handed over by the new Committee without the backing of the proper resolution of the general body of Communidade of Kerim and hence it is illegal. The resolution was passed during that meeting empowering the attorney of the Communidade to take necessary steps for the purpose of declaring null and void the agreement which was signed between Shri Ramchandra S. Vaidya and others allegedly representing Communidade of Kerim on one side and representatives of Industrial Development Corporation on the other, on 27th March, 1989." This resolution was also not recorded in the relevant books of records, since the books were taken away by the Administrator of Communidade on 12.1.1990, just before two days of the meeting, of which the notification was published in the Gazette dated 28/12/90 cited above.

Conclusions:

1. The Committee concludes that since the land in question is under acquisition by the Government it is irregular on the part of the Communidade to hand over the possession of land without the payment of compensation for the same.

Secondly, the notifications under sections 4 and 6 were issued by the Revenue Department under Land Acquisition Act 1894 which mentions that the land is needed for public purpose viz. "Land Acquisition for Industrial Estate/Nylon 6,.6 Project at Keri Vaghurme, Savoi Verem & Khandepar Village of Ponda Taluka". It is, however not understood as to how the Government can acquire land for Nylon 6,6 Project which is almost a private Company because the E.D.C. and public participation has been reduced to almost 20%. The Committee has commented in detail on this issue in the relevant chapters to follow in the report.

2. The acquiring Department i.e. G.D.D.I.D.C. has indicated the rate Rs.2/- per sq. mts. for the land in question in the check list submitted to the Government, but the Committee has a document which shows that sale price in the surrounding areas is around Rs.37/- per sq. mts. Since the Land Acquisition Officer has not since fixed price, and has not issued award so far, the Committee reserves its comments on the same.

3. The Committee has also noticed that there has not been regular handing and taking over of the charge by the new Managing Committee of Communidade from the previous Managing Committee and therefore the transaction of the new Managing Committee appears to be irregular to that extent. It is felt that the Administrator of the Communidade should have settled this issue by using his good offices which could have avoided confusion in the matter.

4. The Administrator has brought to the notice of the Committee that he has submitted his Report to the Government on 8th May, 1990, wherein he has mentioned that the Communidade of Kerim has been ceased to exist/function for the reasons:- that the deficit of the Communidade was distributed amongst the lease holders (Foreiros) thereby relieving from the responsibility of the Gauncars, which is contrary to the Code; that there is no initial primary register of Gauncars;

that the annual registration of joneiros and matriculation of surviving joneiros as provided in Art. 182 and 193 of the Code has not taken place for many years or perhaps never, as no such records are found. Therefore in his opinion the land should be reverted to the Government. Government has not communicated its decision to the Administrator so far. However, the Committee during its examination of witnesses has noted that some of them are Gauncars like, Dr. Deudatta Kerkar, Dr. Sharad Vaidya and Shri Suhas Hudekar, as declared by themselves as Gauncars of Kerim Communidade. The Committee was surprised to note that if the Communidade did not exist, as to how the Managing Committee was Constituted by the Government.

5. There has been considerable delay on the part of the Government to issue the notification to nominate the Committee of Kerim Communidade. In fact the Managing Committee of the Communidade of Kerim for the Triennium 1986-88 has been constituted only on 12th May, 1988. Therefore the previous Managing Committee remains in office till then. Since there is no record to show that the installation of new Committee has been done, it appears that this Committee is not legally substituted as required under Article 52 (1) of Code of Communidade.

6. Normally, for any important decisions, general body meeting of the Gauncars is required to be called. But however in the absence of necessary records to show the existence of the Gauncars the Constitution of the General Body becomes confirming and doubtful.

To sum up:

1) The Construction of the buildings carried out by M/s. Thapar Du Pont Limited has been without permission from the G.D.D.I.D.C. and without having any title to the land.

Secondly, necessary formalities of conversion Certificate (NA) from the concerned authorities has not been obtained prior to the starting of the constructions.

2) The possession of the land has been handed over to TDL without any payment of compensation and without following procedural formalities as per code of Communidades.

PART B

ABBREVIATIONS

A.A	:-	Adipic Acid
BILT	:-	Ballarpur Industries Limited
C.M	:-	Chief Minister
C.P	:-	Continuous Polymerization
CTP	:-	Chief Town Planner
EDC	:-	Economic Development Corporation
EIA	:-	Environmental Impact Assessment
EIS	:-	Environmental Impact Statement
EMP	:-	Environmental Management Plan
ETP	:-	Effluent Treatment Plant
GDDIDC	:-	Goa Daman & Diu Industrial Development Corporation (now IDC)
GOI	:-	Government of India
GSPCB	:-	Goa State Pollution Control Board
HMD	:-	Hexamethylene-Diamine
IDC	:-	(Same as GDDIDC)
LOI	:-	Letter of Intent
NGO	:-	Non-Government Organisation
NIO	:-	National Institute of Oceanography
NOC	:-	No Objection Certificate
NCAER	:-	National Council of Applied Economic Research
PHE	:-	Public Health Engineering
SIA	:-	Secretariat of Industrial Approvals
SSI	:-	Small Scale Industries
TCP	:-	Town & Country Planning Department
TDL	:-	Thapar Du Pont Ltd.
TDSL	:-	Thapar Du Pont Spandex Ltd.
TPA	:-	Tonnes Per Annum
USEPA	:-	United States Environmental Protection Agency

(Note:- Kerim/Querim. Place name denotes the same village in Ponda - Taluka)

B.1   SCOPE OF THE REPORT AND METHODOLOGY ADOPTED.

The *frame of reference* for the purpose of this study report was mainly to look into the Environmental Implications of the proposed Nylon 6,6 project, including its probable socioeconomic impacts. Allied considerations such as the events leading to the proposal to establish the Nylon 6,6 project in its present location, role of the concerned Government authorities and the intentions of the project promoters, also merited due attention to set the necessary preamble to the main investigation.

Methodology Adopted (See part D also)

(I)   Scrutiny of the following 'literature/documents'.

(1)   All the available official documents and correspondence pertaining to the project. (See E)

(2)   Special 'reports/studies' concerning the State as a whole prepared at the instance of the local and Central Govts.

(3)   'Circular/Guidelines' issued by the Ministry of Environment & Forests and Ministry of Industries, Govt. of India

(4)   Scientific journals, periodicals and independent research reports, relevant to the issue of Nylon 6,6 project.

(5)   Relevant non-official 'reports/articles' such as:-

(i) Press 'reports/articles'

(ii) Reports published by national as well as international Non-Govt. Organisations including those devoted to the field of environmental safety.

(6) 'Maps/plans/layouts' provided by the Nylon 6,6 project promoters and concerned Govt. departments.

(II)   Site Visits.

(III) Meetings, discussions and written clarifications sought with the 'heads/representatives' of the following 'organisations/ institutions/departments:-

(i)   Thapar Du Pont Ltd. (E.23, E.28, E.36, E.43-E47 etc.)

(ii)   E. I. Du Pont de Nemours Ltd.

(iii)   BILT

(iv)   Officers of the Chief Secretary, Secretary (Industries) and Secretary (Revenue). (D-5.2, D.5.3, D.5.4)

(v)   Goa State Pollution Control Board.

(vi)   Deptt. of Industries, Govt. of Goa.

(vii) Town & Country Planning Deptt., Govt. of Goa.

(viii) Public Works Deptt.

(ix)   (PHE Division) Govt. of Goa.

(x)   Office of the Labour Commissioner.

(xi)   Deptt. of Irrigation, Govt. of Goa.

(xii) Economic Development Corp. of Goa.

(xiii) Goa Industrial Development Corp.

(xiv) Goa University. (D.5.1.) (E.48)

(xv) National Institute of Oceanography (D.5.1, E.48)

(xvi) Communidade of Kerim.

(xviii) Village Panchayats of Kerim, & Vagurmem.

(IV) Interviews with the general public likely to be affected 'directly/indirectly' due to the proposed Nylon 6,6 project at Kerim.

(V) Synopsis of the responses received from the Members of Public & NGO's complied by the Legislature Department, Govt. of Goa.

B.2   THE BACKGROUND OF TDL'S (THAPAR DU PONT LTD.'S) NYLON 6,6 PROJECT.

B.2.1 The issues involved.

The issues under scrutiny in this report are concerned with the developments after the EDC of Goa applied and obtained a letter of intent for the manufacture of Nylon 6,6 Filament/Industrial Tyre Cord Yarn. The letter of intent led to the formation of a Joint Sector Company, Thapar Du Pont Ltd. (TDL) on the understanding that EDC will get the letter of intent transferred in the TDL's name. E.I. Du Pont de Nemours and Company of U.S.A. on their part signed an agreement of financial and technical collaboration with TDL, for conditional transfer of the Nylon 6,6 tyre cord and fabric manufacturing technology. Subsequently, BILT and EDC of Goa chose the present site at Kerim Ponda, for locating this industry.

Thereafter, starting from the year 1988, events such as the handing over of 88.63 hectares of land at the site through the GDDIDC conversion of land-use, issue of the NOC from the State Pollution Control Board etc. were completed at an unusually and surprisingly fast pace. The TDL promptly went ahead with the developmental works such as digging of tube-wells, levelling of ground, cutting rock faces, constructing various buildings, laying down roads etc. causing concern among the residents of the surrounding area in particular and eco-conscious citizens and environmentalists in general.

These developments brought into focus the possibilities of improprieties on several counts such as:-

(i)   The processes of site selection, land-use conversion and transfer of land.

(ii)   Role of various 'government departments/officials' in granting various 'licences/facilities'.

(iii)   Roles of EDC, GDDIDC, Panchayats, Communidades in site location and land acquisition.

(iv)   Adhoc manifestations of vital issues such as our industrial and economic policies.

(v)   Nature of Nylon 6,6 manufacturing process.

(vi)   Adequacy of effluent treatment 'Plans/processes'.

(vii)   "Backdoor" entry of multinationals.

(viii) Over enthusiasm of authorities at the top level.

These issues have a vital bearing on Goa's economic, industrial and eco-conservation policies for the future. The fallouts of the above relate to the menace of awesome manipulative capabilities of giant business establishments/multinationals and the influencing power of industrial lobbies. Hardcore techno-economic calculation showing scant regard to socio-cultural and ecological repercussions seems to be the 'modus-operandi' of the present project-promoters.

The background of TDL's Nylon 6,6 project therefore, warrants a close and critical analysis.

B.2.2 The Industrial 'backwardness' of Goa.

In its application for the letter of intent dated 19-11-83 (in Annexure 'D'), the EDC identifies 'industrial backwardness' of Goa as one of the factors favoring the establishment of Nylon 6,6 project in the State giving an impression that industries such as Nylon 6,6 manufacturing are indeed indispensable for Goa's industrial development. (E.1)

However, this view is not shared by experts. The industrial backwardness of Goa was a reality in 1970s. The Government of India, as a part of the national policy to correct 'regional imbalances' identified certain areas in the country as industrially backward areas. The criteria were based on parameters such as per capita consumption of electricity, number of industrial workers per lakh of population, contribution of the industrial sector to State income etc. Through the above criteria the entire territory of Goa, Daman & Diu with the exclusion of the area covered by municipal limits of Panaji was declared as an industrially backward area. Consequently, due to concessions and incentives, offered to industrialists the State had a phenomenal industrial growth from 1973. The number of small scale units went up from 702 in 1973 to 3527 in 1987, employing around 26,000 persons. As per 1981 census, the workers in industry and tertiary sector constituted 71.42% of all economically active main workers in the State. (F.4)

The report of the Centre for Policy Research, New Delhi, prepared at the request of the Goa Government confirms the above as quoted below:

"It is in manufacturing that a remarkable change has taken place in Goa. As late as 1971, Goa was identified as an industrially backward area. By 1981, contribution from the manufacturing sector to SDP, percentage-wise, increased four times that of 1960 (from 7.3% to 28.4%). In these 21 years, at constant prices, manufacturing activity increased 16.5 times with an annual growth rate of 14.3%. Even during 1971-81, the growth rate of manufacturing sector (large and small industries) was fairly high (16.39%). Between 1975-76 and 1980-81, the growth rate of manufacturing sector was 13.85%." (P.11)

This excerpt clearly indicates the folly of classifying Goa as industrially backward in comparative terms (F.4).

It has to be noted that this growth, to a large extent, has occurred due to the establishment of labour intensive small scale units. EDC's joint ventures with TELCO, Hindustan Antibiotics Ltd., and its setting up of subsidiary units for the manufacture of auto-components, ceiling fans, wrist-watches, television sets, telecommunication equipments, etc. appeared in tune with the resource-related, infrastructural and ecological realities of Goa, until the decision to pursue the Nylon 6,6 project was undertaken. This major policy-shift was justified under the label of 'industrial backwardness', notwithstanding several other policy options in tune with EDC's own 'expertise/limitations'.

EDC's interpretation and perception of Goa's industrial backwardness, coincides with the ambitious plans of multinationals such as Du Pont for expansion into the growing Asia-Pacific Sector.

B.2.3 EDC's 'historic' decision about Nylon 6,6 and its implications.

Given EDC's considered perception of Goa's 'industrial backwardness' its decision to apply for a letter of intent for manufacturing Nylon 6,6 filament/industrial tyre cord yarn was truly historic.

With this decision, EDC had completely changed the broad technology outlook conceived over the years by 'agencies/bodies' such as NCAER, the Goa State Planning Board, etc. EDC believes that 'there is a substantial scope for manufacturing Nylon 6,6 Tyre Cord/Industrial Yarn'. Why only Nylon 6,6 tyre cord/industrial yarn? There could be a substantial scope for manufacturing hundreds of other items-in small, medium and large scale sectors.

Did EDC arrive at this decision i.e. Nylon 6,6 project, on its own 'assessment/shortlisting/market survey'?

Relevant documents that were scrutinized by us do not support the above. On the contrary they clearly show that M/s. Ballarpur Industries Ltd. (BILT) of the Thapar group had been active before 1983 and the EDC despite knowing its own resource limitations and constraints signed a memorandum of understanding with BILT. This was the first significant step before launching TDL in 1987.

The implications of this memorandum of understanding are far reaching. With one application, EDC ventured into changing the course of industrial development in the State, which was clearly inclined to favour small-scale, non-polluting and labour intensive industries after the bitter experience of Zuari Agro Chemicals Factory. It acted as a policy-making body without any public involvement/legislative control. It could set for itself any limits in terms of the magnitude of the project and complexity of its technology. It could conveniently ignore the draft Regional Plan and the recommendations and guidelines of Task-Force on Eco-Development Plan for Goa which were circulated before 1983.

The EDC relied on and believed in, whatever the BILT supplied as data related to Nylon 6,6 process and project. It did not consider the risks involved as there were no options to cross-check/examine the data supplied by BILT concerning the Nylon 6,6 technology, being a monopoly technology unlike 'Chassis-building' and 'antibiotics packaging'.

Before rushing up the applications for securing the letter of intent for Nylon 6,6 manufacture, EDC as a "full State owned company promoted by the Government of Goa, Daman and Diu to catalyse industrial development," should have been made watchful and responsible, considering the nature, magnitude and likely impact of the Nylon 6,6 technology.

However, there seems to be powerful lobbies bent upon hiding the real nature of the project from public scrutiny since 1983. This view is further strengthened by subsequent developments.

B.2.4 The application for the Letter of Intent and the BILT CHEMTEX nexus.

In its application for securing the letter of intent dtd. 19.11.1983, in annexure-D, EDC claims that it "carried out extensive negotiations with various entrepreneurs for this project." "Amongst the parties that EDC contacted for the association in the assisted sector were M/s BILT, a Thapar group enterprise. After prolonged negotiations with them, the group offered themselves as associates in the assisted sector". No explanation was forthcoming from EDC as to who were the "various entrepreneurs" with whom it carried out "extensive negotiations." The "prolonged negotiations" with M/s. BILT must have begun in 1979, although we have not perused records of that period, i.e. 1979-1983.

M/s. Chemtex Inc., New York were brought into the picture by BILT as technical and engineering collaborators. The memorandum of understanding between the BILT and Chemtex Fibres Inc., New York, clearly establishes the fact that Du Pont would not have given the green-signal to provide the know-how through Chemtex Inc. if they were not confident of locating the project in Goa, which has an ideal facility, namely the Mormugao Harbour, for their expansion plans in the South-Eastern sector of Asia.

The BILT-CHEMTEX memorandum of understanding anticipated plant start-up in the "4th quarter of 1985", that is, within barely two years of EDC's application for the Letter of Intent. How this `plant start-up' schedule was decided is still a mystery because EDC received the letter of intent for manufacture of 6000 TPA Nylon 6,6 Industrial Yarn/Tyre cord as late as 28-2-1985. (E.1).

B.2.5 The changing dimensions of the project.

Scrutiny of the correspondence of EDC, BILT and TDL reveals the changing dimensions of the Nylon 6,6 project. The application for the issue of letter of intent specifically mentions the manufacture of Nylon 6,6 filament/Industrial tyre cord yarn, falling under scheduled industry No. 19(7). However, the letter of intent No.171 (85) dated 28-2-1985 is issued for the manufacture of Nylon 6,6 or Nylon 6 Industrial Yarn/Tyre Cord. (E.2)

The EDC was given the choice of seeking technology for Nylon 6,6 manufacture, but it was already biased in favour of Nylon 6,6. The BILT through CHEMTEX Fibres Inc. had sought Du Pont's technology, but the letter of intent showed a low production capacity for the plant. The Nylon tyre fabric manufacture proposal became part of the project through another letter of intent in EDC's name -No.LI-1052-(1985) dtd. 30-9-1985. (E.3)

The capacity of the plant was enhanced from 6000 TPA to 14,000 TPA for Nylon 6,6 Cord and from 5,100 TPA to 11,900 TPA for Nylon tyre fabric, vide amended letters of intent dated 3-2-1986 and 27-6-1986, respectively. Why this capacity was not envisaged at the first stage of application by BILT-CHEMTEX understanding, is a matter for speculation but it shows that even at this stage EDC was not aware of dilution of its share. By more than doubling the licensed capacity, BILT and Du Pont ensured that EDC would not exercise any control over their operations due to its limited equity participation. (E.6)

Even on technical grounds there seems to be a major discrepancy in the application for the letter of intent dtd. 19.11.1983 and subsequent plans and reports of BILT and TDL.

Form I.L. clause 9 provides details of Raw materials; 'Imported/indigenous', wherein under the heading "Imported", it is mentioned that 7740 metric tonnes of AH Salt (Dry Nylon Salt) costing Rs. 968.00 lakhs will be imported besides 66 tonnes of finish oil/additives etc. costing Rs.12.00 lakhs. Annexure 'A' says that the process is based on Nylon 6,6 Salt (Hexamethylene-dia-ammonium adipate) and that it is received at the plant as a dry powder and is dissolved in hot water in a jacketed mix tank equipped with an agitator. However, the AH Salt does not figure as imported raw material in other documents where the ingredients are shown separately as "Adipic acid" and "Hexamethylenediamine". (E.1)

In the same application, it was estimated that Rs. 30 lakhs will be required for the land as fixed assets, Rs.500 lakhs for buildings, Rs.21 crores for indigenous machinery and Rs.18 crores for imported machinery. It was also claimed that adequate water supply was available and the same was to be drawn from public source. There was no plan for installing own power generating station. There was no proposal to set up any 'SSI/ancillary' units in the project. The process was claimed to be non-polluting. The material movement was conceived to be 'mainly' by road. As far as the imported technology was concerned, EDC claimed that "it is highly advanced and sophisticated and the imported equipment will have inbuilt provision to adequately treat the effluents before discharge........".

EDC was indeed hopeful that state-of-art effluent treatment plant will also be a part of the technology transfer package for Nylon 6,6 manufacture.

However, the picture that we get from the application is totally different from the subsequent developments that are apparent as we analyse the changing and expanding dimensions of the project.

B.2.6 The EDC-BILT agreement (E.5)

The EDC entered into an agreement with BILT on 12-12-86 to promote a Joint Stock Company with Limited Liability in Goa, for production of Nylon 6,6, 'Industrial Yarn/Tyre Cord' and fabrics. In the agreement "it is recognised that manufacture of the products entails technology of a high order which is not available indigenously and will have to be imported..........".

The agreement does not reflect EDC's concern about the magnitude of the project vis-a-vis the safeguards to project the interests of the public by way of major equity participation. On the contrary, it provided a backdoor entry for Du Pont as an equity participant. The EDC Board had cleared the formal agreement promptly on 5th November, 1986 before studying its overall implications. (E.11)

B.2.7 The site selection process.

The site selection process had begun in 1979-80 on the initiative of BILT. We have reasons to believe that the selection of the most suitable site must have been done before applying for the letter of intent. Although EDC submitted that the process began in 1984, no dates are available for the site selection survey carried out by the officials of EDC, Udyog Vikas and BILT's team (D.2.2, (E.28)

The site selection process was based on techno-economic considerations and the survey team indiscriminately visited industrial and non-industrial areas. The land requirement was identified as 500 acres, and EDC or Udyog Vikas did not show any interest in independently working out a realistic estimate of the land required for the project before selection of the site. It seems that they believed the estimates given by BILT team about the land requirements, in toto: Dust-free atmosphere was used as one of the site selection criteria. However, the same sensitivity was not shown about the ecological and hydrological aspects of the surveyed sites.

The EDC report gives an assessment of nine locations, but the BILT report excludes Navelim Cudanem in Bicholim taluka and Cuncolim in Salcette Taluka. As per EDC's assessment the Navelim-Cudanem area was not considered suitable on account of dust problem and 'relatively more distance from the port'. However, the 'relative distance from the port' does not seem to be a factor in the BILT report on locations surveyed. (E.28)

BILT's comments on Colvale-Bardez site are revealing. The Colvale site was found to be a suitable location, but the report says ......"as per the Town & Country Planning Department, this site does not fall into declared industrial area. There may be difficulties in revising their plans so as to convert this area into industrial area. As such, a revision would involve completion of time consuming formalities."

These comments assume importance in the light of the objections raised by the then Chief Town Planner in his letter (E.4) dated 20-11-1985 regarding Kerim Ponda location. BILT was not interested in Colvale site because it anticipated "difficulties" in converting the non-industrial area into "industrial area" but while selecting the Kerim-Site (reserved for orchard in the Regional Plan) as 'the most ideal site', it shows no such concern and fails to solicit Town & Country Planing Department's view before selecting it.

The BILT report says that the land at Kerim site is "barren with practically no vegetation, few trees and no inhabitants ...." a questionable statement. "The same report says that the total area available is 250 acres which is adequate to accommodate the plant and housing colony". While the EDC was looking for 500 acres of land for the project right from the beginning of the site survey, the BILT team was satisfied with 250 acres available at Kerim-site: EDC did not investigate why the land requirement was reduced at the moment. Obviously, it had not worked out the land utilization plan in consultation with BILT before proceeding with the site selection process.

B.2.8 EIA studies overlooked.

Before supporting the BILT's assessment of Kerim site as 'most ideal', the EDC did not contemplate environmental impact assessment studies despite knowing the nature of the technology and the uniqueness of Kerim site. As a State owned body, EDC should have given topmost priority to EIA studies in public interest, but it had no such plan, neither did it put EIA studies as conditional pre-requisite in the agreement signed with BILT.

B.2.9 The Kerim site conversion story.

The lobbying for the acquisition of Kerim site had begun in 1985 much before finalisation of a formal agreement between EDC and BILT. The Chief Town Planner, Shri. J.A. D'Souza, disagreed with the proposition of BILT regarding the Kerim site, approved by the high powered co-ordination Committee, in its meeting on 15-11-1985. He suggested that 'any new industry could easily be accommodated in any one of the existing or proposed industrial estates/areas in Ponda Taluka'. He further opposed releasing new areas in Ponda Taluka for industrial development. (E.4)

His disagreement was based on scientifically sound planning point of view as well as from ecological point of view. The ecological dimensions which he brought to the notice of the Joint Director, Directorate of Industries & Mines are quoted as under:

"Moreover, the location of the industry on the Kerim plateau at a height of more than 150 mts. will have some serious ecological consequences of the surrounding orchard lands. The area is rich in the ground water resources and a few sweet water channels, which should not be disturbed by any organised industrial development on the plateau. Besides the exploitation of the sweet water springs will also adversely affect the thriving arecanut plantations at the lower slopes". (E.4)

Despite these valid objections, the high-powered co-ordination Committee in its meeting in the Chief Secretary's chamber on 23rd June, 1987 directed the CTP to move the file 'within a week' for necessary amendment empowering the State Government to alter the land-use in 'public interest'. It was pointed out by CTP in the said meeting that *Kerim area was marked as orchard in the Regional Plan*. (E.13)

However, notification for conversion of land-use was moved only in 1988, on the initiative of the then Chief Minister Mr. Pratapsingh Rane, as seen from the minutes of the meeting that he convened on 22nd June, 1988 (E.19).

B.2.10. New Policy sidelined.

A major policy announcement was made by the Govt. of India on 17-2-87 by identifying the entire territory of Goa, Daman & Diu as protected district and non-polluting industry district (Letter No.10/157/85-LP). (D.5.4.)

There should have been an immediate review of the Nylon 6,6 project at this stage in the light of this policy. But this was never brought on the agenda of the high-powered co-ordination Committee's meetings held after the 17.2.87 letter.

B.2.11 BILT's request for land.

Interestingly, in his letter addressed to the then Chief Secretary of Govt. of Goa, Daman & Diu, Mr. V.K. Malik, General Manager (Fibre Division) BILT, sought 'guidance' and 'help' in land acquisition. He requested the Government to organise the land acquisition. The cost of the land was sought to be paid for the project in installments with no interest, in effect requesting that the land be allotted to the project on a perpetual lease basis (BILT letter, 9.3.1987). (E.11)

At this stage, there was no mention of the cost or size of the land. But Mr. Malik expected the Government authorities to build the approach road from main highway upto the site without any cost to the project. And he assumed that "*the State Govt. or the local authorities will not put any form of cess on drawing water either from tubewells or river or from any other source at any stage.*" (E.11)

The then C.S. sought the comments of the Revenue Secretary, Secretary Industries, Development Commissioner and Finance Secretary by 30.3.89, as could be seen from the remarks on the said letter.

B.2.12 Objections of the Director of Industries, Govt. of Goa.

We have referred to the letter of Mr. Denghnuna, the then Director of Industries & Mines, dated 2.4.1987, wherein he categorically wrote to the secretary, Industries that ...... "Before giving final approval on the site location for this project, it may be worthwhile examining it from the point of view of ecology, pollution and loss of huge area of 20 lakh sq. mts...." Referring to CTP's comments mentioned earlier, Mr. Denghnuna further remarked..... "We already have in this territory quite a large area which is occupied by highly polluting industries. Should we bring in within the grip of pollution still larger areas by encouraging this industry is a matter for greater study particularly, in the light of the comments of the Chief Town Planner, who has not agreed to support the location of the project at Kerim...." (E.12)

Contrary to Mr. V.K. Malik's expectations about land acquisition, Mr. Denghnuna cited EDC's clear opinion that "Govt. should not acquire the land and the acquisition should be left to M/s. BILT only." Mr. Denghnuna also found that the land asked for by M/s. BILT was unreasonably on the higher side. About M/s. BILT's claims that the Nylon 6,6 industry is of non-polluting nature, Mr. Denghnuna remarked that `*This industry has been categorised by the Govt. of India as an industry of a highly polluting nature'*.

B.2.13 Land-use conversion - Modification of the Regional Plan.

Despite the CTP's objections, M/s. BILT and EDC remained firm on Querim-site for the Nylon 6,6 project. The new Central Policy of 'protected district' (17-2-87) had no effect on their intentions. The suggestions of TCP department about shifting the industry to Xeldem/Xelvona had no effect on the promoters. The only 'hurdle' about Querim site seemed to be its categorisation as 'orchard land' in the Regional Plan.

Notwithstanding the procedural 'hurdles' in possession of the Kerim site, M/s. BILT were consistently demanding extra land for 'future expansion'. They ascertained that "*the project was cleared for being set up at the chosen site at Querim in Ponda Taluka,*" (P.4 minutes of high-powered Co-ordination Committee, 23.6.1987), before taking the next important step, i.e. the incorporation of Thapar Du Pont Limited (TDL). TDL was incorporated on 8.7.1987 under Reg. No.760 of 1987. (E.23)

Meanwhile, in persuance of the discussion in the high powered Co-ordination Committee's meeting on 23/6/1987, the Under Secretary, Industries and Labour addressed a letter to the CTP, on 6.7.87, citing BILT representative, Shri Bakshi's argument that due to hike in the licensed capacity the "*land requirement had gone up substantially*". The CTP was requested to study the `revised' project report with reference to the permissible coverage and FAR and the appropriate land requirement for the purpose was to be indicated. (E.14)

It appears that in principle, the Govt. had accepted M/s. BILT's argument for excess land. However, M/s. BILT used two arguments namely, of 'excess land for increased licensed capacity' as well as "land required for future expansion", notwithstanding serious reservations of the members of the high powered Co-ordination Committee.

TDL received a certificate for commencement of business on 12.8.87 and within a month or so, on 8.9.87 EDC wrote to the Govt. of India requesting the transfer of respective letters of intent with amendments to TDL. Apparently, the process of land use conversion at Querim-site was accelerated following a meeting specially called at the instance of the former Chief Minister, Shri. P.R.Rane. This meeting held on 22.6.1988 was attended by a majority of members of the highpowered Co-ordination Committee alongwith a representative of BILT. The minutes of the meeting indicate that the CTP was asked to work out the land requirement and expedite the procedure for land-use conversion through the appropriate authorities 'immediately'. In the same meeting, the former CM desired that the entire land admeasuring 500 acres may be acquired by the GDDIDC. That the process of changing the notified Regional Plan of the State in order to grant land-use conversion to the site at Kerim gathered pace at the initiative of the former CM, was further confirmed in the meeting held by the House Committee with the representatives of EDC, GDDIDC and Town & Country Planning Department (E.48)

The High-powered Co-ordination Committee in its meeting held on 5.9.88, only confirmed the necessity of the change in land-use of the Kerim site, as decided in the above mentioned meeting held by the former CM on 22.6.88. As per the minutes of the high-powered Co-ordination Committee meeting it was decided to work out a realistic area requirement of the TDL project and go ahead with land acquisition procedure at Querim, through the IDC.

B.2.14 The role of GDDIDC

As a result of a subsequent meeting called by the Secretary (Industries), the IDC proposed to acquire an area of 2584425.00 sq.mts. of land for "Industrial estate/Nylon 6,6" project at Kerim, Vaghurme, Savoi-Verem and Khandepar villages of Ponda Taluka. In the meantime, the Managing Committee of the Communidade of Querim-Ponda was persuaded to grant NOC to the IDC for starting developmental work. The decision to grant NOC appears to have been taken at the former Chief Minister's initiative at his residence on 24.10.88. However, the GDDIDC's letter to the Secretary, Industries (NO.IDC/LND/65/(III)/12431 dtd. 16th Jan.'89) from Dr. P. Deshpande, CEO gives a different date i.e. 24.8.88. Dr. Deshpande writes that `...... a meeting was held at the residence of Hon'ble Chief Minister on 24.8.88 and it was decided to obtain NOC from the Communidade for allowing to go ahead with the developmental work at Nylon 6,6 project, pending the land acquisition proceedings......' (E.25, E.29).

On 27.3.1989, the Communidade of Kerim-Ponda gave the possession of 88.63 hectares of land to GDDIDC pending the land acquisition proceedings. The land belonged to the Survey

No.102, 103/1, 104 part, 139, 140, 143 and 152. GDDIDC's letter of 16.1.89 mentioned that.......
"The Govt. has estimated the requirement of the land for this Nylon 6,6 project as 60 hectares
including land for further expansion............M/s. TDL has indicated the requirement of their land
as 123 hectares bearing the Survey Nos. 102, 103/1, 104, 139, 140, 143 and 152 of Querim Village
and Survey Nos.46, 47 and 48 of Khandepar village. This matter has already been discussed with
the Hon'ble Chief Minister on 13.1.89 and also in the Board meeting of GDDIDC held today, i.e.
13.1.1989....." On 9.2.1989, the Under Secretary (Industries) informed GDDIDC about the
Revenue Department's non-objection for taking the possession of land. (E.30)

The minutes of the 141st meeting of the IDC held on 3rd March 1989, indicate that *former
Chief Minister Shri. Pratapsingh Rane and former Minister for Industries, Shri Shaikh Hassan
Haroon 'graced' it*. Allotment of land at Kerim-Ponda for Nylon 6,6 project was the last item on
the agenda. It was in this (E.32) meeting that the decision *to allot about 130 ha. of* land belonging
to Kerim and Khandepar Communidade *to 'Nylon 6,6' project as required by them was taken*.

It is interesting to note at this point that GDDIDC's letter of 16.1.89 mentioned the land
requirement for Nylon 6,6 project as 60 hectares including land for further expansion; while
M/s TDL had indicated their land requirement as 123 hectares. But the IDC decided to grant not
60 ha. (Govt.'s estimate); not 123 ha. (TDL's demand) but 130 hectares.

The approval of the Govt. to the decision taken in IDC board meeting held on 3.3.89 to hand
over the entire area of 123 hectares, (not 130 ha. as recorded in the IDC Board meeting minutes?)
instead of 60 hectares to Nylon 6,6 project on the conditions that the additional area being released
may be developed by the Company for *afforestation* purpose was communicated to GDDIDC on
9.3.89 by the Industries Deptt. The Company was asked to limit the *construction of the factory*
to the plans approved by the competent authority. (E.33)

B.2.15 Serious omissions

It is surprising that the IDC Board meeting minutes omit the discussion on release of
additional area for 'afforestation' purpose. It will be important to investigate the origin of this idea
because after almost 4 years of controversy over the 'extra land requirement', it seems that an
excuse was invented to release the additional area. The Company had proposed the extra area
requirement for 'future expansion', but it was directed to develop it after release for 'afforestation'
purpose. If that was so, what was the benefit of 'afforestation development' to TDL which would
not have permitted them the future expansion as deserved. On the other hand, nobody seems to
have thought about the afforestation schemes of the Forest Department, which undertakes such
development schemes on Communidade lands. It is pertinent to assume that the 'smokescreen'
of afforestation was raised in a haste to release additional land. On the other hand it was possible
to undertake afforestation without surrendering the area to TDL through either the Forest Deptt.
or the Village Panchayat. Ultimately, the TDL appears to be the recipient of a bonus of 73 hectares
of extra land in the name of 'afforestation' through a clever manipulation, to serve the Company's
interest. It will be interesting to record here that the BILT report submitted has not made any
provisions for landscaping or afforestation in the project cost.

The TDL was informed on the same day, (9.3.1989) by GDDIDC about the Govt.'s approval
to hand over 123 ha. land and was promised that .... "No sooner the possession of land is given
to the GDDIDC the same will be transferred to TDL...." The TDL was given green signal to go
ahead with the development work in the land possessed by the GDDIDC vide proceedings with
Querim Communidade dated 27.3.89. The GDDIDC, in its letter dated 29.3.1989 to TDL (E.34)
further communicated that the physical possession of the land would be handed over to TDL as
soon as the agreement is executed between GDDIDC, Govt. and Nylon 6,6 project.

While TDL was asked by GDDIDC to go ahead with the development work, the Industries Deptt. expected the GDDIDC to start the development work in the said land as per the letter of Industries Deptt., dtd.17.4.1989. GDDIDC had no plans to develop the said land. Its role seems to have been limited to that of a 'Transferring agency' for TDL's Nylon 6,6 project. Records available to us show that GDDIDC never took serious interest to develop the Querim site as an Industrial Estate on its own. (E.35)

The TDL sought GDDIDC's permission on 8.5.89 to proceed with the development work. TDL assured that..... "the developmental work on the site at Querim will be undertaken at their own risk. In case the Nylon 6,6 project does not materialise due to some reason, the land will be handed over back to IDC and they shall have no claims towards the amount they had spent on account of any developmental work...." This was agreed to by the IDC via their letter dtd. 10.5.1989 conveying the decision of the Govt. to permit TDL to continue with the development activities at Kerim, Ponda, Goa for Nylon 6,6 Project at their risk and costs. It was left to the TDL to obtain necessary NOC from the local authorities, Village Panchayat, Town Planning etc., for development works. (E.37)

The Kerim Panchayat in its meeting held on 18.6.89 took a decision to grant construction license to TDL and the TDL commenced its development work immediately, pending completion of land acquisition proceedings. (E.38)

Thus, from the analysis of documents inspected by this Committee, it appears that only due to the intervention of the former Chief Minister, Mr. Pratapsingh Rane, TDL got all clearances pending till June '88 within a year's time i.e. from the date of Mr. Rane's meeting on 22.6.88 to obtaining the construction license on 18.6.89. (E.19-E.38)

B.2.16 TDL's progress on other fronts

It seems that TDL preferred to wait before signing the technical and financial agreement with Du Pont on 18.9.1988. The agreement has to be seen against the background of land-use change of the Kerim site. Only after ascertaining that steps had been initiated by the Govt. to change the land-use of Kerim site, the agreement was signed and application for capital goods import approval was moved at New Delhi, on 26.9.1988.

It is to be noted that the interests of Govt. of Goa were not represented in the TDL - Du Pont agreement as EDC was not a signatory to it. This we feel was a serious lapse on the part of EDC and Govt. of Goa, because this 'autonomy' further encouraged TDL to sign another similar agreement between Thapar Du Pont Spandex Ltd., and Du Pont on 9-11-1988. Without studying the technological and ecological implications of Spandex manufacture, EDC moved an application for the grant of an industrial license for the manufacture of 850 tons/annum Spandex Fibre, on 23.2.1988. This was apparently done under pressure from M/s. BILT. Thapar Du Pont Spandex Limited was incorporated in Goa and all that EDC could do was to be a silent spectator as it had no say in foreign collaboration agreement between Thapar Du Pont Spandex Ltd., and Du Pont. The TDSL moved an application for the *issuance of a letter of intent and approval of foreign collaboration for the manufacture of 800 TPA of Spandex Fibre in the State of Goa* on 7.12.1988 (E.26)

This was definitely a part of TDL's 'future expansion' plan in Goa, i.e. to locate the Spandex-Fibre Plant at Kerim site once the letter of intent was issued either to EDC or to TDSL. As for the progress on EDC's letter of intent application, Mr. Shetye of EDC, said in the House Committee meeting on 31.10.90, that 'it was applied but it was never pursued subsequently'. He further said that '*EDC had made a reference to the company (i.e. BILT) that they can file on behalf of EDC*'. The implications of TDSL's Spandex project and the possibility it being located at Kerim-Ponda will be further discussed elsewhere.

The State Pollution Control Board issued a NOC from environmental pollution control angle to M/s. TDL on 2.2.1990. It was meant to be valid upto *30 days prior to commissioning of* the plant. We have scrutinised the presentation made by TDL to the Technical Committee of the Goa State Pollution Control Board on 25th May, 1989, and discussed various aspects related to the NOC with members of State Pollution Control Board and its technical committee on 8.10.90. Our reservations on this matter have been included in *Chapter B.8.*

B.2.17 The extensions of Letters of Intent.

The letters of intent issued to EDC were extended from time to time. The latest extension was granted on 9th July 1990, for a further period i.e. upto 30.6.1991. EDC had requested the Govt. of India on 8.7.1987 for transfer of the said letters of intent to M/s. TDL. Mr. Shetye of EDC submitted in the meeting held by the House-Committee on 31.10.90, that EDC still possesses the letter of intent and "application for transfer of the letters of intent had been lying with the Govt. of India for quite some time, pending the clearance by the special P.A.B. for this project, ..."(E.49).

It has been assumed by EDC and the Govt. of Goa that the said letters of intent will be transferred to TDL sooner or later, but no inquiries have been made about the cause of the 'delay'. It is pertinent to note that 4 extensions were granted for the letters of intent by the Govt. of India beyond the initial validity period of 12 months as stipulated in Condition 6 of the letter of intent. It categorically says that "on no account will the validity of the letter of intent be extended *beyond 12 months* from the expiry of initial validity period".

The extension granted on 10.8.1989 to EDC's letter of intent No.1052 (1985) puts the following condition:- ".... no further extension of time will be allowed and the letter of intent will automatically lapse in case you fail to obtain an industrial license in lieu of the letter of intent within the extended period. You are therefore advised to comply with all the conditions of the letter of intent within the stipulated time." (Letter from Govt. of India, Ministry of Textiles, No. to EDC, signed by S. Ahmed, Director)". The extension vide the said letter was given upto 30.3.1990 and the stipulated time was about 232 days (E.40).

From records available to us, it becomes clear that EDC failed to obtain the industrial license within the extended period. The said letter of intent should have lapsed automatically as per the condition mentioned above, but surprisingly this was not the case.

EDC made another application on 7.5.1990 to Govt. of India for extension of letter of intent No. 171 (1983) dtd. 28.2.1983 (dates quoted in Govt. of India letter dtd. 9.7.1990). In Govt. of India's correspondence with EDC regarding the issue of letter of intent, we have noticed a few errors i.e. the confusion of dates. The letter of intent No. 171 (85) dated 28.2.1985 which is referred as 171 (85) dtd. 25.2.85 in Govt. of India's letter dtd. 6.4.1988; is again referred as letter of intent No. 171 (1983) dated 28.2.1983 in another letter of Govt. of India dated 19.7.1989. This 'error' was not brought to the notice of the Govt. of India by EDC as could be seen from the letter dated 9.7.1990 mentioned earlier wherein the error is reproduced. The letter of intent held by EDC is mentioned as letter of intent No.171 (1983) dated 28th Feb. 1983 instead of letter of intent No. 171 (1985) dated 28th Feb. 1985. (See E.2 & E.42)

The commission of such "mistakes" on very important documents such as Letters of Intent for large industrial projects, should be viewed seriously and cannot be dismissed lightly as an oversight or a `clerical error'. Even if such "mistakes" are rectified at a later stage, the fact remains, that the possible technical and legal repercussions of the same were `overlooked/ slighted' by the EDC. It may be therefore pertinent to doubt the ability of the EDC to handle complex techno-industrial agreements when they could not ensure simple supervisory skill to scrutinize important correspondence.

B.2.18 TDL and the question of EDC's equity participation

The Economic Development Corporation (EDC) of the State Govt. had applied for and obtained two letters of intent: One for manufacture of 6000 tonnes per year of Nylon 6,6/Nylon 6 cord (L:I: No. 171 (85) dtd. 28.2.85), and the other for manufacture of 3000 tonnes per year of Nylon 6,6 tyre cord fabric (L:I:No. 1052 (85) dtd. 30.9.85).

When EDC applied to the Govt. of India for issue of letter of intent for the manufacture of Nylon 6,6 cord and also tyre cord fabric, it took pains to tell the Govt. of India that EDC is a fully State-owned company promoted by the Govt. of Goa and as such the above projects would be implemented in the joint sector. In both the cases, Govt. of India had indicated that the corporation should hold a minimum of 26% equity in the joint sector undertaking. In accordance with the standard conditions of the Letter of Intent, the project was proposed to be implemented with the following pattern of Share holding:

EDC of Goa	26%
Private promoter	25%
General Public	49%
Total	100%

Initially, the project was to cost Rs. 55 crores but EDC applied and obtained GOI permission to expand the annual capacity of the tyre cord plant from 6000 TPA to 14,000 TPA (Feb., 1986). After that, Govt. of India's consent was also obtained to increase the tyre cord fabric production from 3000 TPA to 12000 TPA. This has correspondingly hiked the costs of the Nylon 6,6 Project to Rs. 200 crores (if not higher).

Assuming the usual 2:1 debt: equity ratio, EDC's 26% share in equity participation works out to Rs.16 crores (Earlier at Rs. 55 crores project cost, EDC's equity participation share was around Rs. 5 crores).

It is only after it had obtained the two letters of intent and approval to increase the capacity of the plants from the Central Govt. that EDC appealed to the Central Govt., to reduce its share in equity participation on grounds that it (EDC), does not possess the required funding capacity. It pleaded that Thapar and Du Pont be permitted increased equity participation, with reduced EDC and Public participation. The new ratio worked out by EDC is as follows:

EDC of Goa	11%
Public	9%
Thapar	40%
Du Pont	40%
Total	100%

Notice the reduced share of EDC and the Public and the heightened role of the Thapar Du Pont combine.

To the question as to why EDC has sought to request its decreased role in equity participation (from 26% to 11%), EDC has replied that it did not have the required capital to invest. This answer appears to be strange for a number of reasons, mainly that it was EDC which had applied to the Central Govt. for hiking up the capacity of the project in the first place. Moreover, the new equity participation ratio proposed for this joint sector project has gone against all norms of public interest as the public shares work out to only 9% equity participation. This 9% public equity participation together with 11% EDC participation works out to a meager total of 20% equity participation. For a joint sector project of this kind, and keeping in mind the EDC's application for the Letter of Intent, the reduction of Govt. and public participation from the earlier 75% to the later 20% is a subversion of all norms of a joint sector project involving public interest and appears to have been engineered to facilitate the back door entry of private individuals to take over what was earlier proposed as a joint sector project. It is no wonder then that the new distribution of equity participation met with the disapproval of the Secretariat of Industrial Approvals (SIA), which also saw it in the above light. Perhaps the EDC knew all along that the Central Govt. may object to any significant divergence from their standard, equity participation policy. It therefore follows that the EDC applied for permission to enhance the annual plant capacity and on obtaining it, pleaded with the Central Govt. to reduce its equity participation and that of the public while at the same time pleading for an increase in the shares of Thapar and Du Pont. There is sufficient reason to believe that the EDC adopted the above methodology in full confidence that the Govt. of India could be persuaded to concede the above demand under the guise of "the inability of EDC to raise the required capital".

EDC's desire to obtain the requisite approval at all costs is reflected in one of its Board meetings (5.11.1986) where it was even suggested that until the letter of intent was converted into industrial license by the Central Govt., the EDC may show its equity participation as 26%. EDC thus seemed to go out of its way to seek Central Govt. approval for the project. Should the changed equity participation ratio be accepted, it is the Thapar Du Pont combine that stands to gain the most. With EDC and the public holding a mere 20% share (of a joint sector project), Thapar and Du Pont would walk away with a lion's share of 80% equity. Further, since the Controller of Capital Issues cannot guarantee that all 9% public shares go to the locals in Goa, Thapar Du Pont and their interests could very well come to possess a good hold of the total equity participation. At one stage EDC had even sought to get away with a token equity participation of Rs. 5 lakhs! One could expect the Thapar Du Pont caucus to virtually control the company. What has been made to appear as a joint sector project, is in reality nothing more than a private venture, shorn of all the external paraphernalia.

B.2.19 The question of land transaction value as share of EDC's equity.

The BILT had sought Goa Govt.'s help as far as land acquisition was concerned. Till June 1988, no thought had been given to the idea of equity participation by EDC in Nylon 6,6 project by taking into consideration the value of land transaction.

In the meeting convened by the former CM, Mr. Pratapsingh Rane, on 22.6.1988, the Secretary (Industries), pointed out that the equity participation by EDC in the joint venture could be through the value of the land to be procured by the IDC for the purpose of the project. This was way before the commencement of land-use change and acquisition proceedings.

In the meeting of the high-powered Co-ordination Committee held on 5.9.88, it was decided that 'the size of the land and the rate to be charged to M/s. TDL will be finalised by IDC in consultation with the Govt.' Then as per the discussions held in the Chamber of Secretary (Industries) on 22nd Sept. 1988, it was decided that 60 hectares of land including land for future expansion be allotted to the company and 20 hectares more should be retained by GDDIDC for downstream industries and SSI ancillaries. Further, it was resolved that the rest of the 500 acres can be acquired and retained by GDDIDC for future use. In the same meeting, it was also decided that land cost to be communicated later may be termed as equity contribution, and that the GDDIDC should acquire the said land.

However, GDDIDC, in its letter dtd. 16.1.89, wrote to the Secretary (Industries) that ....'It may not be possible for this Corporation to take the possession of the land and then to transfer to the Govt. since the land acquisition proceedings have not been completed and the *price of the land has not been fixed yet.*' The above letter further requested the Industries Secretary to 'kindly take possession of the land and allot it to Nylon 6,6 project as *Govt.'s equity contribution*'. In the Board meeting on 3.3.89, the Secretary (Industries) informed ....'that the Govt. has to invest directly in the share capital of the new company of 'Nylon 6,6' project in the form of land and the new company will issue the shares in the name of the Govt. in lieu of the cost of the land transferred to the new company. Further, he informed that the Govt. will issue orders in this respect shortly...'

In pursuance of this meeting, the GDDIDC informed TDL on 9.3.1989 that ...'It has been decided *to treat the land cost as the share capital directly invested by the Govt....*(E.33)

When the acquisition proceedings were being finalised, GDDIDC referred to Industries Deptt. that they may require at least about Rs. 2.2 crores as compensation for the land and requested the Govt. to make the necessary budget provision.

EDC's note dtd. 17th Jan. 1990, giving the history and background of Nylon 6,6 project has the following to say on the various aspects related to the land acquisition, land price, transfer and agreement:

"33.... a meeting was convened in Chief Secretary's Chamber (no date mentioned) and various points were raised as regards:-

i.   the agreement executed by EDC with BILT;

ii. the equity contribution by 'EDC/Govt.' to the extent of 11% amounting to Rs. 6.11 crores, assuming the project cost of Rs. 167 crores;

iii. Budget provision to GDDIDC for acquisition of the land to the extent to the minimum Rs. 2.20 crores;

iv. procedure for transfer of land to the company and consideration of equity contribution by the Govt. by way of cost of land;

v.   the clarifications sought were on the following events:-

a) If the equity contribution is considered by way of cost of land then the project cost would be over burdened with the cost to that extent and the *company may hesitate to consider the said cost.*

b) In case the price-arrived at is agreed upon, then a modified agreement may have to be executed with BILT by EDC incorporating the above procedure for equity contribution.

c) The agreement may have to be executed before finalisation of the award for the price of the land....''

In any case as the BILT project report indicates (Annexure P.2, Page 167), BILT had anticipated only Rs. 62.50 lakhs towards the cost of 250 acres of land i.e. Rs. 25,000/- acre, working out to a very cheap rate of 6.25 Rs./sq.mt. The land cost calculated by BILT was thus just a fraction of the total project cost of Rs. 167 crores or just about 0.37%. This price would not have met the requirement of 11% equity participation which worked out to Rs. 6.11 crores in Jan., 1989. Even going by GDDIDC's estimates, land cost of Rs. 2.2 crores, the EDC would have secured only 3.6% of equity participation instead of 11%. (E.28).

The anxiety of the Govt. as regards the '*overburdening of the project cost by increasing the land purchase value*', appears to be groundless because even otherwise, cost of various project heads would have gone up and since land cost formed only 0.37% of the total project cost, increasing it to even 4-5% would not have made much difference to M/s. BILT as they had already made considerable savings on power and water supply.

On the other hand by undervaluation of the orchard land with dense slope vegetation and sufficient ground water reserve, BILT stood to gain in the long run as pressure on land would increase in Goa. Absence of any scientific work on land capability classification helped BILT to a large extent alongwith the change in the landuse plan, the long range economic implications of which were not foreseen. The only thought which occupied the Govt.'s mind and the only alternative which the Govt. thought for equity participation seems to be - conversion of the land value in equity shares all that too at a very low price. In our opinion, this was an unimaginative management of land resources and economic policy.

B.2.20 TDL's site development work.

It should be noted that TDL commenced its developmental work on 123 hectares land allotted to it without undertaking any Environmental Impact Assessment studies. Since, March-June 1989, TDL has made rapid developments on the site - by fencing the area, building internal roads, clearing a vast area for erecting the main plant, boring tubewells, erecting pumping station and electric transformer and by constructing several buildings on the site. While doing this, TDL has indiscriminately felled large trees, the surface scrub vegetation canopy and exploited the precious groundwater resources. Although, exact quantity of groundwater tapped by TDL for various developmental and other activities need to be ascertained, this was done in an unregulated fashion, without the consent of the authorities. By removing the lateritic outcrop from a part of the site and by changing the stabilized topography, TDL has reduced the water catchment and percolation potential of the site. As for the proposed effluent treatment plant and the effluent discharge pipeline is concerned, absolutely no progress was noticeable when the expert committee members inspected the site on 1.11.1990.

B.2.21 Present Status of TDL

1. The letter of intent No.LI-171 (85) dated 28th Feb. 1985 is presently in the hands of EDC. (E.48)

2. On 8.9.87, EDC wrote to the Central Govt. to transfer the above letter of intent via letter No.EDC/NYL/66/27749, but this is yet to be realised. Hence, TDL does not possess the Letter of Intent as such and has no permission to set up the factory.

3. Without possessing the letter of intent, TDL has gone ahead and begun development works on the site and also constructed permanent buildings such as Hostel cum training Centre and Administrative Block, as part of the infrastructure for the Nylon 6,6 project.

4. TDL has set up these buildings without the required official documents like Land Title Deeds, Non-agricultural Conversion Certificates etc. These are mandatory documents and essential before any construction is undertaken as per the current laws. All this serves to prove that the work done on the site is illegal since the mere claim that the Panchayat authorities have issued the licences is not sufficient.

5. The Goa Industrial Development Corporation (IDC) has recently issued a letter to TDL officials halting all construction works at the said site. (E.48)

B.2.22 Report of the Expert Committee concerning the site visit on 1.11.90.

Location and site characteristics:- (D.1.3)

The proposed site for the Nylon 6,6 factory, located about 8 km. from Ponda town, in Ponda Taluka is a plateau at an altitude of 151 m., having some upland paddy land. As of date, the company TDL has acquired 88.63 ha. of land in Kerim village with further provision of expansion and acquisition of land to the South (Zone E, F) (see Map) of Village Khandepar and Querim.

To the South of the site at a distance of about 4 km. is located the facility of OPA water works along the Khandepar River and to the East of the site at a distance of 2 km. flows the Mandovi river formed by the convergence of two rivers, namely Madei and Khandepar. The area to the East of the site is gently sloping land in the direction of the river; and to the East of zone A is a valley with rich horticultural plantations of' arecanut, coconuts, cashew, pepper consisting of crystal clear springs and human habitation. The area West of the present boundary of the site is one of the most fragile and eco-sensitive zones, with steep slopes. It is a valley with rich green cover of trees, coconut plantations, bamboo plantations, cashew and other horticultural crops, temples, and human habitation.

The area to the South of the site beyond the present acquisition of 88.63 ha. comprises of active agricultural land (paddy fields) flanked by a hill with shrub vegetation. The area to the North of zone A consists of agricultural land where paddy is grown during the monsoons, and dwellings of farmers. This land, that has been acquired by the Govt. for transfer to TDL is both private and Communidade land. High tension lines cut across the site from North to South.

Approach Road to the site:-

The only available approach road to the site is the narrow and precariously winding road from Ponda town through scenic villages. The road passes through agriculturally rich areas which could be seriously affected by the establishment of the plant. Cutting of part of the hillock and widening of the road to accommodate the increase in traffic along this route entails heavy damage to the environment through loss of vegetation and ensuring soil erosion. As such, the likelihood of traffic accidents involving the transportation of hazardous chemicals, raw materials, and finished products is high. As accident involving heavy duty vehicles along the route would cause incalculable harm to the rich vegetation, and human settlements. The possibility of chemicals leaching into the ground and polluting the ground water aquifer is a valid probability.

The question of water runoff:-

As mentioned earlier, the soil is lateritic with patches of paddy land. Lateritic rock being porous, acts as a sponge, and the whole plateau is the catchment area for the rainfall that feeds the groundwater aquifer, ultimately recharging the wells, springs, and temple tanks. This catchment area is now being destroyed by blasting operations for building the Nylon 6,6 plant. The serious alteration of the geomorphological status of this site can have a serious deleterious effect on the quality and quantity of ground water as well as surface water flow. To the West of the present site at a distance in the valley is a natural irrigation lake that supplies water to various horticultural farms in the area. As the lateritic rock surface is replaced by a concrete plain surface that runoff will increase and water recharge rate will decrease. Thus in the not so distant future, the above mentioned tank supplies could be adversely affected threatening local agricultural and horticultural activities.

Tapping of ground water resources:-

TDL managed illegally to drill two tube wells through the lateritic strata. These tube wells were drilled to supply water for construction purposes at the site which presently include the "Administrative Block" and the "Hostel-cum-Training Centre". However, overwithdrawal of water has led, during the summer months, to serious shortage in the valley.

Damage to the natural vegetation:-

Although TDL officials have classified this land as 'E' grade degraded lands, this observation by the officials is far from the truth. We noticed that a number of trees were cut on the location where 'rock/soil' cutting and levelling has been done to install the Nylon 6,6 plant.

Clearance of the natural vegetation of this area has destroyed the possibility of any regrowth - and led to the loss of topsoil. An area of around 60,000 m^2 has been affected by these operations.

Conversion of prime agricultural land:-

TDL officials have in disregard to the guidelines issued by the Ministry of Environment & Forests, Govt. of India, for the setting up of industry 'acquired/proposed to acquire' agricultural land (paddy fields). According to company officials this area is to be used as a Paddy Field Test Farm, but we believe otherwise. As per the map supplied by the company, the effluent treatment plant which appears to have come as an after thought, is presently proposed to be located beyond the 88.63 ha. acquired. The agricultural land could thus be used as a soak pit for the effluents from the manufacturing process. (The case of pollution of wells/springs in Sancoale and Velsao comes to mind in the case of the pollution by Zuari Agro-Chemicals' Bisso reservoir). Alternately, the company officials may decide to discharge the effluent into the valley at the base (West) of zones C,D.

If the effluent is discharged to the East of zone, F, then the possibility exists of the effluent entering into the agricultural zones around, ending up in the ground water, irrigation tanks, and ultimately in the Madei-Mandovi River. Mr. K.S. Pal stated before the House Committee that effluent discharge will occur at the juncture of the Madei-Mandovi river (D.1.1.)

Gaseous emissions from the power plant like No_x, SO_x can seriously affect vegetation, ground water supplies, and human habitation in areas around the factory. (D.1.1.)

Local and community rights:-

For years, people of the neighbouring villages have used these lands (the area that is proposed to be occupied by the TDL plant) as grazing grounds for their cattle. This area provides fodder, within easy reach of their homes, but with the acquisition of this land, and the installation of barbed wire fencing around, the traditional rights of the people have been encroached upon. This leaves no alternative to the people who subsist on animal husbandry but to sell their cattle and enter the cycle of poverty.

The approach road from the main gate to the Nylon 6,6 factory site has been raised above the level of the surrounding areas, paddy fields have been traversed and the natural drainage channels for water have been altered. This has also affected the nocturnal movements of fauna.

The area around the Bhootkam temple, along the Savoi-Querim road also has been enclosed by barbed wire fencing, causing further hindrance to public access.

TDL. company officials present on the site were questioned by members of the experts committee. To the question about the Nitrogen plant, they first expressed denial about its existence, and then pleaded ignorance. They were also questioned about the proposed effluent treatment plant, and gave conflicting reports about the stoppage of work at the site from "just yesterday" to "15 days ago". They claimed ignorance about the equipment to be installed at the site, and were only concerned about constructions such as the "Administrative Block" and "Hostel cum Training Centre".

B.2.23 A brief summary of points presented.

1.1 EDC obtained two letters of intent, revised later, to increase the licensed capacity of Nylon 6,6/Nylon 6 tyre cord and fabric manufacture, in 1985. Subsequently, BILT of Thapar group and Du Pont showed their interest in this letter of intent. The type/magnitude of the technology, the site 'selection/development' process etc. raised several issues demanding probe by the House-Committee.

1.2 The 'industrial backwardness' of Goa is no longer a reality. The EDC's perception of 'backwardness' was based on growth of big industries.

1.3 EDC's good offices were used by M/s. BILT to obtain the letters of intent for Nylon 6,6 manufacture. EDC did not study the implications of importing a new technology.

1.4 EDC's choice of collaborators was prejudiced in favour of Nylon 6,6 patent holders and M/s. BILT.

1.5 The licensed capacity of the project was hiked at the behest of M/s. DU-Pont.

1.6 EDC failed to study the implications of its agreement with BILT.

1.7 EDC towed M/s. BILT's line as regards the site selection despite categorisation of Kerim-site on the Regional Plan as a non-industrial and orchard area.

1.8 EIA studies were not found necessary by EDC, nor such a condition found place in the agreement with BILT.

1.9 The Chief Town Planner opposed selection of Kerim site on valid planning and ecological grounds, offering alternative sites within Industrial Areas.

1.10 The Govt. of India identified Goa as protected and non-polluting industry district on 12/2/87. The policy was sidelined in case of Nylon 6,6 project by Govt. of Goa.

1.11 BILT lobbied with Govt. of Goa for extracting concessions.

1.12 Mr. Denghnuna, Ex-Director of Industries opposed the Nylon 6,6 project stating various reasons.

1.13 The Kerim site was cleared by the High-powered Co-ordination Committee. Pressure was brought on Chief Town Planner to change the land-use plan.

Ex-Chief Minister, Shri Pratapsingh Rane, came into picture in order to expedite the project.

1.14 The Govt. notified change in land-use plan of Kerim and other sites and GDDIDC commenced its role as 'site transfer agents' for TDL. Decision to allot 123 hectares of land was taken by the Govt.

1.15 Discussion part on the 'afforestation of excess area' was found omitted from IDC Board meeting minutes.

1.16 TDL concluded agreement with Du Pont without EDC's participation. Incorporation of TDSL shows Du Pont's expansion ambitions. EDC fails to grasp the implications of Spandex project.

1.17 EDC's letters of intent received 4 extensions. The letters failed to meet stipulated conditions.'Errors' in the letters show deficiencies in EDC's functioning.

1.18 EDC was almost shunted out from Nylon 6,6 project due to lowered equity participation. The 'backdoor-entry' of M/s. Du Pont in Goa is confirmed.

1.19 Govt. of Goa gambled with precious land resources by undervaluing the land and by proposing to convert the land price into EDC's equity shares. BILT's motives are overlooked.

1.20 TDL makes rapid progress on the Kerim site without any concern to ecological and environmental damages. Exploitation of ground water, free of cost, in an unregulated manner is overlooked by the authorities.

B.2.24 Conclusions.

(1) Despite knowing its own limitations, EDC at the behest of M/s. BILT applied for the letter of intent for Nylon 6,6 technology.

(2) EDC had done no 'studies/assessment' on its own about Nylon 6,6 technology but preferred to depend totally on the material supplied by BILT.

(3) EDC compromised the public interest by accepting low-equity participation.

(4) EDC showed no concern for EIA studies before selecting the site for the project.

(5) EDC failed to grasp the implications of the changing dimensions of the project in terms of area requirement project cost, equity share and the entry of multinationals such as M/s. Du Pont.

(6) The selection of Kerim site, a non-industrial area, was done by sidelining the Regional Plan.

(7) The Town & Country Planning Deptt. was pressurised to change the land-use plan of Kerim site at the initiative of the then Chief Minister.

(8) Excess land was allotted to the project on fictitious, unreasonable and unconvincing grounds.

(9) The then Chief Minister, Mr. Pratapsingh Rane, took special interest in the project as evidenced from the developments in 1988-89.

(10) Mr. Denghnuna's remarks were ignored completely and the Industries Secretary during 1988-89 expedited the project.

(11) The GDDIDC was exploited by Govt. of Goa as a 'land transferring agency' ignoring the earlier plan to develop Kerim site under GDDIDC's control.

(12) The then Chief Minister, Shri Pratapsingh Rane, took personal interest in getting NOC for the possession of land from Kerim Communidade.

(13) The Development work by TDL at Kerim site was neither regulated nor supervised by the Govt. or other authorities.

(14) The project implementation plan was hastened despite the 1987 declaration of Goa as 'non-polluting industry district'.

(15) Criteria used, if any, for (a) site survey (b) site selection (c) site and land capability evaluation (d) land price determination (e) granting NOC from environmental angle were incomplete, unscientific, inadequate or incompatible.

(16) TDL was allowed to proceed without any review on the matter of progress of letters of intent transfer.

(17) EDC remained a spectator to the incorporation of Thapar Du Pont Spandex Ltd. and plans to set up Spandex Fibre plant in Goa.

(18) Nylon 6,6 project is a part of M/s. Du Pont's ambitious expansion programme in Asia as shown by incorporation of TDSL.

(19) The environmental fragility, ecological vulnerability, increasing population density, limited geographical area, heavily strained infrastructural utilities and uniqueness of landscape, society and culture (threatened by migrants, slums and polluting industries) were some of the factors overlooked by EDC and Govt. of Goa before deciding about the project.

(20) There is a room for drawing the conclusion that non-existence of statutory industrial policy and vulnerability of highly placed authorities, may lend a helping hand to industries like BILT and multinationals like Du Pont, to get a foothold in Goa.

(21) The highly secretive nature of Nylon 6,6 process and technical data have been favourable factors for BILT and Du Pont in withholding information on all aspects.

(22) It is further to be noticed that no such project exists in whole of Asia, like TDL's Nylon 6,6 project in Goa.

B.3 The question of industrial policy and ecodevelopment.

B.3.1 Policy issues related to Nylon 6,6 project.

Nylon 6,6 project's conception began from the EDC's Letters of Intent. How EDC can indiscriminately apply for letters of intent is a basic policy issue inviting scrutiny. As a fully State-owned body, EDC's decision making should be in consonance with the State's economic and industrial planning. The emerging industrial growth pattern in Goa and the advisability of various options for the future have been 'studied/reviewed' on many occasions. Hence, broad guidelines for selection siting and development of industries are available, although a statutory industrial policy has *not* been formulated. (F.1)

Policy issues cannot be dictated by emotional and political considerations. The often quoted rationale for inviting any big capital intensive industry in Goa, is the felt need to create employment opportunities and thus solve the so called "serious" unemployment problem in the State. But this may purely be a superficial statistical guesswork. Today, several sectors of Goa's rural economy are threatened due to unbalanced urbanisation and other developments displacing hundreds of workers from their traditional highly sustainable means of employment creating artificial, unemployment. Besides, unplanned and incompatible educational growth leads to excessive skilled manpower generation which remains unemployed. The very fact that an estimated 2,20,000 people from other States have migrated to Goa for permanent settlement, during 1961-81, clearly shows that (F.4) employment opportunities were available in Goa, but not to the choice of the local unemployed. Blanket industrialisation is not a solution to this problem. What is needed is a long-term policy of skilled (local) manpower generation, utilisation and efficient management.

A Master Plan for utilisation of the surplus educated manpower available locally should be developed. Quantitative but non-productive 'employment generation' programmes ultimately put additional burden on the State, which can be seen from the saturation in Govt. services leading to inefficiency and increasing non-plan expenditure. On scrutinising the relevant facts, it is hard to accept that the 'solution to the unemployment problem' was the driving logic behind the welcome given to the Nylon 6,6 project. An example we could cite is the BILT report. Going only by BILT's well documented claim (E.28) "The total number of the workforce for the proposed plant is foreseen at 1032, out of which the total skilled, semi-skilled and unskilled labour is 346, 48 and 422 respectively. It is proposed to hire most of the skilled workers from Goa and they would be given due training before being inducted into the operations."

From this passage, it is clear that 'workers from Goa' (not necessarily those of Goan ethnicity) will have to compete for 'most' of the 346 skilled workforce. Also, it is pertinent to note that a project costing Rs. 167 crores could promise to employ only 346 local skilled workers, without defining the 'skills' necessary.

If 'employment generation' was the prime consideration, EDC had the alternative to pursue industries which are known to be labour-intensive and non-polluting. EDC's policy appears to be that of applying Industrialisation models of large States like Maharashtra, Gujarat, U.P. and W.Bengal photostatically to the tiny State of Goa, which is much smaller in size than any of the coastal districts of Maharashtra or Karnataka. *At the same time, States like Maharashtra after facing the pollution threat are reconsidering the policy about the polluting industry.* (Financial Express news item, 8.11.1990).

And EDC failed to work out its own policy tailormade for balanced industrial and economic development of Goa. Such policy would have automatically eliminated large and polluting industries incompatible with Goa's ecology, topography and demography. Such policy would have led to sustainable development as envisaged in the Regional Plan: 2001 A.D. proposals.

Also, it cannot be ruled out that EDC's decisions about Nylon 6,6 project were modulated by large industrial lobbies such as BILT and Du Pont for whom Goa is like any other industrial State conveniently and wrongly labelled as 'backward area'. This is further strengthened from the BILT project report which says..... "Industrialisation is one of the most important methods of developing backward and inaccessible areas..."(E.28). However, the report makes a case for large, polluting industries only.

B.3.2 Nylon 6,6 and existing ecological concerns.

There are two diametrically opposite views about industrial development of Goa:

(a) 'Industries/activities' like mining have already caused eco-devastation in Goa. People have basically 'tolerated' pollution from factories like Zuari Agro Chemicals, MRF, Ciba-Geigy etc. A few more industries will not make difference. Nylon 6,6 project is one such industry, possibly with effluent control.

This is the well-known short-term development view.

(b) Eco-devastation by mining/other industries, burgeoning 'real estate/construction' business threats to bio-diversity, large-scale influx of population, increasing pollution of 'air/ water/soil', deforestation, soil erosion etc. has already made Goa's eco-systems fragile and vulnerable. Besides controlling the on-going environmental damage, steps should be taken to protect and improve important traditional industries (cashew, salt industry, toddy tapping, fishery) and agriculture and stop the infiltration of large and capital intensive, polluting industries.

This is the long-term sustainable development view. (F.2, F.3, F.4, F.14)

People having view (a) want quick results and show little concern for eco-conservation. People having view (b) show a humanistic consideration and are concerned about ecological threats.

Most people having the view (a) represent the universal group which is responsible for 'ozone hole', 'acid rain', 'global warming', 'pollution due to hazardous wastes' as well as 'oil spills' and 'rainforest destruction', that are today threatening the very existence of our planet. View (a) may be suited to industrial societies but not to a very small eco-dependent society prevalent in Goa.

Industries like Nylon 6,6 therefore cannot fit in Goa's ecological matrix, due to their magnitude, nature of technology and layout.

B.3.3 Expert views on Goa's industrial development. NCAER Report.

Goa's unique setting was realised by NCAER, when it prepared a techno-economic survey of Goa, Daman & Diu in 1963-64. It suggested, after a review of industrial structure in 1960, several industries which could be set up in Goa. These industries were classified under agro-based industries, live-stock-based industries, forest-based industries, mineral based industry, textile industry, chemical industry, metal based industry and other small industries. (F.5)

Even at a time when 'environmental/ecological' aspects were mostly ignored, iron and steel because of Goa's vast ore reserves, and paper and pulp, because of State's forestry potential, were the only large industries considered by the Council's experts. Comparatively, small industries such as industrial explosives (due to their use in mining), soaps, paints and varnishes were recommended under Chemical Industry. The projections of this survey were made upto 1974-75.

After the bitter experience of polluting industries like Hindustan Ciba-Geigy and Zuari Agro-Chemicals, etc., the experts gave a fresh thought to industrial planning. The latest views are reflected in the report 'Economic Development of Goa through the Application of Science & Technology' prepared for the Govt. of Goa by the prestigious Centre for Policy Research (New Delhi), and published in October, 1988. The report categorically says..... "Goa's industrial index shows predominance of pesticides, urea etc. whose impact on ecology is disastrous. Another group of industries, together with construction and mining have increased the flow of immigrant labour, with their shanty towns and slums. *The State will have to be on guard lest it is infested with large pollution belching or slum creating industries.*" (P.80) (F.4)

Regional Plan (2001 A.D.) for Goa State.

As pointed out earlier, Nylon 6,6 project has not been examined from the angle of Goa's Regional Plan proposals, which shows that a broadbased statutory plan could be sidelined easily in the interest of giant projects. The Regional Plan aims at industrialisation without ecological or environmental disorder, through judicious control of location and type of industry as well as adequate treatment of industrial effluents. We have referred in particular to the proposals of the Regional Plan, having a bearing on the locational, environmental and technical aspects of Nylon 6,6 project to be located at Kerim, Ponda and our conclusions are as follows:- (See F.1)

(1) The Nylon 6,6 project breaches the strategy of land utilisation in Goa (P.19)(2) and (3), by proposing to occupy the land meant for orchards.

(2) On Page 37, the Regional Plan states that...... "So far, as industrial location is concerned, it is unsafe to allow industries in the catchment areas of fresh water streams...." By locating itself on a high plateau, a major water catchment area on Mandovi river, as well as of ground water aquifer of agricultural importance, Nylon 6,6 project has breached this policy.

(3) Chapter 6,6 of the Regional Plan lays down a policy for industrial development and lists 17 proposed Industrial locations. By easily opting out of these planned locations, Nylon 6,6 has made a mockery of a statutory plan.

(4) On page 62 under recommendations for infrastructural development, the Regional Plan lays down specific guidelines for EDC and IDC, which if analysed in the context of the Nylon 6,6 project put EDC and IDC in poor light.

(5) The limitations of the working of State pollution control Board is clearly anticipated by the Regional Plan which says... "It is to be noted that even though the projects have been cleared subject to adhering to the stipulated minimum standards of industrial effluents, all treatment schemes are undertaken by the units individually. Hence, a new approach has to be devised where by the State authorities can sufficiently control and monitor the discharge of industrial effluents".

This should also be seen in the light of the conditional NOC granted by the State Pollution Control Board to TDL on 2.2.1990. We have discussed the role of this Board in Chapter B.8.

(6) Considering the uniqueness of the State's cultural ethos, the Plan categorically states:

... "It may be emphasized here that adequate safeguard of the environment and ecological interests of these small and beautiful districts is absolutely vital to its development in other sectors, tourism in particualr,. The industrial development will have to be essentially oriented to this vital need..."

The invitation to Nylon 6,6 project does not take into account this concern.

Report of the Task Force on Eco-Development Plan for Goa

The recommendations in the Report of the Task Force on Eco-Development Plan for Goa, prepared by Planning Commission, New Delhi, under the Chairmanship of Dr. M.S. Swaminathan in March 1982, were ignored in granting clearance to the Nylon 6,6 project. (See F.2)

The project was granted land on the Querim Plateau. The Task Force has recommended that all the rocky lands on plateaus be exploited for agro-industries. Also, other recommendations on ground water conservation, water catchment area conservation, prevention and control of water pollution etc. made in this report, have not been considered in clearing the projects.

B.3.4 Conclusions

We have sufficient reasons to conclude that the Nylon 6,6 project could enter Goa because EDC and the State Govt. ignored the views of the experts and neglected the Regional Plan provisions as well as recommendations of the Task Force on Eco-Development Plan for Goa convened by the Planning Commission. EDC functioned in this case as a quasi-Government body shaping Goa's industrial future and ecological destiny. Assumed 'employment generation' seems to be the logic, in clearing the Nylon 6,6 project in the absence of a clearcut statutory industrial policy statement and master plan for balanced development of the State.

B.4 ISSUES RELEVANT TO THE LOCATION OF ANY INDUSTRY

B.4.1 Incompatibility of Nylon 6,6 project

The arguments of Du Pont and TDL have been based upon their experience of Richmond plant in U.S.A. But Goa is not Richmond and James river where Du Pont's release their treated waste water cannot be compared to life-line rivers of Goa i.e. Mandovi and Zuari.

The question of importing technology is not just related to its state-of-the-art nature, but also to its magnitude and compatibility if we consider the unique cultural ecology of various regions of India. Goa has such an unique cultural ecology. Richmond - U.S.A. has an industrial ecology and people are engaged solely in manufacturing activity. There are no orchards in or around Richmond which provide the only means of sustanance to communities. Neither, as per best of our information, the pollution infested James river provides fresh fish to the surrounding localities. As is well known 'fish/fish products', and for that matter all food, in the U.S.A. is supplied in a centralised and standardised manner to all the corners of the country, through a well-organised transportation and marketing system. Communities in developed countries such as U.S.A. seldom depend on their local food sources for sustainance.

The question of dismantling and exporting the existing line of Nylon 6,6 production from Richmond, U.S.A. to a tropical country like India and to a tiny State like Goa has to be answered after a deep analyses of Goa's cultural ecology. We are inclined to believe after examining the layout of the Richmond plant, an aerial photograph of which was circulated by Du Pont officials in the 9th October, 1990 meeting, that they have been thinking in terms of 'Technology transplantation'. The Querim area which they have been developing would be possibly modelled after Richmond. When multinationals do such transplantation, normally, least concern is shown to its impact on cultural ecology of any region.

Considering the unique but vulnerable landscape of Goa and its fast dwindling natural resources, technology transplantation exercises will ruin the cultural ecology of this small State in a few years. Technology of the magnitude of Nylon 6,6 manufacturing can disturb the equilibrium of various interlinked ecosystems. Goa's land and aquatic ecosystems are interwoven in a biological sense. Their interdependence has kept this State's landscape, rivers and life-systems healthy. (F.2, F.3, F.14, F.15, F.17).

The promoters of this project have perhaps assumed that Richmond is Goa and if it is not so, at least a part of it could be engineered as a model of Richmond by technology transplantation. This 'black-box' philosophy would have been compatible with highly industrialised areas in some States of India, i.e. Baroda, Kanpur, Calcutta, Bombay etc. None of these cities have the cultural ecology which Goa could boast of. The inhabitants of these cities have become immune to any technological transplantation. Even if TDL or Du Pont were to locate the Nylon 6,6 plant in any of these cities nobody would have probably objected. A 'Richmond' near Trombay or Vapi would not have made any difference to industrially immunised local communities. But the cultural ecology of the tiny State of Goa cannot be immune to such technology transplantations. On the contrary, the pollution from mining sector, the bitter experience of big factories like Zuari Agro-Chemicals, Hindustan Ciba-Geigy etc., have made the people of Goa more sensitive to the future threats.

If we remove the internationally famous, all weather Mormugao natural harbour from Goa's map, Du Ponts and Thapars will lose interest in locating their projects in Goa. This clearly means that for them strategic techno-economic thinking is more important than future of an endangered and threatened society. By location of this plant amidst the virgin, scenic surroundings the seed of destruction of Goa's cultural ecology will be sown by TDL and Du Pont.

The self-sustaining, self-governing village communities of Goa - (the Communidades) are part of Goa's cultural ecology. Through mass labour over the years, the Goan settlers have topo-engineered the land for orchards, bamboo-groves, cashew plantations etc. Bandharas or mini-dams were built for irrigation. Springs and fountains were protected and conserved. Stone-fencing was done on hill-slopes to curtail soil erosion. Plateaus having yet unexplored grassland flora were reserved as traditional grazing areas. Holy trees were carefully nurtured and protected. (F.8) (F.7)

In techno-economic calculations, these traditions, their cultural significance, economic contribution to the community etc., have no place. In the board-room, industrialists may see a map of Goa, the Mormugao Port, the Inland Waterways and discuss 'most suitable sites' - again a 'Black-box' hardcore profit making opportunistic, and exploitative approach. The Nylon 6,6 project is not just erection of a few buildings and a plant. It is a whole township, right in the midst of a horticultural community. While the Goans may have to beg for a small piece of communidade land and the housing problem may assume serious dimensions, the TDL proposes an industrial township on cheaply acquired communidade land. Considering the skyrocketing land prices in Goa and increasing population density, the scenario in 2001 A.D. could very well be imagined. TDL's housing plans, the township scheme could turn out to be at the cost of thousands of shelterless people of Goa. (F.1)

Nylon 6,6 project is therefore not only incompatible to Goa but its profit motive, dis-regard for ecological concerns etc., makes it a real threat to our unique ecology. (F.1, F.2)

B.4.2 The need for E.I.A.

The E.I.A. is a stipulated condition laid down by the National Committee for Environmental Planning & Coordination, created in 1972, which advocated that all projects should undertake an E.I.A. and meet the standards imposed by the water and air pollution control Boards. (F.2, F.3)

Consequently, the Ministry of Environment & Forests, Govt. of India, has also made it clear that all development projects require an Environmental Impact Assessment (EIA) study prior to site selection and investment decisions. The EIA is a procedure for bringing out the potential effects of human activities identifying the possible positive and negative impacts on the environment, resulting from a proposed project. EIA is meant for inter-comparison of the development options and screening of alternate sites for locating the projects. This is followed by Environment Impact Statement (EIS) preparation, which is a final analysis to an EIA. Finally, an Environment Management Plant (EMP) is prepared which is an implementation plan for mitigation, protection 'and/or' enhancement measures recommended in the EIS. The EMP presents in details how these measures should be operated, the resources required, and the schedule for implementation. It is intended that in the EMP, the implementation status of protection measures will be elevated to a level suitable for incorporation in the design phase of the proposed project.

As per the circular of Department of Industries, Govt. of India, Ministry of Industries (Deptt. of Industrial Development, Circular dtd. 17.2.87), the Eastern & Southern part of Goa along the Western Ghats is declared as a 'protected district' from the point of view of environmental protection from industries. The circular recommends certain non-polluting industries (list (2) of the above circular), as the type of industries which can be considered in this region. Large industries such as Nylon 6,6 are rightly excluded from this list. Besides, the Regional Plan 2001 AD for Goa has also demarcated the Kerim site as an 'orchard area'. E.I.A. studies are therefore *crucial* and *essential before* any policy decisions are taken at the Local or Central Govt. levels to denotify this area for *any* industrial purpose, and particularly so for a large chemical industry such as the Nylon 6,6 project.

B.4.3 The Regional Plan 2001 AD and industrialisation criteria

1) Strategy for conservation as stipulated in Regional Plan 2001 A.D., prepared through the provision of TCP Act 1974, and approved in October 1986, has been compromised whilst contemplating the proposed TDL Plant for Nylon 6,6 manufacture.

2) The entire proposal of setting up TDL's Nylon 6,6 plant in Kerim has to be seen against the background of the Regional Plan proposals, specially, considering those that dictate the policy for industrialisation.

3) The Nylon 6,6 manufacturing plant does not meet the Regional Plan requirements in the following manner:

    a) Technology for manufacture of Nylon 6,6 is imported and the nature of industry does not fit with the policy of the Regional Plan.

    b) Land Use plan/pattern as envisaged in the Regional Plan does not include chemical industries like Nylon 6,6.

c) The Plan mentions that, "the land resources are of a non-renewable character and as such, excess land utilisation strategy is to take measures to make best possible use of land and to increase its production."

d) Any industry of the scale of Nylon 6,6 has to satisfy the guidelines provided in the Regional Plan, which says that, "Industrial estates areas, comprising the Organised Industrial estates where most of the proposed industries are developed, should be localised as far as possible".

e) The Regional Plan has not provided for any extra pollution loads in the Mandovi and Zuari basins apart from the existing ones from mining activities, and hence the location of the TDL plant itself does not fit within the policy for water pollution formulated in the Regional Plan.

f) On Page 37, the Regional Plan categorically states that "so far as industrial locations are concerned, it is unsafe to allow industries in the catchment area of the fresh water stream".

g) In Chapter 6,6 under industry, the Regional Plan proposal is quite clear that it does not allow a plant of the order of magnitude of TDL's Nylon 6,6 at Kerim (Page 55-63 and Page 51 Map).

B.4.4 Criteria as per the studies conducted by NIO

(1) The NIO report prepared at the behest of the Central Pollution Control Board (F.15) has categorically concluded as follows:

(1) Urban and industrial development upstream of the rivers *should not* be extended beyond Piligao. Tidal flushing in this area is low, and there is the possibility of effluents concentrating in the bottom sediments and pollutants accumulating in benthic fauna, aquatic plants, etc.

(2) Parulekar, Ansari and Ingole, Scientists from the Biological Oceanography Division of the NIO, in their studies reported in the Indian Journal of Marine Sciences, have advised *against* any extra load in the river system of Mandovi and Zuari by way of any soil-run-off or industrial effluent discharge. The mining activities, as they have shown, have already damaged the river ecosystem. Location of Nylon 6,6 or any other new chemical industry with discharge point in the river may lead to the extinction of estuarine living resources.

The relevant comments of these experts reproduced from their research paper entitled "Effect of mining activities on the clam fisheries and bottom fauna of Goa estuaries" (F.14) are as follows:

"....Mining activities are about double as much along the Mandovi river than along the Zuari river (Anonymous 1979) and accordingly, the ecosystems in Mandovi estuary, receive the maximum adversity, due to mining rejects. Kamat and Sankaranarayana (1974) observed high value of 40.3 mg/1 of particulate iron in the near bottom water at Ribandar as compared to 6.6 mg/1 at Banastarim and further reported that about 70,000 tonnes of iron, in particulate form, gets annually deposited in Mandovi river. Based on a 1977-78 study, significantly high concentration of iron and manganese in the sediments of Mandovi and Zuari river, with moderate concentrations in the inter-connecting Cumbarjua canal have been reported (Anonymous 1979)...." (F.15)

".... Besides the overall decrease in the dissolved oxygen concentration, other obvious reasons for the decline in the clam resources are due to the immense increase in the quantity of suspended solids and structural deformation of bottom deposits ..."

"....The red clay particles, both in suspension as also settled on the bottom deposits alongwith the lateritic cobble and pebbles strewn in the clam beds are of terrigenous origin, and have entered the estuarine environment through land run-off from the mining rejects and due to spilling, handling mishaps and washings from mechanized barges, transporting iron ores, from mine head to the shipment point. Such massive inorganic inputs, estimated to be about 70,000 tonnes of iron, in particulate form, getting deposited annually in the Mandovi river (Kamat and Sankaranarayana 1974), has resulted in the considerable reduction of the assimilative capacity of the clam bed ecosystem at Ribandar and serious ecosystem instability at Banastarim clam bed. These deleterious man-made changes though gradual are recurring in nature and unless abated, the total extinction of estuarine living resources, is evident...." (F.17)

B.5   CHARACTERISTICS & UNIQUENESS OF KERIM AND ADJOINING REGION

B.5.1 The neglect of baseline studies.

Although broad geological, minerological, hydrological and botanical data are available with respect to most of the laterite plateaus or orchard lands, detailed baseline studies have not been carried out from the environmental angle.

In this regard, the opinion of the experts of the Geological Survey of India, Mr. A.R. Gokul and A.K.R. Hemmady, is worth quoting. The duo says in the abstracted paper 'The environmental studies in Goa: A framework' (1982): "Goa has been exposed to environmental pollution for quite some time past. The environmentalists are strindently advocating that before it is too late some preventive steps should be taken and corrective measures introduced". While expressing the need for multidisciplinary baseline studies from the environmental viewpoint they stressed that ...."In order to understand the factors that cause the environmental pollution, quantify as far as possible their effects and delineate remedial action, a multidisciplinary team comprising ecologists, engineers, geologists, mining engineers, landscape planners, health and district administrators have to work and synthesize the data. It calls for preparation of a variety of maps such as lithological base maps showing the rocks grouped according to their capacity to store and discharge ground water, hydrological map, land use map, inland and water pollution map, marine pollution map showing the locations of human habitation industrial activity etc., according to the magnitude of their potential for causing pollution..." To the best of our knowledge, no such multidisciplinary studies have been carried out for the Kerim site. The site was converted into an industrial area without studying the land capability and its full economic and productive potential. (F.3)

B.5.2. Assessment of the groundwater resources. (F.7)

For the computation of our groundwater resources an infiltration factor of 300 mm for 80% of the geographic area has been considered. The figures (1977) are as follows:

Sr.No	Geogr.Area	(3)	(4)	(5)	(6)	(7)	(8)
1.	Ponda 7679.7 Ha	6143.7	1843	1290	519	772	40%
2.	Bicholim 7192.1 Ha	5753.6	1726	1208	95	1113	8%

Note (3) = area taken for recharge Ha.   (6) = Existing net draft Ha M.
(4) = Gross recharge in rainfall Ha M.   (7) = Groundwater available Ha M.
(5) = Recoverable recharge 70% of crops, Ha M.   (8) = Stage of groundwater development.

The Mangueshi-Mardol-Priol valley with an area of 0.91×10^6 sq.m. has a groundwater storage capacity of 9.555 million cubic metres. In this valley, there is very little pre and post monsoonal fluctuation of the water levels as evaporative losses and seepage is very small. Wells dug into the lateritic aquifer of depth 5-6 m have a discharge rate of 3-5 litres per second, which is the same for a shallow tube well of 10^M draw down.

Systematic groundwater studies were carried out in some parts of Ponda taluka in 1970-71 by the groundwater division of the Geological Survey of India. Successful bore holes located in the lateritic topographic depressions yield between 4000 to 10000 litres per hour. Springs are common in this area and the discharge is about 15 to 30 lpm. The chemical quality of the groundwater is good except in the area where the tidal water enters through rivulets into the plains. The aquifers of this region are recharged seasonally by the monsoonal precipitation from June to October. Most of the springs gain water from, rather than lose water to the aquifers (F.3.)

B.5.3. The principal river basins draining the Kerim region.

It is important to know the drainage system (D.1.2.1, F.3) of the rivers near Ponda Taluka, keeping in view the plans of the TDL to discharge 'treated' effluent downstream.

Mandovi River Basin: This river rises in the Karnataka State and meets the sea near the city of Panaji. This has two main branches: Madei and the Khandepar river (the TDL intends to discharge effluents close to the confluence of these rivers.)

Madei Rivers: Rises in the Ghats of Khanapur Taluka of Karnataka State at the altitude of about 600 metres and runs for about 30 km. before entering Goa. This is a perennial river with a summer *discharge of about 850 litres per second* near its meeting point with the other branch. The important tributaries of the river are:

(i) *Surla River* (nadi), a non-perennial river forming down from the Surla village (altitude 700 m) in the Ghats with a part of the catchment in Karnataka meeting the Madei near the Nanorem village.

(ii) *Veluz River*, wholly lying in Sattari (Goa), a non-perennial river meeting the Madei river near the town of Valpoi. And the

(iii) *Ragada River*, wholly lying in Goa meeting the Madei near the Ganem village. The latter is perennial in its last reaches discharging about 50 litres per second in the summer. The area drained by the Madei river with its tributaries is 600 sq.km. The tributaries have catchments in Goa as follows:

    (1) Surla nadi   - 75 sq.km.

    (2) Veluz   - 105 sq.km.

    (3) Ragada   - 175 sq.km.

The length of the Madei river in Goa is about 40 km., that of the Surla nadi, being 18 km. and of the Ragada is 33 km. (F.3)

The Khandepar River: The Khandepar river has its origin in the Ghats of Karnataka, but most of the catchment is in Goa. The river is perennial and carries about 750 litres per second at Opa. Its main tributaries are (1) Callem river (2) Dabhal river, both flow wholly in Goa. The former flows perennially with a small discharge and meets the main river upstream of the Kirlpal bridge. The other runs dry during the month of April and May, meets the Khandepar river at Nirankal. The Khandepar river drains with its tributaries an area of about 400 sq.km., and its length in Goa is about 60 km.

The Zuari River Basin: The Zuari river is formed by the joining of two rivers, Selaulim and Uguem of Sanguem taluka. Both are perennial rivers, carrying about 300 1/sec discharge in the summer months. The length of the Selaulim river upto Sanguem is 35 Km, with a catchment area of 200 sq.mts. Its important tributary is the Kushavati river, which is perennial with a flow of about 400 litres/sec during the summer months (F.3)

WATER REQUIREMENTS

When questioned about alternative arrangements for water for the TDL plant should the Selaulim Dam water not reach the people of Margao and Vasco cities *K.S. Pal* said: "The only alternative arrangements left for us is to tap water from the foot of the OPA water works. There is a leakage over there and the water is getting wasted so they have erected an artificial lake, we can pump the water from there instead of it being wasted."

B.5.4 Uniqueness of Kerim site and adjoining region

The site is a plateau at a height of 150 mts. above main sea level, perhaps, the highest plateau in Goa. It has a 'pure/fresh' air, tranquil surrounding and enchanting scenic beauty with views of distant green hills, winding river courses and deep green valleys. Rest of the land is relatively at a lower level, mostly consisting of grasslands intermixed with bushes, sparse trees, pockets of morod paddy lands and few patches of dense vegetation. The "Morods" or upland paddy fields are used for monsoon paddy cultivation. In general, the overall site can be classified as pasture land. The land cannot be termed as degraded, the way TDL describes it. Except for paddy cultivation, most of the site was a virgin land not affected by human activities from topographical point of view. Cutting, bulldozing, filling for road construction and building constructions undertaken by the TDL have now deformed the landscape, conceivably for the first time in its history.

Immediately, at the periphery of the site, the land slopes downwards and thick vegetation starts. It includes natural vegetation, cashew plantations and bamboo plantations in the upper reaches of the slope. At the lower parts of the slope and in the valley, are the villages of Kerim, Savoi-Verem, Vagurmem and part of Khandepar. These areas are profuse and thick with extremely productive 'arecanut/coconut/horticultural' plantation, having multiple cropping system. The rich bio-diversity of this zone include forest species, medicinal plants and wild relatives of our cultivated plants. The cultivated plants in the plantation system are Bamboo, Coconut, Arecanut, Pepper, Cardamom, Mango, Jackfruit, Pineapple, Birla madd (Caryota ureus), Cashew, Jamun (Syzygium cuminii) etc. The area is also rich in perennial water sources such as, springs, tanks, streams, and lakes. *One of the streams originating from this lake (just a hundred metres from the periphery of the proposed site) passes through the villages of Priol, Velling and Marcaim*, which are, again, agro-ecologically rich. The stream ultimately drains into the river Zuari after feeding an irrigation lake and rich agricultural lands on its way. Other streams drain into rivers Khandepar and Mandovi, coconut groves associated with rich low-lying paddy fields occupy the lowest topography levels of the landscape in the region. Agriculture and horticulture has been the occupation of this region for centuries.

The Ponda region in general with its forest cover is a contiguous part of the Western Ghats ecosystem, and hence rich in its diversity of plant and animal species. There are many species that are confined to this region alone. Much of the hilly terrain still has virgin forests that supply fuelwood, wild fruits, honey, mushrooms, medicinal plants and a variety of timber for the local people. A rich wild life of about 100 and odd species of birds, small mammals, reptiles of different types etc. is also found in the region.

The geological formation both at the proposed Nylon 6,6 plant site proper, and adjoining areas is unique, consisting of a lateritic soil composition with underlying layers of crystalline and metamorphic rocks, that belong to the precambrian age. The partly exposed lateritic rocks are of sub-recent origin, have a high iron content and are rich in aquifers. The crystalline and associated rocks vary widely in their water bearing capacity. The fractured porosity, degree of weathering and the topographical setting plays a dominant role in controlling conduit and storage function of these formations. The depth of the dug wells tapping weathered jointed crystalline and associated rocks vary from 2.8 to 15 m. with depth of water table ranging from 1.5 to 13 metres below the ground level. (F.3)

The laterites are the most important water bearing rock formations covering more than 60% of the area in Goa. Besides being inherently porous, the laterites are highly jointed and fractured which increases their water bearing capacity. *The topographic setting of the laterites has a definite say in the groundwater bearing potential. Kerim site has an ideal setting in this respect.* The aquifers are locally conceived as hollow spaces beneath the rock surfaces which are full of water, and thus vernacularly termed as "Pokalthemals".

Perhaps, it is this peculiar environment that must have contributed towards the high aesthetic sensitivity and the rich cultural ethos of the region. The area within a radius of 7 to 8 kms. from the plant site, engulfs the rich cultural zone of Goa. Most of the famous temples of Goa lie in this zone. It is this area which has contributed to the nation more than 50% of Goa's top most vocalists, singers, musicians, artists and writers. Also, it is this area that is well known for contributions in the educational field. Two of the three Sanskrit Pathshalas in Goa are in this area only. The home of the late Dada Vaidya who started the modern educational movement in Goa is just 1 km. from the plant site. Late Smt. Kesarbai Kerkar, a singer renowned all over India, belongs to the Kerim village, and the home of the singing phenomenon of India, Lata Mangueshkar, is just 5 kms. from the site.

If the proposed Nylon 6,6 plant is allowed on the Kerim plateau, which influences the whole 'Kerim/Ponda' region, it will *adversely* affect the rich socio-cultural heritage, highly productive agro-horticultural ecosystem, abundant 'ground/surface' water resources and diverse wild life of the region described above.

B.6   THE MANUFACTURING PROCESS AND CONNECTED ISSUES.

B.6.1 Infrastructure sought by BILT for the Nylon 6,6 Plant

In a letter dated 9th March, 1987 addressed to Chief Secretary (Govt. of Goa), Mr. V.K. Malik, General Manager Fiber Division of BILT stated: (E.11)

"(1) We seek your guidance and help of the Union Territory in the following matters:-

(A) *Land acquisition*:- It is requested that the land acquisition is organised by Govt. authorities, land costs to be paid for the project in installments with no interest, or the land to be allotted to the project on perpetual lease basis."

Over the years, a sudden increase in the quantum of land required for the Nylon 6,6 plant has occurred, illustrated with 2 cases:-

(a) In one document, the total land area required is shown as 129000 m² with the following break-up: ISBL-40000m²; OSBL-20000m²; offices and administration-5000m²; (E.28) Residential colony-40000m²; Roads-24000 m²;

(b) In another document (D2.2) on TDL's land utilisation plan, areas are shown as

Zone A = 288300m²;   Zone B= 68100m²;

Zone C = 63850m²;   Zone D = 206045m²;

Zone E = 106005m²;   Zone F = 499700m²;

With a total area of 1232,000m² (D.2.1.) or about 10 times of (a) above.

"(B) *Investment Subsidy*:- Almost all States give an investment subsidy, normally a subsidy of 15% will be given on the fixed investment on land, buildings, machines, etc. to a maximum of Rs.15 lakhs and can be increased to Rs.25 lakhs in special cases.

(C) *Power*:- Exemption from electricity duty for 10 years for backward areas declared as such by the Govt.

(D) *Sales Tax Loans*:- Interest free sales tax loans is to be made available to this project.

(E) *Access/Approach Road*:- Approach road from the main highway upto site to be built by Govt. authorities *without* any cost to the project.

(F) *Power Tariff*:- Concessional power tariff to be made available for this project. The concession in power tariff requested is 25% of the present rate applicable to such industries in the State. It's requested that the concession in power tariff will be made available to this project for 10 years from the start up of commercial production.

(G) *Powerlines to the project*:- Since the project is to be located in a backward area and the Govt. has agreed to make available the power required for this project, its requested that the cost of laying the powerline be borne by the Govt.

(H) *Water*:- Its assumed that the State Govt. or the local authorities will not put any form of *cess* on drawing water from either *tubewells* or *river* or from any other source at any stage".

B.6.2 Reflections about the water requirements of Nylon 6,6 process.

Shri K.S. Pal of TDL, informed at the House-Committee meeting on 9.10.90 that water supply from Opa Water Works was possible only if the Selaulim water scheme came on stream, remarked: "The only alternative left for us is to tap water from the foot of the Opa Water Works. There is a *leakage* over there and the water is going wasted, so they have erected an artificial lake - like, we can pump water from there and get it instead of wasting water". (E.48)

To control the influx of tidal current, which is slight upto Opa, an engineering firm from Madras installed a barrier during the Portuguese regime. To control the leakage under this barrier, another one was put further downstream and it is to the zone between these two barriers that Shri. K.S. Pal was referring to. In this context, it should be noted that this is good quality potable water that requires just filtration and disinfection before onward supply to households. Further, *it is pertinent to point out again that the PWD (PHE) is already drawing 24 MGD of water as against the capacity of Opa Water Works being only 16 MGD*. Given the above facts and the likelihood that the water supply from Selaulim project (to Vasco) may not be available in the near future, it 'is/was' preposterous and irresponsible to contemplate the use of a vital drinking water source for meeting the enormous needs of a 'large-scale' chemical industry, that *too free of charge*. When further questioned, TDL officials remarked that "there have not been any baseline studies such as geomorphological-hydrological studies *before* the installation of the tubewells. Shri. K.S. Pal said, "No". We have not done it. We have used the benefit of the Hydrological (Irrigation) Department of the Govt. of Goa and they have shown us in their map which are the veins of water in that particular area. Underground veins of water do not interfere with any other veins of the springs". (E.48)

That, this blatant, sweeping and casual statement made by Shri Pal is far from the truth, can be seen from the fact that a number of wells and springs in the valley close to TDL's tube wells, experienced a water crisis this summer, (1990).

B.6.3 Raw materials involved in the Nylon 6,6 process:

Raw materials such as Adipic acid and HMD needed for Nylon 6,6 manufacture cannot be 100% pure as claimed by Shri. K.S. Pal of TDL. In the BILT application (E.28) appendix-3, page 33m under specifications for AA and HMD, the following chemical impurities are present:

Adipic (A.A.):

Caproic acid and Succinic acid

Hexamethylene diamine (HMD):

Epsilon amino capro nitrile, Hexamethylene imine, Ammonia, 1,2 Diamino cyclohexane, 2 Methylpenta methylene diamine, 2 Amino ethylcyclo-pentyle amine, Tetra Hydro-azepine.

B.6.4 Other utility requirements of the Nylon 6,6 process (E.28)

- Electricity 1500 KW
- Steam
- Dowtherm (Diphenyl and Diphenyl oxide) 1.55 mm kg. cal/hr.
- 1.5 mm kg.cal/hr
- Nitrogen 0.6m³/min at STP
- Compressed air 7 kg/m² 45m³/min
- Water (Refrigeration - 650T; DM-80¹/min;
- Filtered - 7501/sec; Cooling- 19m¹/min)
- Freon glycol system.

B.6.5 Nylon 6,6 technology and process component as per BILT and its CG application:

Du Pont, BILT and TDL officials have highlighted the various aspects of the state-of-the-art technology for the manufacture of Nylon 6,6 in the BILT report, Capital Goods Import application documents, etc. However on perusal of these documents and other 'source' documents we have arrived at the following conclusions:

About the Technology:

(1) The Nylon 6,6 technology is not the most recent, and state-of-the-art. Du Pont, admitted reportedly that it has developed a high strength polymide fibre that will improve the durability and performance of tyres and mechanical goods.

This new product named 'Hyten' is a monofilament fibre that is 38% stronger than polyester cord and 10% stronger than conventional tyre cord.

(2) There is a serious discrepancy in transfer of technology noticed between the remarks of the letter of Mr. L. Ciporin, (Director of Technology Du Pont Far East), in his letter dated Feb. 1st, 1988 (E.16) where he says that, 'Du Pont does not contemplate releasing the design and specifications of this equipment', and the Memorandum of Understanding between BILT and EDC submitted alongwith the Letter of Intent dtd.19th Nov., 1983. (E.1)

(3) It is indeed difficult to follow the arguments put forward by the promoters that modifications and upgradations of the recent years will be compatible with equipment of the mid 1900's when one cannot quantify its age. E.S. Woolard, Chairman of Du Pont has admitted in his address to the World Resources Institute on 12.12.1989, that many of the plants built in the 1950's and 1960's need to be upgraded to incorporate new technology or to correct problems that Du Pont didn't *know about* or couldn't solve until recently. Our apprehension is that since the age of this equipment cannot be quantified, the plant from Richmond could be one such case.

About the machinery:

(1) There is a contradiction between the admission of H. Luthra, Director of TDL (E.23) in his letter dated 26.9.88 under the subject 'Refurbishment of Equipment' wherein he says, "there have been so many upgradations and replacements during the last 5 years that it is impossible to quantify its age."

(This letter was written to the Secretariat for Industrial approvals) and Mr Vijay Malik's statement to the House-Committee on 9.10.90.

(2) Using data in the BILT report (1988) we have computed that

   (a) The cost of the fiber plant is Rs.2394.25 lakhs.

   (b) The cost of the fabric plant is Rs.657.39 lakhs.

   (c) The cost of the old machinery in the fiber plant is Rs.855 lakhs or *about 40% of the total cost* of the machinery for this plant.

(3) Misleading data has been provided in different instances concerning the 2nd hand machinery for the TDL plant. H. Luthra, Director of TDL, remarks that, '....it is established and certified that the residual life of the second hand equipment is *greater than 20 years'*.

Whilst the Chartered Engineer's Report (E.23) has the following remarks, "Present condition of machinery is good and expected residual life *is around 20 years*."

Du Pont in promoting Nylon 6,6 technology has made the ambitious claims that this technology is non-polluting and safe. This claim has been repeatedly made by Du Pont, BILT and TDL officials in various correspondence as well as during the proceedings with the House-Committee.

The preparation of Nylon 6,6 tyre cord is not simply the mixing of Adipic Acid and Hexamethylene diamine as we are made to believe but involves the following steps with waste generation:

(1) In the salt preparation stage activated carbon is a waste, it is used to remove colouring matter. Adipic acid dust is vented to the atmosphere. Added to the salt solution are polymerization catalyst (Phenyl phosphoric acid), antioxidants, stabilizers and proprietary ingredients (Ti O_2).

Nylon salt spills do occur.

(2) The mixing of adipic acid and hexamethylene diamine to form Nylon 6,6 polymer is a reaction where 100% conversion of AA and HMD molecules cannot thus be achieved, so HMD appears in the waste stream together with impurities present in these two ingredients mentioned in Table No.1, including toxic Hexamethylene diamine. Du Pont has given no indication how this will be detoxified or recovered.

(3) In steps of the continuous polymerization process gel formation occurs, which requires the need for dual separators and finishers for switching vessels before gel build up in the vessel significantly affects the process.

(4) H. Luthra, Director of TDL, claims in his letter (E.28) to the Secretariat for Industrial Approvals that "there is no byproduct. The reaction between the ingredients and polymerization is complete and no monomers are left in the process and/or product. Hence, there is no need of a monomer recovery unit". This contradicts the claim put forward by Ashoke Chatterjee, Project Engineer Du Pont (E.28) in point (8) below.

(5) In each of the steps for the continuous polymerization process, process emissions, emissions of Dowtherm vapour, and discharge to the waste streams occur, these are outlined below:

a) Evaporator and Reactor are mentioned to have a diamine recovery system with assessories, under the notice to Indian manufacturers, in Indian export bulletin of Dec. 26th, 1987. However, the diamine recovery system has not been mentioned under the list of equipment of indigenous equipment against specific inquiry. As this technology is not available in India, and the diamine recovery system and accessories does not also find mention among the list of old or new imported equipment.

This explains why TDL claims that *Diamine Carbonate is harmless.*

(6) In the proforma invoice for new and refurbished imported equipment note that the relief valves for release of emissions in the Reactor, Flasher, Separator, Finisher and Dowtherm system, are not new equipment but refurbished ones. There is also no mention of any pollution abatement devices like catalytic oxidation unit or scrubbers.

(7) Dowtherm a eutectic mixture of Diphenyl and Diphenyl oxide will be released into the atmosphere via dowtherm relief valves.

(8) In the spinning section under 'Air Quenching System', in the proforma invoice for refurbished equipment, Ashok Chatterjee, Project Engineer of Du Pont, mentions the need for monomer exhaust fan with ducting, exhaust fan for hot tube and instrumentation alongwith control panel. For the monomers, in the BILT report Page M-7 of process emissions, there is no abatement device whilst in TDL's letter Ref. No.TDL/HC/90-91/2, a scrubber has been added.

(9) A comparison of page M-7, Annexure M-1 BILT Report of process emissions, and TDL's letter TDL/HC/90-91/2, will reveal the glaring discrepancies between projected emissions in lbs/hr at Goa. A further comparison with the proforma invoice for refurbished and new imported equipment indicates that TDL is not interested in controlling process emissions and following US standards or Indian ones yet to be notified. (E.28; E.43).

MACHINERY

- *Vijay Malik:* "Nothing is old, it is purchased as either new in Japan or Europe or in USA, and as per the Guidelines laid down by the Government of India no equipment can be imported which is more than 7 years old, and it is accepted by the Government."

- *Vijay Malik:* "Du Pont has no better machines."

- *Vijay Malik:* "It is modern type of machinery as whenever there is a change it is replaced. In fact some of the machines which are coming to us is as old as only 3-4 years."

- *Vijay Malik:* "...And as I have said earlier, that it is 2nd hand machinery."

- *Vijay Malik:* "The life of the plant depends on how we will maintain the plant. Normally it is 25 years and more than 25 years not less than that."

---

(10) In the spinning machines assembly, hot tube emissions will occur through the hot tube assembly; waste yarn will be generated in the Yarn Handling and Rewinding System; and emissions from the Oil Heating System, may also occur. (E.28).

(11) The Goa State Pollution Control Board in their NOC (E.41) No.4/6/89-PCB/859 dated 2.2.90, have mentioned that 2nd quality product should not be burnt or otherwise disposed on site. But TDL in the notice to indigenous manufacturers requires the following equipment for their spinning pack and pump shop:

(a) Lindberg type 364830-E125 electric furnace, for burning polymer from packs. (E.23, E.24)

(b) Electric furnace for burning polymer from meter pumps. No mention has however, been made in any document about the nature of the emissions due to burning of polymer. In another (E.28) document it is mentioned that the waste 2nd grade polymer would either be incinerated or be dumped in a land fill.

B.6.6 Facts about the Nylon 6,6 process gathered from other US agencies including USEPA.

The high rate of polymerisation to be achieved is possible only under extremely precise and carefully controlled conditions of temperature and pressure. Theoretically, cent percent polymerisation may appear possible but in actual practice, it is *not so*. Even the most stringent and judicious supervision of the highest kind cannot ensure complete polymerisation. There is always scope for raw material waste, however, tiny a proportion it might seem to be. Secondly, there is the question of the hazardous nature of the *Raw Materials* used in the process. The EDC's Letter of Intent for Nylon 6,6 project (E.1) states that the Raw Material to be imported is *AH Salt*. The significance of this is discussed in details elsewhere in this report. Though this aspect is played down by the representatives of TDL, it is a fact that both the raw materials used, i.e. Hexamethylene Diamine and Adipic Acid have been enlisted as Hazardous substances by U.S. Health authorities and, in both cases, extensive care and protection is demanded in their handling and use (D.4.1).

Though TDL representatives maintain that these 2 raw materials (Adipic Acid and HMD) would be imported into Goa in finished form, prudence suggests that such statements should not be taken at face value. Economic considerations in the future could very well dictate their production 'at/near' the site of the Nylon 6,6 manufacturing plant. This could be extremely problematic since the ingredients which go into the making of these raw materials are themselves hazardous too.

For manufacture of Adipic Acid, chemicals such as Benzene, Cyclohexane, Cyclohexanol, Cyclohexanone and Nitric Acid are used. (All these are enlisted as hazardous on the U.S. Hazardous Substances fact sheet). So also, the manufacture of Hexamethylene Diamine, involves Acrylonitrile which is in turn used in the manufacture of Adiponitrile, a precursor of Hexamethylene Diamine, also classified as hazardous in the U.S. list. (D.4.1)

RAW MATERIALS	REMARKS
For Nylon 6,6	
1. Hexamethylene diamine	Hazardous substance
2. Adipic Acid	Hazardous substance

INGREDIENTS	REMARKS
For HMD	
1. Acrylonitrile	Hazardous substance
For Adipic Acid	
1. Benzene	Hazardous substance
2. Cyclohexane	- do -
3. Cyclohexanol	- do -
4. Cyclohexanone	- do -
5. Nitric Acid	- do -

The information available through other Nylon 6,6 manufacturing plants in the United States, discloses quite a few chemically hazardous substances used at various stages in the production process of Nylon 6,6 and are listed as under:

(i) Cadmium sulfide (ii) Lead acetate (iii) Cupric acetate (iv) Potassium iodide (v) Phenyl phospheric acid (vi) Titanium dioxide (vii) Carbon dioxide (viii) Methanol and (ix) Asbestor.

These have been indicated in the following tabular form:

ADDITIVES	REMARKS
1. Cadmium sulfide	Hazardous substance
2. Lead Acetate	- do -
3. Cupric acetate	- do -
4. Potassium Iodide	- do -
5. Phenyl phosphoric acid	- do -
6. Titanium dioxide	Hazardous substance
7. Carbon dioxide	- do -
8. Methanol	- do -
9. Asbestor	- do -

A summarized description of the production process, with the different process stages involved and the effluents given out, follows:

Nylon 6,6 Resin production:

Nylon 6,6 is produced by the reaction of Adipic Acid and Hexamethylene Diamine. Each of these contain 6 carbon atoms, hence the 6,6 nomenclature. The dibasic acid groups on the Adipic Acid molecule combine with the amine groups of the Hexamethylene Diamine molecule, resulting in the elimination of a molecule of water after the formation of an intermediate salt. An exact 1:1 molar ratio of reactants is necessary in order to form the repeating group which characterizes Nylon 6,6. While both batch and continuous operations are possible, economic conditions favour *continuous polymerisation operation* integrated with spinning equipment. The various stages are:

(i) *FEED PREPARATION STAGE*: Relevant Features:

Function: The first step for preparing Nylon 6,6 is neutralising adipic acid with hexamethylene diamine (HMDA) in methanol or water. The salt solution must then be decolourized with activated carbon before use to remove impurities which would discolour the product polymer.

Waste Streams: Decolourizing results in liquid and solid waste streams. Effluents contain spent carbon, diatomaceous earth and some nylon salt. Quantitative estimates of 14 kg. (30lb) of carbon and 2.9 kg. (6.3 lbs) of Nylon salt per 0.9 Mg (one ton) of Nylon 6,6 produced are reported by one reference for a plant producing 14 Mg. (30,000 lb) per year (F.10, F.11)

(ii) *EVAPORATION STAGE*: Relevant Features:

Function: The aqueous suspension of nylon salt is fed to a steam heated evaporator operated in a continuous mode for concentration. One source specifies the use of an agitated thin film evaporator.

Operating parameters: The concentrated slurry is generally 50 to 60 per cent nylon salt but it may contain as high as 75% solids. The bulk of the water is removed in the continuous method. A temperature of 110 degrees C (230 degrees F) is reported in the use of a thin film evaporator.

Waste Streams: The water vapour removed by evaporator is condensed and sent to the sewer. The liquid waste stream contains upto one percent HMDA and is one of the major sources of BOD in the aqueous waste from the plant. Additional contaminants in the waste water are reported by one source as 2.4 kg. methanol, 4 kg. nylon salt and 1.4 kg. of other impurities (including glutaric acid, succinic acid, acetic acid, 1.2 cyclohexadiamine) per 0.90 Mg (one ton) of Nylon 6,6 produced. An EPA summary of emissions based on replies to questionnaires indicate an emission of 0.000333 kg. of particulates and aerosols per kg. of Nylon 6,6 produced. These particulates and aerosols contain HMDA, adipic acid, nylon salt, nylon polymer, cyclo-pentanone, halide and sulfonamide and are responsible for the "blue haze" formation attributed to the Nylon 6,6 process.

(iii) *POLYMERIZATION (CONTINUOUS) STAGE*: Relevant Features:

Function: Additives such as acetic acid and titanium dioxide alongwith the dewatered monomer from the earlier stage are fed to tank reactors, tubular columns or thin film reactors. The reaction mixture is subjected to elevated temperature and pressure to effect polymerisation. Water produced by the reaction is removed as steam. Additional water of reaction is removed by reducing the pressure to atmospheric pressure, which is a flashing step. The vapour streams consisting of contaminated steam may be scrubbed with water to reduce atmospheric emissions. Acetic acid is added as a chain terminator and delustrants such as titanium dioxide (Ti O^2) are fed to the process stream.

OPERATING PARAMETERS: Reaction temperature according to one source is 233 degrees C (450 degrees F) and reactor pressure is about 1.5 MPa (200 psig). The flashing step is accomplished at 160 degrees C (320 degree F) and atmospheric pressure.

WASTE STREAM: The water removed as steam forms a liquid waste stream of ouled condensate. If scrubbers treat the vapour stream, the scrubber water also becomes a liquid waste stream. Atmospheric emissions of particulates and aerosols (including HMDA, adipic acid, nylon salt, nylon 6,6 polymer, cyclopentanhalide and sulfonamide) are estimated as 0.00212 kg. from reactor and 0.0011 kg. from the flasher per kg. of nylon 6,6 produced. These are the materials believed to be causing the "blue haze" formation. Another source indicates emissions of O.1 kg. (2.6lb) of HMDA per 0.90 Mg (one ton) of Nylon 6,6 produced.

(iv) *PRODUCT PREPARATION STAGE*: Relevant Features:

Function: In some continuous operations, the polymer goes through a finisher at elevated temperature to assure complete polymerisation. Molten polymer from a continuous process may go directly to spinning operations. The polymer may also be cast and pelleted as in the Batch Method to form a resin product.

Operating Parameters: Finishing takes place at a temperature of 280 degrees C (540 degrees F).

Waste Streams: The vent from the finisher contributes emissions of particulates and aerosols estimated at 0.044 g. per kg. of Nylon 6,6 produced. This stream is normally not scrubbed.

CREDIBILITY

- *Sam Singh* (Du Pont): In 50 years of experience we have not seen or heard of any bad effect on the people or on the environment. So it is not showing you the good side and hiding something. I extend my invitation to come and see any of the 5 plants." (in the U.S.)

- *Sam Singh*: "Du Pont is very, very credible, as you can see how many different organizations have called Du Pont as a safe company."

- *Sam Singh*: "We do not operate our equipment worldwide even for a second, if it does not meet with environment or safety standards."

- *Sam Singh*: "...and this plant is the safest plant."

- *Sam Singh*: "We are not talking of theory on a piece of paper. We are talking about the practical experience of 50 years of safe operation where not a single incident of environmental pollution has been noted. That is why I was taken aback when you (Chairman Mr. A.N. Naik) said otherwise. I mean it with all sincerity as I am the one from Du Pont who is going to live in Goa."

- *Rita Heckrotte* (Du Pont): "You will not find an incident with this plant, You will not....we stand by our records."

NOTE I:

In pelleting and flaking procedures, pneumatic conveying methods and dry blending procedures are potential sources of particulate emissions. The once through cooling water for the casting section forms a liquid waste stream containing polymer fines. One U.S. plant indicated that this waste stream is generated at the rate of 0.14 m³ (36 gal)/ min. No indication of the plant capacity was given. Another U.S. source indicated that a portion of this waste water may be used in the cooling tower for condensing. Casting scrap forms a solid waste stream which is reportedly incinerated. One plant reports incinerating 0.003 kg. Nylon scrap per kg. produced, but no data is given on the composition of the incineration gases.

NOTE II:

"BLUE HAZE"

An environmental problem may exist in plant localities due to the formation of a "blue haze". This is caused by particulate and aerosol emissions from various vents throughout the operation. According to one source in the U.S. waste-water emanating from Nylon 6,6 production process is 0 to 152.3³/Mg. Raw waste load is reported to include BOD: 1 to 135 kg/Mg: COD 1 to 300 kg/Mg; and suspended solids, 0 to 8 kg/Mg.

Some Reflections:

The extensive use of chemically hazardous substances in the production process has been noted. The constituents of the waste streams in the various stages of production have also been shown, alongwith the presence of a "Blue Haze", in plant localities, caused by particulates and aerosol emissions from various vents.

Though TDL representatives preach the absence of any major point source air emissions, experts warn that *fugitive emissions* may be a significant environmental as well as worker health hazard. The magnitude of impact of these emissions is a function of stream constituents, process operating parameters, engineering and administrative controls and maintenance programmes. Additionally, employees may be exposed to monomers, catalysts and other additives during the handling and packaging of raw materials and final product. Then there is the real problem of disposal of solid wastes and liquid effluents. The expected volume of water waste disposal per day is in the region of 1000 m^3 and the TDL plans to discharge its liquid effluent after "treatment" into the Madei river at Khandepar. This could cause serious adverse effects on marine life and endanger human as well as `animal/cattle' life downstream. The presence of gaseous emissions would also pose an environmental threat to the surrounding areas. The Westerly winds would carry the emissions towards the populated areas of Savoi-Verem, Vagurme and Pale. Harmful effluent seepage into the earth could also result into the poisoning of sweet water spring in the Kerim Plateau region for miles around. The harmful consequences on human, animal and plantation life could be substantial.

B.6.7 Conclusion:

Contrary to the claims of the TDL, the Nylon 6,6 manufacturing process involves the following:

(1) Indiscriminate, unwarranted, dangerous and cheap use of our vital natural resources such as river water presently already overused for drinking purposes, ground water being presently utilised for sustaining one of the richest 'agricultural/horticultural/forestry' watersheds in the State, prime agro-horticultural land-scape and power supply.

(2) Use of hazardous chemical raw materials.

(3) High probability of TDL venturing into the local manufacture of the above cited raw materials (Adipic Acid and HMD) which is much more dangerous from the pollution point of view.

(4) Potentially dangerous and significantly large quantities of solid, liquid as well as gaseous pollutants are produced at every stage during the manufacturing process.

B.7   THE VALIDITY OF NYLON 6,6 PROJECT'S EFFLUENT TREATMENT CLAIMS

B.7.1 The licensing conditions related to pollution control.

The preconditions laid down by the Government of India concerning environmental pollution in the Letter of Intent issued to any industry, are as follows: (E.2, E.3)

1) The State Director of Industries has to confirm that the site of the project has been approved from the environmental angle by the competent State authority.

2) The entrepreneur commits both to the State and Central Government's that he will install the appropriate equipments and implement the prescribed measures for the prevention and control of pollution.

3) The concerned State Pollution Control Board has to certify that the proposal meets with the environmental requirement and that equipments installed or proposed to be installed are adequate and appropriate to the requirements.

The effluent treatment process will have to meet the above conditions stringently.

B.7.2 Salient features of Nylon 6,6 technology vis-a-vis pollution control.

TDL's Nylon 6,6 project has to be analysed with respect to the above conditions in the context of the specific manufacturing technology. Hence, one has to consider the following:

(1) Nylon 6,6 is a trade name of Du Pont for Polymide Fiber. But TDL considers it as a chemical product.

(2) Nylon 6,6 manufacturing process is a closely guarded technology. (E.23, E.24, E.28, E.16)

(3) The raw materials required for Nylon 6,6 including the additives, finishers etc. will be imported.

(4) Hexamethylene diamine and adipic acid, the basic ingredients, have not been used on a large scale by fibre industry or any other industry, in India.

(5) There is no way to cross-check the information provided by TDL or Du Pont as regards the intricacies of the chemical process, technical components involved, composition of effluents, emissions, etc.

(6) The effluent treatment, waste disposal and emission control processes for Nylon 6,6 have been standardised by Du Pont and hence are specific to their own manufacturing technology.

(7) Effluent treatment, waste disposal and emission control know-how for Nylon 6,6 production does not exist in India.

(8) Since Nylon 6,6 is a new material to be manufactured in India, specific effluents and emission control, regulations will have to be applied to it. The existing general regulations are inadequate to cover the range of effluents and emission components, such as Diamine Carbonate. (D.2.3, D.2.4, D.2.5)

(9) Du Pont's disseminate their state-of-the-art waste management and environmental restoration services through a separate concern namely, 'Du Pont Safety and Environmental Resources'. The so called 'state-of-the-art technology' for effluent treatment, claimed by them for Nylon 6,6 process is thus a separate marketing item. To import it, separate agreement may be necessary. (E.22)

(10) State-of-the-art effluent treatment plant is an integrated component of the Nylon 6,6 manufacturing unit. The manufacturing process and effluent treatment plant, therefore, are based on the same technical specifications and equipment configuration. (E.48)

B.7.3 Claims about the non-polluting nature of technology.

In its application for Letter of Intent, the EDC based on the information supplied by BILT claimed that ".....the technology that we are going to get is highly advanced and sophisticated and the import of equipment will have built in provision to adequately treat the effluents before discharge ....besides whatever little discharge is there will be as per I.S.I. standards ...." (E.1)

TDL mentions some of the salient features of Nylon 6,6 (their application dated 26.9.88) as follows:

"f) Du Pont Nylon 6,6 technology is closely held and involves proprietary equipment and design.

g) Du Pont process is non-polluting and safe''. (E.23)

TDL also claims that ... "The process for manufacture of Nylon 6,6 is so designed that no environmental pollution will arise. The process is non-polluting and free of any environmental hazards''.

These claims have been made on the assumption that the manufacturing plant will incorporate state-of-the-art effluent treatment technology involving 'proprietory equipment and design'. The claims were analysed critically with respect to all the documentary and other information available to us. The discrepancies found are detailed below.

B.7.4 Discrepancies in various versions of effluent treatment process.

At least six versions have come to our notice after analysing various documents and after examining Du Pont's claims as well as the plant layout. The versions are as follows:

Version 1: This is found in the capital goods import application made by TDL in September, 1988. The information given in the application (dated 26.9.88) as an appended document gives some aspects of effluent treatment plant. (E.23)

Version 2: This is found in the presentation made to the Technical Committee of Goa State Pollution Control Board, on 25th May, 1989. It appears as a continuation of the note on Nylon 6,6 subtitled 'Manufacturing Process':

Version 3: This is found in the document mentioned in "Version 2" above, entitled `Exhibit 1': Indian Nylon Venture Waste Water Treatment Scope: Major Equipment. (D.3)

Version 4: This is found in the BILT report (Jan.1989) in the section on environmental factors and in other sections (E.28).

Version 5: This version is based on the presentation made by Ms.Rita Heckrotte of Du Pont before the House Committee on 9th October, 1990 at the Conference Hall, Secretariat, Panaji. The Version is also based on the replies given to various questions raised by the Members present and the discussion that followed (E. 48).

Version 6: This is based on our study of the technical drawing giving scaled dimensions of various types of works at the proposed site Kerim (Ponda). (D.1.3, D.2.1.)

As per *Version 1*, the state-of-the-art effluent treatment technology will be available to TDL in India. It is claimed that "Du Pont process is non-polluting and is safe", and the envisaged "Nylon 6,6 Fibre manufacturing technology that would be coming to India will be a most modern state-of-the-art technology currently being practiced by Du Pont in U.S.A., or elsewhere in their own plants" and "it will be providing for the first time continuous polymerisation, coupled with spinning and spin drawn system not yet available in India". It is also claimed that "the process for manufacture of Nylon 6,6 is so designed that no environmental pollution will arise".

The idea that is given in the said capital goods import approval application is that of "state-of-the-art effluent treatment technology" to be supplied to India by Du Pont. However, it does not form part of the plant import package that is being given in the application. If the effluent treatment plant does not form part of the equipments to be imported as capital goods, then it means that the same may be procured from India or from other sources excluding Du Pont. But, in a notice directed to indigenous manufacturers and published in the "Indian Export Bulletin" by TDL on December 26,1987, *we do not find any reference to equipments related to state-of-the-art effluent treatment plant*. At serial No.25, of the said notice, only 3 items are mentioned: (1) TOC analyser (2) flow measuring instruments (3) kjedahl unit, which are analytical instruments mostly used for checking the quality of `wastes/effluents' generated.

Since no specific information and detailed sketch of the promised 'state-of-the-art' effluent treatment process technology is available in this document, we are inclined to believe that, in reality, there are *no* plans to install an effluent treatment plant as an Integrated part of Nylon 6,6 manufacturing unit.

As per *Version 2*, we have been led to believe that recycling units, dikes, equalisation vessels, aeration vessels, abatement equipment etc. will be used as components of the proposed effluent treatment plant. It is claimed that .... "*The treatment system is based on a design operating in the U.S.A. Vessels will be above ground and will be similar to Du Pont's Nylon 6,6 plant in the US*".

It is clear from this claim that the treatment system is not exactly the one that is being employed in the USA but '*is based on a design*'. It will not be the same but '*similar*'. This shows the uncertainity about the exact configuration of the effluent treatment plant at Kerim site. From this version, we may conclude that if the state-of-the-art effluent treatment plant is not being imported, the serious technological gap will be filled by designing the ETP based on the configuration of the U.S.A. But the state-of-the-art technology would remain as a proprietory secret of Du Pont.

In the same presentation, part 'M' entitled 'Environmental Factors', gives information on the effluent treatment plant and environmental monitoring which is taken from the BILT report (January 1989). Here, some more components come into picture. They include emergency holding tanks, guard pond, centrifuge and monitoring stations. The list of components given at two separate places in the same presentation document shows that a sort of 'patch work' planning has been done about the effluent treatment process which obviously is ambiguous, unclear and, consequently, appears fictitious.

In *Version 3*, we could visualise a flow diagram of the waste water treatment plant after going through the list of major equipments given under Exhibit 1. However, on close scrutiny, we found that this exhibit is of foreign origin and the listed equipments like Belt Filter Press, Polymer Feed Facilities, etc. have not been mentioned in Version 1 & 2. Neither do they form a part of import package.

The buildings mentioned in the above exhibit (Page 2) such as 'Belt Filter/Polymer Building' and 'ECR/ICR' have not been indicated in the earlier versions as a part of the effluent treatment plant. The instruments mentioned in the exhibit except flow metres are excluded from earlier versions.

Figure 1 which is a part of the Exhibit 1 and entitled 'Indian Nylon Venture Waste Water Treatment Facilities', 'tank alternative', when analysed comparatively, was found to be inconsistent with the flow chart found in the same presentation, related to Version 2. (compare D 1.4, D.3 Fig.1)

If Version 2 and Version 3 are compared, the discrepancies are quite serious, because this was the documentation used by the decision makers of State Pollution Control Board and its technical Committee, to grant a NOC to TDL, on 2.2.1990. Although, the technical Committee of the Goa State Pollution Control Board could be taken for a ride by TDL, our analysis indicate that the effluent treatment plant has *not* been given any serious thought.

As regards Version 4, on closer examination of the BILT report to cross-check the facts related to the effluent treatment plant, we found that no efforts have been made to procure the major equipments from indigenous suppliers. There is no provision to construct buildings as mentioned in Version 3. There is a provision of only Rs.34 lakhs in Annexure J.2 under 'Indigenous Equipment', Section 2.8. *Effluent Treatment Plant for Factory and Residentials, Disposal Pipeline Pumps, Cake Trolleys*. It is to be noted that pipeline pumps and cake trolleys have been grouped together with the effluent treatment plant for the factory and residential facilities. If these equipments were to be procured from indigenous suppliers, no details have been made available. Besides the notice given by TDL was also silent about this aspect as mentioned in Version 1.

This report further mentions in serial No.1.19 that Rs.12 lakhs will be spent on the civil works of effluent treatment plant. Considering the civil works and the cost of equipments, the amount provided for the effluent treatment plant comes to Rs.46 lakhs.

We noticed that the company has not thought of laying an effluent discharge pipeline to release the treated waste water in an environmentally sound way, and the planning of the envisaged effluent treatment plant appears to hang on some alternate release and discharge point within the premises.

It is pertinent to note that while the company has provided Rs.950 lakhs for captive power generation facilities, only Rs.46 lakhs are allotted to the effluent treatment plant which obviously is not based on the so called 'state-of-the-art' technical specification of Du Pont.

In the BILT report (Annexure 1.3 under 'Du Pont Technical Information' at 'G') we have the *'Description of effluent and recommended treatment for disposal'*, meaning obviously that only description of effluents and treatment for its disposal will be recommended as a part of the technical information and knowhow supplied by Du Pont.

In Annexure I.4 of the same report, we found that *no* specific engineering information related to the effluent treatment plant has been given as a part of technical knowhow package agreed to by Du Pont. Similarly, under 'plant & machinery' (Section J), where information is given about the capital goods to be imported, no mention is made about the import of equipments related to the effluent treatment plant. The information provided pertains to only the manufacturing plant equipments to be acquired by TDL from the existing Du Pont manufacturing facility in the U.S.A.

Considering the inconsistencies described above, we have no alternative but to conclude that the entire effluent treatment plant scheme is incomplete and uncertain.

Version 5 apparently is the most up-to-date version (E.48) available to us. This refers to the slide presentation by Rita Heckrotte of Du Pont before the House Committee on 9th October, 1990 at the Conference Hall, Secretariat. Among other things, it mentioned that TDL proposes to install a 5 km. long pipeline to discharge the treated effluents in Mandovi river. The description of effluent treatment plant presented in this meeting, when compared to earlier versions, did not bring out any new facts but on the contrary has put before us several question marks:

(1) Whether the equipments shown in the flow charts will be imported or procured internally?

(2) Whether the modified scheme including the 5 km. pipeline will be presented to the concerned authorities and if so, when?

(3) Whether the Indian technical knowhow would be comparable to the state-of-the-art effluent treatment plant technology used by Du Pont?

(4) Whether the proprietory and secret state-of-the-art effluent treatment plant 'design/ fabrication/manufacturing' technology will be supplied to TDL without a separate agreement?

(5) Whether the effluent treatment 'design/technology' claimed to be in operation at Richmond, USA, would be compatible in a tropical, humid and monsoon prone climate prevalent in Goa.

No satisfactory answers were given in the said meeting attended by Du Pont's representatives regarding the above aspects. As for the cost of the effluent treatment plant, Mr. Vijay Malik of TDL submitted that it will be Rs.5 crores. This we found is *not* in agreement with earlier versions and the cost of laying the 5 km. long pipeline is yet to be taken into account separately.

Version 6 is based on our study of technical drawings and observations made on-the-spot during site visits.

From the technical drawings and figures given under TDL's land utilisation plan, it can be noted that the dimensions of the effluent treatment plant are not only inconsistent with all the previous versions but even the land where the said effluent treatment plant is supposed to be built is yet to be acquired. The drawings do not indicate any linkage between the manufacturing plant and the proposed effluent treatment plant and unless the input route is drawn, it is difficult to visualise how the waste water and the effluents will be treated.

In the BILT report (page 159, Section M), it is stated categorically that *pollution treatment/ treatment facilities to treat waste water, air and solid waste will be taken up before commencing production.*

However, while it can be seen from the site developments that the installation of manufacturing plant has been given top priority, there is absolutely no indication of any preparations for erecting the effluent treatment plant.

From the scale of the effluent treatment plant, its location on the site and the non-priority given to its basic development work, it follows that TDL may not at all be serious about the proposed effluent treatment plant. The ETP 'paddy field test farm' as shown in the drawing consulted, shows that the sludge is likely to be dumped in the said area which is a fertile 'morod' paddy field. Also, it should be pointed out that the mention of this so called "paddy field test farm" is missing in all earlier versions described above.

Ultimately, when all versions are analysed, it can be concluded that the claim of state-of-the-art effluent treatment technology being a part of the Nylon 6,6 manufacturing unit, is a *hoax* shrouded by discrepancies, inconsistencies, gaps conflicting statements and 'adhoc/casual' treatment of such an important issue.

Nylon 6,6 manufacturing process and the state-of-the-art effluent treatment plant are complimentary and specific to each other. Any other combination or configuration will be a gamble ruining the environment, ecology and health of the people in this State.

B.7.5- Other revealing observations:

(1) Comments on discrepancies noted in the Land Utilisation Plan and the flow chart given in BILT report. (D.1.4)

The flow chart of the Effluent Treatment Plant shows several equipments namely, lifting sump, equalization tank, emergency holding tank, aerator tank, clarifier, guard pump etc. Most of the equipments occupy a large area excluding that required for their supervision and maintenance. However, the Land Utilisation Plan shows that only 1200 sq. mts. of land will be reserved for the Effluent Treatment Plant. If so, the question remains as to which design is correct and reliable.

(2) Comments on drawing No.1014/2001 entitled "Master Plan" dated 2-8-1989 of the T.D.L. Project

1. The analysis of Master Plan drawing shows that the main plant building will be constructed at a height of 149-153 metres.

2. On all the sides there is a smooth slope.

3. The effluent treatment plant area shown in this drawing does not match with the description given in other documents such as the BILT report.

4. There is no underground or over-ground connection shown between the main manufacturing plant and the effluent treatment plant.

5. No outlets are shown on the effluent treatment plant design, to discharge the effluents by underground or overground pipelines.

6. The drawing shows that a disproportionately large area has been acquired for the said project.

7. A big area entitled "paddy field test farm" could be clandestinely used for dumping waste material, sludge or even untreated effluents.

8. No central sewerage treatment plant has been indicated for colonies I and II.

9. No water intake pipeline has been indicated for the manufacturing process.

10. The area under Zone F (area:499,700 m^2) where TDL plans to have the effluent treatment plant, horticulture farm, nursery, etc. the land is characterised by an undulating and rocky terrain with a natural drainage, that can facilitate the effluents to flow by gravity into the Madei-river, and, on way, seep through the porous laterite strata into the ground water aquifer.

11. No drainage channels have been indicated for laboratory wastes, boiler water blowdown, sanitary wastes, clean condensate, storm water and fine water, and oil spillage from oil storage tanks. One valid fear is that of rain water, spillage, run off, etc. being diverted into the natural valley in the West, which is rich in springs, areacanut plantations, coconut plantations and horticultural farms.

(3) Insufficient area earmarked for E.T.P.

From the land utilisation plan given by Thapar Du Pont Ltd., which gives zone areas in sq. mts., terrain and primary use, the Effluent Treatment Plant is shown in Zone 'F' (D.2.1)

Zone 'F' contains R & D Centre, Dipping plant, Conning Department, Colony Quarters type 'F', Children Park, Playground, Effluent Treatment Plant, Horticultural Farm and Nursery. As per the above plan, the effluent treatment plant will be confined to an area of 40 x 30 mts. i.e. 1200 sq. mts. This is hardly 0.24% of zone 'F' and 0.01% of the total area.

Further, considering the total area under Fiber Plant, Fabric Plant and Polymerization Plant as provided in Zone 'D', it could be seen that the effluent treatment plant area is just about 5% of the same. As of date details regarding the specifics and efficiency of the treatment process are vague. One wonders whether this size of the effluent treatment plant can handle the quantum of wastes which would be produced.

It can thus be concluded that for a plant of the magnitude of Nylon 6,6 which requires a matching state-of-the-art effluent treatment technology the Effluent Treatment Plant has been given a poor consideration in the land utilisation plan of T.D.L.

B.7.6 - Conclusions

1) Nylon 6,6 manufacture and its effluent treatment process is a proprietory secret and it appears that only the aged and undated manufacturing equipments will be exported by Du Pont to India.

2) The compatible and integrable effluent treatment technology for Nylon 6,6 process has not been developed anywhere in Asia and the Du Pont process is specific and proprietory.

3) The Thapar's have no capability to manufacture the state-of-the-art effluent treatment technology for Nylon 6,6 on their own.

4) The application for import of capital goods *exclude* all components related to Nylon 6,6 effluent treatment technology.

5) The various provisions of TDL's estimates do not match with realistic estimates of installing state-of-the-art effluent treatment technology.

6) It can be concluded that the company gives top most priority to complete all civil and technological work related to the manufacturing unit expeditiously, and only secondary and hesitant references are made to the Effluent Treatment Plant.

7) Since many versions of planning, designs and layout of the Effluent Treatment Plant have been submitted by TDL, at various stages, we are forced to conclude that the Company is not serious in giving due importance to treatment of raw effluents. All available documents also indicate that TDL's claims of installing a state-of-the-art effluent treatment plant cannot be believed. Hence, such an 'incomplete/doubtful' proposal cannot be allowed to move ahead.

B.8 - THE ROLE OF THE GOA STATE POLLUTION CONTROL BOARD (GSPCB)

The powers of the State Board according to the Water (Prevention & Control of Pollution) Act, 1974, have been specified as follows:

(a) to plan a comprehensive programme for the prevention, control or abatement of pollution of streams and wells in the State and to secure the execution thereof;

(b) to advise the State Govt. on any matter concerning the prevention, control or abatement of water pollution;

(c) to collect and disseminate information relating to water pollution and the prevention, control or abatement thereof;

(d) to encourage, conduct and participate in investigations and research relating to problems of water pollution and prevention control or abatement of water pollution;

(e) to inspect sewage or trade effluents, works and plants for the treatment of sewage and trade effluents and to review plants, specification or other data relating to plants set up for the treatment of water works for the purification thereof and the system for the disposal of sewage or trade effluents or in connection with the grant of any consent as required by this Act;

(f) to lay down, modify or annul effluents standards for the sewage and trade effluents and for the quality of receiving waters (not being water in an inter-State stream) resulting from the discharge of effluent and to classify waters of the State:

(g) to evolve economical and reliable methods of treatment of sewage and trade effluents, having regard to the peculiar conditions of soils, climate and water resources of different regions and more especially the prevailing flow characteristics of water in streams and wells which render it impossible to attain even the minimum degree of dilution;

(h) to lay down standards of treatment of sewage and trade effluents to be discharged into any particular stream taking into account the minimum fair weather dilution available in that stream and the tolerance limits of pollution permissible in the water of the stream, after the discharge of such effluents;

    (i)   to make, vary or revoke any order-

        (i)   for the prevention, control or abatement of discharges of waste into streams or wells;

        (ii)   requiring any person concerned to construct new systems for the disposal of sewage and trade effluents or to modify, alter or extend any such existing system or to adopt such remedial measures as are necessary to prevent, control or abate water pollution;

(j) to lay down effluent standards to be complied with by persons while causing discharge of sewage or sullage or both and to lay down, or modify annul effluent standards for the sewage and trade effluents;

(k) to advise the State Govt. with respect to location of any industry, the carrying on of which is likely to pollute a stream or well;

(l) to perform such other functions as may be prescribed or as may, from time to time, be entrusted to it by the Central Board or the State Govt.

Given above are some of the important functions of the State Pollution Control Boards as per the Water Act. Similarly, the Air (Prevention and Control of Pollution) Act 1981, also specifies functions of the Pollution Control Boards.

From all that has been given above, it is clear that the Goa State Pollution Control Board holds a position of paramount importance/responsibility as far as guaranteeing the protection, preservation, conservation and maintenance of the environment is concerned. It should have been the bounden duty of the State Pollution Control Board, therefore, to have exercised its powers and discharged its responsibilities to the best of its abilities, more so, in issuing the NOC to a large Chemical Factory such as the Nylon 6,6 project. Since such a plant does not exist anywhere in India or for that matter in Asia, it was imperative that the study of possible chemical and pollution hazards should have received the careful and studious consideration it deserved. In carrying out its duty to issue NOC to the Nylon 6,6 project, the Goa State Pollution Control Board was bound to analyse the matter critically and indicate its directives by clear, stringent and comprehensive directions in the NOC to be issued. However, the NOC given by the Board belied all these expectations, being a very superficial and naive document.

When one goes through the No Objection (E.41) Certificate issued by the Goa State Pollution Control Board, to Thapar Du Pont Limited for production of Nylon 6,6 Tyre Cord at Kerim, it is surprising at the first instance that the NOC for a huge chemical project should consist merely of one page and half. The NOC should have been a detailed document covering many aspects provided and required by the relevant pollution control acts.

The said NOC, is found to be full of lacunae and hence unacceptable as a valid document due to the following reasons:-

1. One of the main functions of the State Pollution Control Boards is to advise the State Government with respect to the suitability of locations vis-a-vis the proposed industry so as to minimize the possible environmental damage in general and the pollution of air, water and land in particular. This is clearly mentioned in the Air Act, 1981 and the Water Act, 1974. Nowhere in this NOC given by the State Board, the proposed location of the Nylon 6,6 plant has been specified.

2. It does not specify the standards for stack emissions likely to be discharged from the Nylon 6,6 plant nor does it make any mention of the likely pollutants involved in stack emissions.

3. It does not specify the hazardous substances involved in the process of Nylon 6,6 manufacture nor does it prescribe any 'regulations/precautions' for their handling.

4. By merely stating that the mode of transport of hazardous material should be by river, the Board feels that it has discharged its duties. It has not considered the fact that to reach the factory premises at the proposed site, at least part of the journey by road is inevitable. It has also not considered the transportation alternative when the barges do not operate during the monsoon. Other dangers on the transportation front, that have been ignored are:

(i) the unsuitability of the existing roads for transportation of heavy vehicles carrying hazardous chemicals.

(ii) the possibility of accidents involving hazardous chemicals and the precautions to be taken in this regard. (See Map D.1.2.1. (2a))

5. The Board also ought to have specified the maximum amount of each of the hazardous materials that could be stored at any given time within the factory premises.

6. It has failed to specify the pollutants in the treated effluents and fix the qualitative and quantitative standards for the same.

7. The general standards stipulated in item No.5 of the NOC are meant for effluents discharged from small-scale industries, mining, sewage, etc., and not for a large, Nylon 6,6 type of highly polluting industry. Since the Govt. of India considers this industry as highly polluting, the Goa State Pollution Control Board was duty bound to certify that the equipments proposed to be installed to treat the effluents and stack emission were adequate and appropriate to convert raw effluents and stack emissions to standards acceptable for their final discharge into the environment.

On the contrary, the Board has not even bothered to check the doubtful validity of TDL's claim that they will install a state-of-the-art effluent treatment plant. If it had done so, the Board would have discovered the *unreliability* of TDL's claims as has been determined by this report. In short, the Board has given the full benefit of doubt to the Company's unilateral claims and none to the people of Goa.

8. It does not even specify the location of the outlet for the discharge of effluents and the desired characteristics of the receiving ambient water body. This specification is *indispensable* since the 'qualitative/quantitative' standards for discharge of treated effluents are to be laid down based on the quality, current use and dilution potential of the receiving ambient water body. Also, no standards have been laid down for the receiving ambient water body.

9. It merely mentions that the domestic and industrial effluents should be treated separately. No detailed specifications, nor any design of the proposed effluent treatment plant and its approval is included in the document.

10. Similarly, the NOC merely directs that Low Sulphur High Speed diesel should be used as fuel, without identifying the likely emissions and without prescribing any treatment and disposal 'standards/procedures'.

11. It stipulates that second quality product should not be burnt or otherwise disposed on site. At the same time, it fails to indicate as to how it should be disposed. So also, it does *not* stipulate any condition for disposal of solid waste.

12. In condition No. 8 of the NOC, it is stated that the National Institute of Oceanography could survey the stretch of river where the treated effluents will be discharged. This appears to be a highly unethical suggestion since the Chairman of the Technical Committee of the GSPCB, responsible for the NOC, is himself from NIO.

CONCLUSION:

On detailed perusal of the NOC granted by the Goa State Pollution Control Board, it is clear that the document is very superficial and fails miserably in upholding the mandate given to the Board by virtue of the Water (Prevention & Control of Pollution) Act, 1974 and Air (Prevention & Control of Pollution) Act, 1981.

B.9   THE CREDIBILITY OF DU PONT, THAPARS AND TDL.

In seeking to promote the Nylon 6,6 project in the small and fragile State of Goa, EDC authorities have merely gone by Thapar's and Du Pont's high sounding claims that the Nylon 6,6 plant is totally non-polluting and that Du Pont Company has creditable reputation, in the U.S.A., not only as far as environment protection is concerned but also as far as workers safety and health safety are concerned.

EDC has failed to procure necessary and important information about the foreign collaborator it had entered into an agreement with. What is to be criticised severely is the fact that it did not think it is necessary in the first place.

Information obtained from reliable sources in the United States, viz: National Wildlife Federation, Environment Protection Agency, and others has served to expose the negative side of Du Ponts and dispel their claims of an impeccable reputation on environmental, health, and worker safety fronts. A compilation of relevant information is given below.

B.9.1 - Factual report compiled by National Toxic Campaign Fund of U.S.A. (D.4.2).

[The Du Pont Company, officially known as E.I. Du Pont De Nemours and Company, produces and releases into the environment, into our water and air, many thousands of pounds of deadly toxics each year. These toxics cause immeasurable harm to the environment, to Du Pont workers and the public health. Some of the releases by various facilities operated by Du Pont, the chemicals involved and their effect, will be detailed in what follows.

The Du Pont Company has and continues to play a critical role in opposing essential ozone protection legislation. The failure to achieve comprehensive and expedited ozone protection measures, a failure which in no small way should be attributed to Du Pont, will likely result in an environmental catastrophe. The Du Pont Company's role in the production of chlorofluro-carbons (CFCs), a major ozone depletor, its promotion of CFCs in the face of overwhelming evidence of the dangers posed, and its continuing fight to block much needed ozone protection laws, will likewise be discussed in this memorandum.

The activities of Du Pont in opposing stronger protective standards covering benzene and acrylonitrile, both of which are highly dangerous chemicals, also merit review. Inadequate standards for benzene exposure will admittedly cause a quantitatively knowable increase in cancer occurrences, especially for workers who regularly come in contact with it. For Du Pont officials and company lawyers, fighting against sufficient benzene standards and other toxic chemical exposures appears not to present any personal difficulties. Perhaps this is because it is not company management nor lawyers who will be exposed to unsafe levels of benzene, but average workers. Du Pont's unswerving willingness to prioritize for profits rather than the safety of its workers and the community characterizes its mode of operation historically.

I. Du Pont produces and releases into the environment thousands of pounds of hazardous toxic chemicals yearly.

The National Wildlife Federation, an American based environmental group, has put together a list of the five hundred largest releases of toxic chemicals in the United States. The information used to put together *The Toxic 500*, has been collected from data compiled by the United States Government, namely, the Environmental Protection Agency (EPA) pursuant to U.S. law. In 1986, environmental and labour activists, led by the National Toxics Campaign, convinced Congress to improve chemical safety by enacting a Reauthorization to the Superfund Act (which is dedicated to the classification and clean up of toxic waste-sites throughout the nation) and as a part of the Reauthorization, the Community Right to Know Act. The Community Right to Know

Act created a "Toxics Release Inventory" which discloses the annual emissions of certain especially dangerous chemicals. The Toxic Release Inventory provides the basis for the information that follows. The laws reporting aspect became effective starting July 1, 1988. At that time, major industrial facilities were required to submit annual reports to the EPA and State agencies. Those reports cover information on the release of over 320 toxic chemicals. Facilities must submit TRI data under the following conditions: 1) they have a Standard Industrial classification code; 2) employ more than ten people and; 3) manufacture, import or process 75,000 lb$_2$/year, and 10,000 lb/year of chemicals used in any other manner. The law requires facilities to report their identity, and all offsite locations to which toxic waste has been transferred.

The National Wildlife Federation, using information reported to the Toxics Release Inventory Data (TRI or TRID) has put together a ranking of toxic releases as follows: 1) the 500 largest releases of toxics by facility; 2) the 500 largest releases of toxics; 3) the 500 largest releases of known and probable carcinogens; 4) the 100 largest releases of known and probable carcinogens, detailed summary; 5) the toxic air 100; 6) the toxic water 100; 7) the toxic land disposal 100; 8) the toxics injection 100; 9) the largest 100 toxic releases to publicly owned Treatment Works (POTW) and 10) the toxic metal 100. All figures are for 1987, since that was when reporting first became mandatory. I will only provide information which concerns the activities of Du Pont. Du Pont maintains a prominent position in the toxic five hundred club.

Several Du Pont operations were identified within the table of the 500 largest emitters of toxics, but I'm only going to include those that placed within the top 100 and they are as follows:

[] Du Pont's Johnsonville, Tennessee plant was ranked #17 and emitted 72,474,201 pounds of dangerous Toxics.

[] Du Pont's Delisle Plant in Pass Christian, Mississippi was ranked #28 and it emitted 52,797,120 pounds of toxics into the environment.

[] Du Pont's Louisville Works plant in Louisville, Kentucky released 26,113,000 pounds of toxics. This plant was ranked # 49th.

[] Du Pont's Memphis, Tennessee plant, ranked #68 emitted 18,611,386 pounds of toxics.

Under the category of the 500 largest releases of known and probable carcinogens, Du Pont's Towanda, PA. plant ranks third and has emitted 7,746,150 pounds of known and probable carcinogens. The principal carcinogen released at this facility is Dichloromethane. Dichloromethane, also known as methylene chloride, is a clear liquid used as an industrial solvent and paint thinner. It is also used in the aerosol and pesticide products and in the manufacture of photographic film. It is probably a carcinogen; in animal studies, chronic exposures leads to throat cancer and impairment in the functioning of the liver and kidneys. In humans, chronic exposure results in memory loss. Acute exposure results in respiratory tract irritation, sluggishness, intoxication, lightheadedness, nausea, headache, tingling in the limbs, unconsciousness and death.

The Du Pont plant in Johnsonville, Tennessee was ranked # 23 out of 100 for the largest facility of toxic releases to the air, emitting 10,234,001 pounds. Its plant in Pass Christian, Mississippi placed #30 and emitted into the air 7,997,027 pounds of toxics. Several other Du Pont facilities were placed within the top 100 for air toxic emissions. Various Du Pont plants rank within the top 100 for toxic releases into the water and the largest toxic releases into the land. Under the category of the top one hundred releases of toxics into the ground by injection, Du Pont had no less than four facilities in the top 15, three of their facilities rated in the top ten. The Du Pont plant in Memphis, Tennessee was identified as ninth among the largest 100 for toxic releases into publicly owned treatment works, discharging some 13,065,270 pounds. The Delisle Du Pont facility in Pass Christian, Mississippi was classified as #13 of the top one hundred releases of toxic metals, putting out close to 10,000 pounds.

II. Du Pont has impeded efforts to halt the production of CFCs and Protect the ozone layer.

CFCs have been widely used in a number of different consumer and industrial products, including: aerosol sprays, as coolants in refrigerators and air conditioners, as blowing agents in the production of plastic foams (styrofoam), and as solvents to clean electronic components. CFCs are destroying the ozone layer which protects the earth from dangerous ultraviolet (UV-B) radiation.

According to conservative projections by the EPA, ozone erosion is likely to cause 3 million to 15 million cases of skin cancer in Americans born before 2075; "some 52,000 to 252,000 of those patients are likely to die from the disease." Melanoma, a more deadly form of skin cancer accounts, currently for 4 percent of all skin cancers and 65 percent of all deaths related to skin cancer. EPA estimates that ozone depletion will lead to an additional 31,000 to 126,000 melanoma cases among US Caucasians before 2075, resulting in some 7,000 to 30,000 additional deaths. The incidence of skin cancer among Americans has increased 83 percent over the past seven years. Ozone depletion will cause cataract victims to be stricken earlier in life, making treatment more difficult. Victims in the underdeveloped part of the world will have a more difficult time receiving treatment or having the funds to pay for it and thus will be more vulnerable to incidence of blindness.

UV-B appears to depress the human immune system, imperiling the body's ability to resist attacking organisms, such as tumors and rendering the body more susceptible to infectious diseases. Of course, the destruction of the ozone layer causes great harm to almost all animal species, sea life and agriculture.

Du Pont and Imperial Chemical Industries are the two largest producers of CFCs in the world. Du Pont has been a leader within the CFC industry to block efforts at halting CFC production and ozone protection laws. Bill Walsh and Eric Johnson, from US Greenpeace have performed a detailed study of Du Pont's efforts at blocking ozone protection laws and CFC restrictions. They have observed:

"To delay the implementation of CFC restrictions, the CFC industry has challenged the findings of objective scientific studies, contradicted scientific findings with industry-sponsored studies, and continually called for more time for research."

Though much credible evidence exists which corroborates the effects of CFCs on the ozone layer, spokespersons from Du Pont persistently challenged the data. In June of 1971, two chemists from the University of California at Irvine, F.Sherwood Rowland and Maria J.Molina, first published in *Nature* magazine, evidence of the theory linking CFCs to ozone depletion. Spokespersons from Du Pont were quick to respond to initiatives aimed at stopping the production of CFCs, asserting:

"There is no experimental evidence supporting the chlorine ozone theory. To the contrary, a study by London and Kelly indicates that the concentration of stratospheric ozone has actually increased during the past decade."

-- Du Pont, 1974

"No ozone depletion has ever been detected, despite the most sophisticated analysis.... all ozone depletion figures to date are computer projections based on a series of uncertain assumptions."

-- Du Pont, 1979

The above quotation illustrates Du Pont's continuing practice of casting aspersions on the increasing amounts and acceptance of data linking CFCs to ozone depletion. In 1985, scientists discovered a giant hole in the ozone layer above the Antarctica. The CFC industry, following a pattern set by Du Pont, denied any relationship between the destruction of the ozone layer and CFCs.

"At the moment, scientific evidence does not point to the need for dramatic CFC emission reductions. There is no available measure of the contribution of CFCs to any observed ozone change. In fact, recent observations show a decrease in the amount of ultraviolet radiation from the sun reaching the United States."

-- Du Pont, March 1988

Du Pont used the above argument to delay regulations of CFCs while simultaneously announcing it would end production of them by the year two thousand.

Another tactic used by Du Pont and the CFC industry to slow regulations on CFCs, has been to argue for more time consuming research prior to actual restrictions on CFCs.

"We at Du Pont feel that such legislation aimed at regulation is unwarranted at this time... Rather, a comprehensive experimental programme should be initiated to determine whether the hypothesized reactions in fact take place."

--Du Pont, 1974

As early as June 1975, a blue ribbon governmental task force composed of representatives from seven Cabinet departments and five govt. agencies concluded that it was time to restrict the production of CFCs "unless new scientific evidence is found to remove the cause for concern." Predictably, Du Pont asserted that the US Govt. had insufficient evidence to support the restrictions and called for further studies over atleast a three year period.

While Du Pont lobbied against Govt. regulation of CFCs it, alongwith the industry, unleashed a sophisticated media campaign designed to lull the public into thinking there was nothing to be concerned about. This pattern of behaviour reflects poorly on Du Pont's sense of its own corporate responsibility to the rest of us. It seems that the company cares for little except the unimpeded flow of its profits.

III. Du Pont has shown a pattern of callous disregard for the health and safety of its workers by opposing safer chemical exposure standards and in exposing them to unsafe amounts.

In 1977, the Occupational Safety and Health Administration (OSHA) proposed a prudent standard for exposure to benzene. Strong evidence existed which linked benzene to leukemia. In August of 1976, then Director of the National Institute of Occupational Safety & Health (NIOSH) (the research and scientific wing of OSHA) submitted a criteria document to OSHA which stated: "It is apparent from the literature that benzene exposure continues to be reported... (thus) no worker (should) be exposed to benzene in excess of 1 part per million. The document acknowledged that the risks of leukemia were such that no safe level could properly be established. Workers felt that the proposed exposure standard was still too high and filed a lawsuit opposing it.

The Chemical Manufacturer's Association, an industry front for which Du Pont is an active member and the American Petroleum Institute vigorously protested the 1 ppm standard. In fact, industry was successful in legally defeating the 1 ppm standard. This will cause a numerically calculable increase in the number of leukemia deaths due to benzene exposure.

Du Pont's use of Acrylonitrile (AN), a long suspected carcinogen, resulted in many deaths and illnesses. Dr. Sam Epstein observed in *The Politics of Cancer*, that:

"On May 23, 1977, the medical director of Du Pont reported, on the basis of preliminary epidemiological studies, that he had identified sixteen cases of cancer, with 8 deaths occurring between 1969 and 1975, among 475 workers exposed to AN from 1950-1956 in the company's textile fiber plant in Camden, S. Carolina. This was nearly 3 times the incidence of cancers that would have been expected in a similar group of exposed workers."

Dr. Epstein suggests that the finding of illness and death suffered by the workers could have been anticipated. This is because the chemical structure of vinyl chloride, understood as a known carcinogen by the industry since the early 1970s, was nearly identical to AN.

The Du Pont chemical complex in Belle, W. Virginia was found to be the source of unhealthy amounts of nitrosamine in the urban areas of Belle and Charlestown, W. Virginia. According to Dr. Epstein, Nitrosamines "are a large group of chemicals, many of which are found in air, food, and water and most of which are highly carcinogenic to a great range of organs in all animal species tested." Equally disturbing, Professor Epstein relates that little work has been done on the detection and measurement of nitrosamine in water. High concentrations have been found in effluent from sewage plants treating wastewater from the Du Pont plant in Belle, W. Virginia. Incredibly "the intake for the drinking water supply of the Du Pont plant was about 500 feet downstream from where it discharged its effluent into the Kanawha River".

Du Pont has also been involved in the manufacture of pesticides. Pesticides can also be nitrosated to form nitrosamine. High concentrations of nitrosamine were discovered in randomly selected samples of commonly used pesticides in the mid-1970s. One of those pesticides was Trysben or Benzac, manufactured by Du Pont for commercial and residential use. During a congressional hearing on the matter, Du Pont attempted to minimize public health concerns over the use of its pesticides.

In August of 1975, high levels of nitrosamine in the air, around Du Pont's Belle, West Virginia plant prompted an investigation. Events surrounding testing of the facility and Du Pont's explanation of the results led to a congressional hearing in May of 1976. The hearing was to be filmed by CBS. Though invited to testify, Du Pont representatives declined, claiming short notice. However, Du Pont managers did attend as spectators and were ordered to testify "when they were found passing notes to the press offering to field questions...at the noon recess".

During hearings held by the Deptt. of Labour in 1973, Du Pont admitted regular destruction of workers' records, including workers exposed to carcinogens at the workplace.

Moreover, Manufacturing Chemist Association (CMA), an industry research group regularly employed by Du Pont admitted that it discovered the carcinogeneity of vinyl chloride in 1972. The discovery was based on studies of the liver in rats. CMA purposely withheld the information for a year and a half, "until the human evidence could no longer be ignored".

At the time Epstein wrote *The Politics of Cancer*, New Jersey had the highest cancer rate in the country. Not surprisingly, New Jersey industry manufactures every known chemical carcinogen. Salem County, New Jersey stands out as having the highest national death rate from bladder cancer "possibly related to the location there of a concentration of chemical industries, including a giant Du Pont organic chemical complex..."

It seems as if everywhere Du Pont carries on the business of producing chemicals, its workers and the community suffer from unusually high rates of cancer.

IV. Du Pont has a long history of opposing workers attempts to improve their conditions through organizing.

Poor working conditions symbolized by the arrogance and caprice of Du Pont management, motivated Du Pont workers to come together in Philadelphia, Pennsylvania in 1975. Dozens of workers from several Du Pont plants came together to share common experiences of harassment by Du Pont Management. The workers asserted that the harassment was deliberate, part of a larger campaign to crush the organising drive of the United Steel workers. The percentage of unionized workers at Du Pont was quite small. Later that year in September, Du Pont laid off two workers in Virginia who had been active organizers and critical of company policy.

In February of 1976, Du Pont workers from Richmond, Virginia hosted a large organizing rally of Du Pont workers from all over. Consumer and environmental activist Ralph Nader was one of the feature speakers. Remarking on Du Pont's propensity for converting to the corporation, the inventions made by workers on their own time, Nader labelled the practice "suppression of freedom of speech". Dr. Sidney Wolfe, another key speaker, noted that Du Pont workers suffered disproportionately from workplace deaths. He charged the company with conducting "human experimentation". Essentially, the company calculatingly exposed workers to dangerous levels of chemicals to see what the effect would be. Nader further charged that big companies like Du Pont had the money and the technological capability to make their workplaces safe, but instead spent their time fighting regulations.

On another note, Du Pont officials were hauled in front of a senate Subcommittee in 1976 to explain why the company's foreign subsidiaries were greasing the palms of foreign governments to promote Du Pont's business. Between 1973 and 1975 Du Pont subsidiaries had paid out $337,000 dollars in illegal payments.

Irving Shapiro, Du Pont's Chief Operating Executive, went on the public relations offensive on the issue of illegal foreign payments. Over sixty other companies had admitted to similar unlawful payments. This made the public cynical of secretive corporate dealings. Addressing a Boston audience on this matter, Du Pont's Shapiro, remarked:

"If trust and respect are lacking it is not just because of recent well publicized misbehaviour by some companies; it is also because for years we in business have not taken the public into our confidence ... Going public is not painful and it helps to dispel the aura of suspicion."

However, Gerard Colby, author of *The Du Pont Dynasty*, noted "(for) people in Latin America, on the other hand, Du Pont's not going public, could be very painful, even deadly. Du Pont's subsidiary in Latin America produced a pain reliever Valipirone. The drug is not sold in the United States because it may cause a fatal blood disease, and a condition of severe depression of the marrow of the bone. The Federal Food and Drug Administration and the American Medical Association determined the drug to be very dangerous and cautioned that it should be used only as a last resort when all other drugs fail. In apparent contradiction to Chairman Shapiro's dictum about public disclosure, Du Pont neglected to inform Latin American users about the drug's dangers. The Du Pont Chairman once proclaimed: "one could not justify shipping to another nation a product that is inherently unsafe".

Du Pont's method of doing business, its unscrupulous tactics, are well illustrated by its operation of a multi million dollar textile and paper dye's plant which dumped highly polluted water into a once pristine water supply. Gerard Colby tells the story in *The Du Pont Dynasty*:

"There, on the banks of the Manari River that flows placidly into the Caribbean, cows and chickens belonging to local farmers began to die, and the one hundred fishermen who know little else in life but to fish began noticing that the once clear green colour of the river was turning black. When red sores began showing up on the fishermen's skin, they took their case to the EPA to protest a discharge permit (it had granted Du Pont to dump in the river).

"Du Pont which had been attracted to the area by its rich spring of pure mineral water, responded with Shapiro tactic number one. "We have tried very diligently to serve the community" said plant manager N.J. Irsh, "yet we are the guys who have gotten into trouble." When local public interest lawyers pointed out that all that technology promised Puerto Rico 76 million gallons of contaminated water rather than purification devices, Shapiro tactic number two was implemented: Du Pont, taking advantage of employment fears while the island was going through a severe economic depression, threatened to shut down and throw 350 residents out of work."

In 1976, Du Pont staked out a leadership position, in the all out attack by corporate America, against the Environmental Protection Agency (EPA). In June of that year Du Pont challenged the legal authority of the EPA to reduce the content of lead in gasoline. Du Pont's strategy was to delay regulatory decisions through time consuming litigation.

Workers at Du Pont's plant at Belle, West Virginia suffered 206 fatal cancers of the eye, throat, skin, brain and face in less than a twenty year time period. The company blamed the high rate on where the workers lived, not the fact of where they worked. Du Pont's own director of environmental affairs, forced to testify at a Congressional hearing when his presence was discovered by a number of workers, admitted that the cancer rate for workers at the plant was higher than the rate for the general community. The union's safety chairman, Earl McCune, disclosed a probable cause, in that the plant "discharged its wastes in the river just five hundred feet from where it took water for drinking by its employees."

Du Pont then undertook its own study of the cancer rate of its workers at the Belle, West Virginia plant in comparison with the general population. Not surprisingly, the Du Pont report concluded that the cancer rate among its workers was twenty one percent lower than the general population. After studying the Du Pont report, Dr. Michael Shimkia, a health expert from the University of California described it as "a deliberate attempt to mislead" and "a public relations show job". The National Institute of Cancer and NIOSH both dismissed the methodology and conclusions of the Du Pont report with contempt. Dr. John Finklea of the National Institute of Cancer told the sub-committee that for Du Pont "to publicly congratulate itself on its low cancer rate, is not merited, is misleading to the public and a disservice to workers".

Since 1968, Du Pont has been in the business of dumping more than 2 million gallons of toxics into the ocean, off the coast of New Jersey, weekly. Shellfish in the area were showing high concentrations of heavy metals as a result. At a hearing hosted by the EPA, on the issue of Du Pont's toxics ocean dumping, Harry Kelly, Mayor of Ocean City, New Jersey protested Du Pont's earning of profits at the expense of the community. He proclaimed, "if Du Pont couldn't find anything better to do with its Waste", the company should "send its poisons to stockholders with their dividend checks." Du Pont was granted a two year extension on its ocean dumping. The company successfully argued that without the extension they would have to landfill the waste.

Further important aspects of Du Pont's operations, which reflect poorly on the company's sense of ethic and responsibility for providing a safe and healthy workplace, deserve illumination. Mr. Dave Ortlieb, of the International Chemical Workers Union, testifying at a public meeting being conducted by OSHA on occupational exposure to pesticides at the Du Pont plant in Charleston, South Carolina made a startling statement. The purpose of Mr. Ortlieb's testimony was to get OSHA to set standards restricting the use of medication, provided by industry to mask hazardous exposures. His account tells of Du Pont workers in Laporte, Texas being routinely given medication "to temporarily mask the early symptoms of pesticide poisoning". Workers were then sent back to the job where exposure continued. The Du Pont operation at Laporte, Texas produced methomyl insecticides. The exposure problem occurred in a department which formulates methomyl. Methomyl is described in the Du Pont Material Hazards Card as highly toxic when inhaled, ingested or swallowed. Two grams could be a lethal dosage.

Du Pont also pumped 1,542,970,400 pounds of hazardous waste into the ground, under LA. Under ground injection has resulted in hazardous accident. As the St. John Citizens for Environmental Justice testified:

"Accidents have happened, such as that in the Tenneco plant in Chalmette, where hazardous ooze that had been injected underground came unexpectedly bubbling to the surface. The waste can travel miles before it emerges to the surface, potentially threatening much of our area. *Du Pont is now opposing DEO regulations to require monitoring for groundwater and the migration of contamination, which have already been delayed since 1986.*"

Lastly, Du Pont has been profiting greatly from its operations in Louisiana, while the citizens suffer the consequences in the form of a polluted environment and sickness from poisoning. Du Pont released 2,645,782 pounds of toxins and 66,208 pounds of carcinogens into Louisiana in 1987. Many local citizens attribute the abnormally high incidence of breast cancer to Du Pont's butadienne emissions. Du Pont's fabulous profits, 2 billion in 1987 were helped along by the fact that it pays zero taxes on $117 million dollars worth of property it owns in St. John's Parish. It is unconscionable for a company making that much in profits not to contribute to the local tax base.]

-Ross Bluestein

The Du Pont Company tries to project itself as one of the world's safest companies - "98 times safer than the U.S. industry average". It claims to be noted for its extensive programmes for protecting and enhancing the environment .... and "to enhance the quality of life for people who work at the company....". It is even claimed "A Du Pont employee is 19 times safer at work than at his/her home". So much for Du Pont propaganda. Let us now turn to a few yet striking U.S. press reports which will give us some idea of how Du Pont functions in the West.

From Wall Street Journal: Nov.2, 1977:

"Last May Earl McCune, a Lab chemist at Du Pont Company's chemical plant here became alarmed at the apparently large number of cancer cases among his fellow workers. He suspected the cause was the chemicals to which he was exposed to at the plant.....he decided this time to take his complaint directly to the federal Government.

"Soon after the hearing, Du Pont made a complete survey of cancer incidences and deaths at the Belle plant since 1956. The study uncovered 195 cancer incidences using statistics on active employees alone. Using statistics on active and pensioned workers 206 cancer deaths were found".

Occupational Safety and Health Reporter, May 1987:

"A jury awarded nearly $1.4 million in damages on May 8th to 6 current and former employees who claimed that Du Pont company physicians failed to inform them of asbestos damage to their health. A jury had found that an employer had knowingly withheld medical information from employees on damage to their health allegedly caused by asbestos".

Chemical Marketing Reporter June 11, 1990 p.5
ISSN: 0900-0907

"......The Citizen Action Report found that in 1988, American manufacturers dumped 3.5 billion pounds of toxic chemicals into the environments of ten states: Louisiana, Texas, Ohio, Indiana, Illinois, Tennessee, Michigan, California, Pennsylvania and Florida. The five leading companies nationwide in total releases were *DU PONT*, Monsanto, American Cyanamid, Shell Oil and BP America.

More than 1.2 billion pounds of toxic chemicals (more than 50 percent of the total 2.4 billion pounds) were released into the air of ten states: Texas, Ohio, Tennessee, Louisiana, Virginia, Utah, Indiana, Illinois, Michigan and New York. The five leading companies in the air emissions category were Amax, Eastern Kodak, 3M, General Motors and *DU PONT*.

Journal of Commerce March 16, 1990. p. 7a
ISSB: 0361-55 1

DU PONT has voluntarily admitted its chemical dumping at its Gary, Indiana plant has poisoned 36 spots and may have contaminated groundwater, the Grand Calmet River and even Lake Michigan. It began assessing the site in 1989, due to inquires made by State regulators, but began its study of plant operations 4 years ago. Of the 36 poisoned sites, 13 are active, 22 are closed and 1 is part active and part closed. Some 16 are considered high risk, 10 moderate and 10 low risk. The dumping began nearly 100 years ago.

B.9.2 - The dearth of information in the Indian context

Elaborate and properly documented information such as the above in the U.S.A concerning the functioning of the industrial sector is scant in India. Indian statistics on injuries and death due to direct effects of chemicals or on their indirect and long-term impact on health are highly inadequate. However, those that exist show that the chemical industry in India kills more workers every year than any other industry (F.19) The Bhopal disaster has brought home the hazards of toxic substances with full force. But, several relatively minor disasters and 'air/water/land' pollution due to regular discharge of 'effluents/emissions' are quite common in our country. Such minor disasters and everyday pollution may cause equally severe damage to human life and environment, but attract less public attention compared to large disasters (eg. Bhopal) only because the number of 'deaths/injuries/toxicities' is *small*.

Due to the extremely poor data-base, improper documentation of accidents and virtual black out of reliable information about the diseases caused among workers by exposure to very small amounts of toxic chemicals in vapour or gaseous form in the work-place, systematic regulations on the front of chemical safety are absent in India. An accidental death in the U.S.A. is defined as one which occurs within a year of the accident. In India, accidental deaths are generally those which occur immediately or soon after the event and get reported to the police or agencies like the Factory Inspectorates and Employees State Insurance Corporations. A number of accidents routinely occur during storage, handling and transport of chemicals and hazardous products but again these are not available in a documented form.

B.9.3 - Credibility of Thapars.

As explained above, due to the lack of information, it is very difficult to probe into the actual working of the Indian industries on the 'human safety/environmental' front. However, a few available facts listed below may be pointers of Thapars' questionable credibility:

(1) Thapars have opted to import second-hand machinery at high cost with scant consideration for its environmental, ecological and safety implications for workers and people in general. For instance, Thapars' project proposal for an Acrylic fibre plant in Himachal Pradesh was recently rejected by the Central Government because it involved used machinery. Similarly, Thapars' have already set up and commissioned a second-hand plant for the manufacture of colour television tubes (CFTs). This plant was purchased from Finvalco, a Finnish Company under technical collaboration with Teba (another Finnish firm) and Hitachi of Japan in 1986-87. Now,

in the case of the Nylon 6,6 project mediated by the Thapars' it is confirmed that a multi-crore component of the machinery to be imported from Du Pont is second-hand and undated.

(2) A recent accident (1.11.88) at Cortalim, Goa involving a road tanker carrying Chlorine gas from BILT (Thapar Group), Karwar to Hindustan Ciba-Geigy plant at Khorlim, Goa, can be cited as another incident casting doubts about Thapar Group's reputation. The tanker overturned close to residential area releasing Chlorine in large quantity, causing one death and extensive damage to human health, vegetation and 'agricultural/household' property. However, both BILT (Thapars) and Hindustan Ciba-Geigy refuse to admit any 'responsibility/liability' for the accident. The victims are yet to receive any compensation and Writ Petition (No.72 of 1989) has been filed in the High Court Goa, on behalf of the victims.

The information pertaining to Du Pont and Thapars narrated above gives us ample reason to seriously doubt their tall claims of commitment to 'environmental/human' safety.

B.10 CONCERNS ARISING OUT OF DU PONT'S INDEMNITY AGREEMENT

B.10.1 - Indemnity for Du Pont.

According to the Technical and Financial Collaboration Agreement signed between E.I. Du Pont Nemours and Company (U.S.A.) and Thapar Du Pont Limited dated 18th September, 1988, (D.6) the special clauses 5.3, 5.4, 5.5, 5.6, and 5.7 are quoted below:

5.3 TDL shall hold Du Pont and its representatives or Assignees harmless from any claims made in the Republic of India against representatives of Du Pont or its Assignees alleging bodily harm or death sustained as a direct result of, or in direct connection with, the performance of this Agreement.

5.4 Du Pont shall not incur or be subject to any indirect, contingent or consequential liability or damages, including, but not by way of limitation, any delays or loss of time in putting the plant into operation, or loss of profits or loss of product caused by delays.

5.5 Du Pont Technical information transferred to TDL pursuant to this Agreement is, information requested by TDL and Du Pont accepts no responsibility or liability in respect thereof, except to the extent expressly provided by in this Agreement.

5.6 Du Pont shall not be liable in any manner whatsoever to TDL or to any third party for any loss or damage caused to person or property, including to members of the public as well as to the person or property of any employees or TDL directly or indirectly caused by any act or omission of TDL or its servants or agents and the TDL shall indemnify Du Pont against said liability.

5.7 Du Pont shall not be liable under any circumstances whatsoever to any third parties including members of the public on any account whatsoever due to any accident at the plant or any act or omission of TDL, including its agents, representatives and employees, except as may be expressly provided in this Agreement. Any loss, damage, claim, demand suit or proceeding whatsoever if made against Du Pont by any third party shall be defended by TDL at its cost and expense and TDL shall indemnify and keep indemnified Du Pont and its personnel against the same at all times; provided, however, if any such loss, damage, claim, demand, suit or proceeding arises on account of proven negligence of Du Pont, TDL reserves to itself all rights, recourse and claims as provided herein or which arise hereunder or in accordance with the agreements entered into between TDL and Du Pont in persuance hereof.

The above mentioned clauses indicate that Du Pont Nemours and Company (U.S.A.) has been indemnified from all liabilities in case of bodily harm or death or any sustained loss caused to persons, property or to the employees or to members of the public due to the Nylon 6,6 project. Further Articles 11.1 and 11.2 of the same Agreement state that any arbitration of the two parties is to be held in London, England. It is further stated that the arbitrators shall apply law of U.K. and such rules of International Law or as may be applicable and thus absolves itself of any claims of whatsoever nature made in Republic of India against representatives of Du Pont.

In the light of this, it is clear that Du Pont has been cleverly indemnified and will not be judged according to the laws of our land, India. Attention should be drawn to the fact that Du Pont will be the foreign collaborator in this project whereby TDL will be 'acquiring/importing' old and some new equipments from abroad. The old refurbished component of the machinery will be supplied by Du Pont from the United States. This refurbished component amounts to at least 40% of the total costs of the new and old machinery for Nylon 6,6 tyre cord fibre plant to be imported. Given the fact that Du Pont is supplying the equipment, and also the categorical claims by Du Pont representatives that the Nylon 6,6 plant in the United States is totally pollution free and non-hazardous, involving no problems nor dangers to the environment and human life, it is *very strange* that such an agreement indemnifying Du Pont should have been made.

Further, the arbitration-in-England, Clause 11.2, is highly impracticable to the possible victims in case of a tragedy, to secure timely and just redressal. Attention is hereby drawn in this context to a Supreme Court Judgement (965 Writ Petition Civil No.12739 of 1985 and Civil Writ Petition No.26 of 1986 D/17-2-86) and also the Supreme Court Judgement (982 Civil Misc. Petn. No.6263 of 1986, d/10.3.86), given in 1987 by Chief Justice, P.N. Bhagwati, D.P. Madan and G.L. Oza J.J. In this case, the Honourable Judges ruled that in case of injury or death to the workmen or harm caused to the people living in the vicinity of the chemical plant due to leakage (in this case, the Shriram Food and Fertilizer Plant, where there was leakage of dangerous oleum gas resulting in loss of life and health hazards to the victims), it is not only the officer or officers of the actual management of the plant (Shriram Food & Fertilizers) who will be personally responsible for the payment of compensation to the victims but also the Chairman and the Managing Director of the Parent Company (Delhi Cloth Mills Ltd.) who would also be liable. The Supreme Court of India by this land-mark judgement imposed absolute liability on the *Parent Company* to compensate the harm done to the victims.

The sole aim of Du Pont in signing the technical and financial agreement with TDL seems to have been not only to indemnify itself but also by contracting that arbitration should be done in London, Du Pont seems to have sought to take the matter out of the purview of the Indian Courts

---

LIABILITY

- *Vijay Malik*: "TDL will see to it that all transport, storage is done safely and in an environmental manner, we have said this right through the meeting and probably will be ending the meeting by saying this and nobody has run away from the responsibility."

- *Sam Singh*: "The answer is TDL" (with reference to accidents.)

- *K.S. Pal* (TDL): "TDL will be responsible."

- *K.S. Pal* (TDL): "TDL has taken the corporate liabilities on itself, and it will meet those liabilities."

and away from the liability implied by the above mentioned Supreme Court Judgement: It can be similarly and categorically implied that by advocating the conduct of any arbitration proceedings in London, Du Pont has, also, chosen to stay away from the normally, unbiased and stringent, judgements given by U.S. Courts for protecting the interests of the victims of industrial tragedies.

B.10.2 - Du Pont's option to terminate their partnership with TDL

According to Article 17 of the Technical and Financial collaboration agreement dated 18th September, 1988 signed between E.I. Du Pont de Nemours and Company and Thapar Du Pont Limited;........... "Should Du Pont at any time, in its reasonable judgement, conclude that because of future legislative and judicial developments (in India) the public liability, risks do not justify its continued participation as a share holder in TDL, it shall so notify BILT and subject to the approval of the Reserve Bank of India, BILT, shall within a period of 30 days thereafter purchase Du Pont's shares in TDL at the prevailing market price for the said shares. Should Du Pont invoke its option, it would of course, continue to meet its obligations to TDL as a supplier of raw materials and technology"...... The implication of this Clause clearly *gives Du Pont the entire pleasure* to decide matters at its own free will and according to its own interests. The choice is given to Du Pont, according to its own reasonable judgement to determine at any future time, whether it wishes or not to continue its participation in TDL. In case of Du Pont opting to withdraw from TDL, the only option next is given to BILT, and only to BILT, to purchase Du Pont's shares in TDL at the prevailing market price for the said shares. Though Nylon 6,6 is a so-called `joint sector' project, no mention is made of the role and interest of the public in equity participation. The public are totally excluded from any shares in case Du Pont should decide to pull out. The reference to the future legislative or judicial developments in India, seems to have been made keeping in mind the recent Supreme Court land mark Judgement in the Shriram Food & Fertilizer case.

The above cited facts lead us to conclude that Du Pont's entry into the equity share participation and as the supplier of 'technology/raw materials' to the TDL project is solely due to the fact that Du Pont considers the terms and conditions beneficial to its interests. It is more likely that Du Pont's decision to transfer its technology and project to our soil is only to take the *undue* and *maximum* advantage of our *less stringent* and often *ineffective* environmental protection laws and legislations and thus maximise their profits at the cost of our environment and economy.

B.10.3 - Learning from the Bhopal experience (The aftermath)

Besides launching a global and concerted campaign to exert pressure on Union Carbide Corporation (UCC) and the Govt. of India (GOI) International Coalition for Justice in Bhopal (ICJIB) launched its own investigations on the performance of UCC and GOI in the wake of the Bhopal disaster. The results of ICJIB's investigations were released worldwide, in July, 1987.

Further, in a report entitled 'We Must Not Forget', also released worldwide in July, 1987, ICJIB identified five major lessons emerging from the Bhopal tragedy and its aftermath (F.22) These include:

(1) Corporate irresponsibility in recklessly endangering the lives of workers and people in neighbouring communities via. exposure to highly toxic and hazardous substances and processes.

(2) Corporate ability to evade responsibility for harms inflicted, as well as to defraud victims of corporate misconduct, via tactics like reducing assets (and in some cases, even filing for bankruptcy) and substantially diminishing the ability of corporations to meet a just and adequate settlement or an award of damages accorded by the Courts in ensuing litigation.

(3) Corporate ability to fabricate and promote misinformation via aggressive public relations exercises, as well as to exploit the unequal access to the mass media by corporations as compared to the victims.

(4) Corporate ability to co-opt and indeed suborn professionals (like doctors and lawyers) in the Third World and elsewhere via "fees" that are exceedingly lucrative and tempting.

(5) Bureaucratic apathy, governmental irresponsibility and the lack of public accountability in attending to the needs of victims of disasters like those of the Bhopal tragedy, especially those involving Trans-National Corporations (TNC) operating high risk industrial plants in Third World countries.

At another but related level, the New York based United Nations Centre on Transnational Corporations (UNCTC) has, in the wake of the Bhopal disaster, identified the following important issues in the light of the role of TNCs in the production, storage, transport, handling or regulation of hazardous substances:

(1) The extent to which TNCs should adopt identical safety standards at home and in host countries, regardless of the laxity of local legislation.

(2) The rationale for locating high-risk and pollution-intensive production facilities in areas characterised by unskilled labour force and ignorant squatter communities.

(3) The responsibilities of TNCs and Govts. in permitting the use of otherwise safe products which become dangerous under the prevailing local conditions.

(4) The comprehensiveness of local environmental legislation and the ability of local authorities to implement it stringently.

In this context, the UNCTC has also documented a wide range of TNC misconduct, including the following:

(1) Loose environmental control by the *parent company*.

(2) Variations in the quantity and quality of environmental control personnel working in the different national subsidiaries.

(3) Adoption of environmental impact assessments in project planning *only when* the host country is concerned about such matters.

(4) The export of products banned or restricted in their countries of origin.

(5) The export of hazardous wastes to Third World countries where environmental awareness and legislation are still incipient.

(6) Concentration of environment related R & D efforts in their home countries.

(7) Non-diffusion of pollution control technologies which are formulated and adopted in one country to similar operations in other countries.

(8) Practising "double standards" with regard to occupational health and safety criteria (F.22).

Most of the above mentioned concerns are relevant to the proposed Nylon 6,6 project. With regard to some of the other lessons to be learned from the Bhopal tragedy, American journalist, Stuart Diamond, has underscored the significance of the following (F.22):

(1) That hazardous production facilities pose added risk in Third World countries, where skilled labour and public awareness are sadly lacking - special training is needed to compensate for such additional risks.

(2) That public education is critical in Third World countries as the general population seldom comprehends the hazards of toxic substances - repeated drills and clear warning signals are needed.

(3) That rural area in Third World countries should not be used to test complex new technologies.

(4) That many parts of the Third World are growing rapidly without any zoning laws-suitable buffer zones should be established around potentially hazardous industrial plants.

(5) That cultural differences between foreign investors and host countries should be taken into account, and suitable preventive maintenance more thoroughly implemented.

(6) That host governments should closely monitor the operation and management of potentially hazardous industries, enforcing strict and timely sanctions for safety lapses.

(7) That when entering into agreements with TNCs, Third World governments should consider importing only these technologies that can be safely handled in the long run - it may also be necessary to amend national laws which mandate the complete handing over of industrial plants to local management.

It is of paramount importance that the bitter lessons learnt from our past industrial tragedies, and documented unequivocally by Institutions and Individuals of international repute (documented above), should be carefully studied and analysed *before* embarking on a pathway of haphazard and indiscriminate industrialization. These facts also *underscore* the hidden dangers and thus the illadvisability of allowing large chemical industries such as the Nylon 6,6 project in tiny, socio-ecologically rich and fragile regions, such as Goa.

B.11 ENVIRONMENTAL, SOCIO-CULTURAL AND ECONOMIC IMPACTS OF PROPOSED NYLON 6,6 PROJECT.

B.11.1 - Threat to the environment.

The TDL venture at Kerim plateau proposes to discard its effluents in river Mandovi which is connected further downstream to river Zuari through the Cumbarjua canal. It is therefore imperative to emphasize that Zuari and Mandovi are the lifelines of the State of Goa. The rivers are the mainstay of estuarine and other river-based fishing activities in the State, practically throughout the year. In 1978-79, at the request of the Central Pollution Control Board, which was then charged with the responsibility of controlling pollution in the State, the NIO undertook a detailed study of Mandovi and Zuari river basins. In this study report (F.20), the NIO had recommended that any urban and industrial development, upstream of river Mandovi should not be extended beyond Pilgao. They further suggested that although the water quality beyond Pilgao was good, the water masses in this region do not seem to be in a very active state of movement both horizontally and vertically. *This means that the major part of any pollutant* released in this zone of the river would either settle at *the bottom or remain in suspension*. This fear is pertinent to the conceived Nylon 6,6 project considering the apparent plan of TDL to discharge the effluents in the above mentioned zone of the river Mandovi. The possibilities of harmful pollution effects due to the Nylon 6,6 plant are very high considering the following facts:-

(1) Even under the assumption that the Effluent Treatment Plant is found essentially successful in converting the 'effluents/emissions' to acceptable qualitative standards, the large volume of effluent discharged (1000M^3/day) involved in the Nylon 6,6 process can have significant 'cumulative/accumulative' effects on shellfish which is available abundantly in

'Mandovi/Zuari' river systems. The shellfish is known to bio-accumulate toxic concentrations of some metals (eg. Cu) which ultimately enter the human food chain.

(2) There are a number of cases, in our country as well as other developing countries, involving:-

(i) Clandestine stoppage of Effluent Treatment Plant for reducing production cost.

(ii) Frequent malfunctions of the Effluent Treatment Plant due to lack of expertise, faulty maintenance, defective machinery, lack of spares, power supply problems etc.

Considering the possibilities mentioned above, it need not be emphasized that if the Nylon 6,6 plant is allowed at its proposed location in Kerim, our prime 'drinking/irrigation' water sources and other biological resources in this riverine region would be seriously affected. Besides the probable seriousness of the damage to the riverine flora and fauna in the vicinity of the possible effluents discharged point, the biological life elsewhere in the river system could also be adversely affected by the possibility of spreading of the pollutants along the route of river Mandovi and into the river Zuari through the Cumbarjua canal. Furthermore it is important to note that both Zuari and Mandovi rivers also serve as our major inland waterways to transport large quantities of iron and ferromanganese ores in barges to the harbour, and hence, are already under pressure due to the sedimentation of ore rejects and oil pollution.

The NIO report cited above, had also rightly advised the State Govt. to exercise extreme caution to ensure that 'solid/liquid' wastes from factories are not discarded in these rivers as the water quality could deteriorate jeopardizing human health and consequently the livelihood of thousands of native fishermen depending on these rivers. Since the 'traditional/conventional' (life style of the people in the region is based on the ecologically fragile networks of rivers interspersed with low-lying paddy fields, the location of any large industry discharging its effluents in inland waters would also pose a significant threat to our low-lying paddy fields).

The likely pollutants and different 'soils/water' pollution possibilities, due to the proposed Nylon 6,6 project at Kerim, are as follows:-

(1) Mineral oils and greases due to cleaning and washing of plant equipments.

(2) Domestic discharges including sewage.

(3) Effluent generating out of the use of 'catalyst/anti-oxidants/delustrants' such as Titanium Dioxide, Phenyl Phosphoric Acid, Acetic Acid, etc.

(4) Spent activated Carbon, Diatomaceous earth, Nylon salt 'succinic/glutaric' acid, 1,2 Cyclohexadiamine, *Hexamethylene Imine*, Blow down of the cooling tower, Condensate etc.

(5) Other solid wastes such as monomers, gels, oligomers, nylon fibres etc.

(6) The continuous discharge of compounds of Nitrogen may lead to eutrofication of river water thus depleting the oxygen from the water.

(7) The continuous discharge of suspended and other solids in the rivers gives rise to siltation and turbidity affecting clams, shellfish and other benthic organisms adversely.

B.11.2 - Effects on 'ground/surface' water resources.

The TDL has dug two bore wells on the site. Although it is claimed that the pumped water is used for construction, its repercussions on community water supply requirements have not been looked into by the TDL. However it may be noted that the Irrigation Department, at the request of the Town & Country Planning Deptt., had undertaken a preliminary study of the ground water resources at the Kerim site, in which they had made it clear that any ground water use beyond what is required for construction purposes, may seriously jeopardise the ground water resources presently being used by scores of farmers all around the slopes of the site. *It is also pertinent to note that as soon as the TDL started using the ground water from Kerim site for their construction purpose, the population in the nearby villages at the lower slopes found shortages of water in their wells.* If this problem is not tackled on an urgent basis, it is feared that the wells in the adjoining villages near TDL plant would dry out in time. As 80% of equity of the TDL is controlled by Thapar & Du Pont combined, and the Goan Public may partly be represented in the overall 9% public equity share, it seems unfair that the ground water reserves being used by the local population is contemplated for serving the growth and development of a purely private enterprise.

As 25% of the TDL complex will be covered by constructions (buildings), the ground water recharging capacity of the commanding TDL site, which feeds all the thickly planted agricultural slopes and forests around it, would be significantly affected. This could have adverse effects on the ground water reserves of the region, affecting both human life and vegetation in the Ponda taluka. Besides, any gaseous (eg. Sulphur dioxide), liquid or solid effluents being accidentally, or otherwise, discharged in and around the plant area, will ultimately find their way into the ground water reserves through seepage, or in the surrounding watershed through runoff, specially during the heavy monsoon season. Similarly, other contaminants like spent fuel discharges or oil spillage from the captive power plant, could also find their way into the ground water and watershed systems. This could cause the pollution of wells in the adjoining villages, again causing serious health problems to the community. The contamination of water with carcinogens (eg. Benzopyrenes) found in spent 'fuels/oils' cannot be ignored either.

EFFLUENT DISCHARGE

- *K.S. Pat:* "It is the practice all over the world while fixing the location of chemical plants that you draw water upstream and that you throw the effluents downstream. The reason for that is two fold. No. 1, the effluents get the benefit of natural oxidation, which in fact makes the quality of the effluent better. It does not cause pollution. Second part why it is thrown downstream is, it gets the benefit of dilution on the downstream side."

- *K.S. Pat:* "The discharge point that we are considering is that the confluence of the river Kandepar and the river Mandovi."

During the summer months, many villages in Goa suffer from a shortage of water supply for human consumption. The present capacity of Opa Water Works is 16 MGD. *However, it is reliably learnt that the PWD (PHE) is already extracting about 24 MGD of water* for meeting the drinking water needs by unjustly depriving many farmers of the irrigation water which they have been using traditionally. While this aspect needs a thorough investigation, it is rather surprising and scandalous to note that the water requirement of the Nylon 6,6 plant is proposed to be drawn from the Opa Water Works. The Nylon 6,6 plant requirement is estimated to be 2500 C.M. per day which is equivalent to the requirement of a population of 30,000. A Senior Engineer of the PWD (PHE) is already on record stating that unless Selaulim water reaches Vasco, it is impossible to meet the water needs of Nylon 6,6 plant through the Opa Water Works. It is anybody's guess as to when the Selaulim pipeline will supply water to Vasco on a sustained basis. It is worthwhile to note in this context that part of the pipeline already laid for the purpose is highly defective and can fail at any moment.

It will be pertinent here to sum up some of the views expressed by C.G.Desai of Central Water Commission in his paper "Surface Water Resources for Goa's Development" presented during the September, 1981 Seminar on "Earth Resources for Goa's Development". (F.3)

(1) The present water supply plant catering mostly for domestic use is not adequate to meet even the present industrial water supply.

(2) The estimated water requirement for industries by 2000 A.D. would be 30 million gallons/day which would be met from the *Selaulim Water Supply Scheme only.*

(3) The pollution of water by industry being *located near the source of water* is another menace to be taken care of for properly guarded water utilisation. This is particularly so because of small size of territory with isolated patches of suitable land for location of industry and problems requiring special attention because of its danger to fish life, etc.

Opinions of experts like Mr. Desai have been sidelined to approve the Nylon 6,6 project, which will create water-scarcity if Opa Water/downstream water is exploited.

B.11.3 - Serious discrepancies in TDL's claims about effluent composition.

The TDL is *not* clear either about the nature of the influent into the Waste Treatment Plant, or the characteristics/parameters of the treated effluents prior to discharge. This is quite clear from the glaring discrepancies indicated in the following table:-

Parameter	Influent	Treated effluent	Influent	Treated effluent	Tolerance limit
Ph	8.3	6.5-8.0	8.3	6.5-8.0	6-9
TSSmg/l	120	50	96	46	92
BOD_5mg/l	450	20	380	23	28
COD mg/l	650	250	560	120	230
TKNmg/l	80	NA	66	26	91
Ammonical nitrogen mg/l	20	NA	-	5	46
Phenol mg/l	0.1	NA	NA	NA	NA
NO_3-N mg/l	15	NA	NA	NA	NA
Flow gpm	NA	NA	169	169	Not Ltd.
Temp.°C	NA	NA	25-35°	25-35°	40
D.O.	NA	NA	2	2	-
Oils and greases	Mgk WA	NA	-	9	9.2
Free ammonia	NA	NA	-	3	46

Note from the varying figures given by BILT application and the TDL letter No. HC/90-91/2 in case of parameters Total Soluble Salts (TSS), BOD, COD, TKN, Ammonical Nitrogen and temperature. *It appears that these figures are a mosaic from different sources suitably adjusted for emphasizing that the proposed Nylon 6,6 project is non-polluting and safe.* At the same time, it is clear that no 'factual/analytical' data and records have been obtained from other similar plants existing elsewhere for giving unambiguous information, for reasons best known to the promoters of the project. (See also D.2.3, D.2.4, D.2.5)

B.11.4- The captive power plant and pollution possibilities.

The power plant is one of the most critical units in the manufacturing process for Nylon 6,6. On the basis of TDL's information, *it is clear that in case of a power failure for even a fraction of a second, there may be serious trouble.* Momentary fluctuations in power will severely affect the process, as well as the supply of utilities to different components. Thus, it is acknowledged that a steady power supply without any fluctuations is an essential pre-requisite for Nylon 6,6 manufacturing process. As the local electricity grid cannot be expected to supply power with the high standard of efficiency demanded by this process, the proposal to establish a power plant based on coal (Grade A) and later switching the same to Low Sulphur-High Speed diesel type arose. Generation of power using LSHSD, will ensure reliable power supply to the company but will have an adverse effect on the ecology of the surrounding areas.

It is pertinent to note that the process of captive power generation for this plant was omitted in Du Pont's presentation to the House-Committee on 9.10.90. Further, although it is mentioned that various pollution abatement devices will be used to control emissions of SO_x, NO_x soot, mist, particulates, etc., these have not been categorically specified.

Apparently, there is a contradiction between the information given in the BILT report (page G-4) on utilities (power) and that in TDL's letter (Ref.No. TDL/HC/90-91/33). (Compare E.28 & E.45)

Transportation of LSHSD oil.

About 0.5 -1% of the fuel oil is left in the holds of the tankers as all the fuel oil cannot be removed by pumps. Residual oils washed into the river due to the cleaning of tankers will lead to river related pollution.

Emissions of SO_x, NO_x, soot, particulates etc.

Surprisingly, the power plant emission figures given by TDL appear to be far too low. One report estimates the same as 80 lbs SO_2, 11 lbs of SO_3 and 14 lbs of NO_x per hour. A simple calculation indicates that over 318 tons SO_2, 4 tons of SO_3 and 56 tons of NO_x will be vented into the atmosphere every year inspite of the claimed abatement devices. The reaction of SO_3 with moisture of the air produces Sulphuric acid mist which is harmful to the human respiratory system and vegetation.

The *withering SO_2 gas affects the mucosa and the cilia of the throat, bronchial tubes and lungs* with the resultant damage turning into chronic bronchitis over the years. Alongwith this comes the varying degrees of lung depression with the heart being affected resulting in pulmonary heart disease and pulmonary emphysema. Of course, this slow pathological degradation of the body may lead to a slow and lingering death.

Plants are affected before any cognisable damage occurs to the human population. Studies conducted by the United States Public Health Service indicate that during one year 36% of the plant life in the country was adversely affected by continuous SO_2 exposure at a concentration of only 0.01 ppm. In other words, power stations that are using low sulphur fuels containing 1.5% sulphur produce SO_x in concentrations of about 900 ppm and the related amount of nitrogen oxides to the tune of about 300 ppm. These nitrogen oxides are usually found in the form of NO and NO_2 compounds. NO_2 reacts with hydrocarbons in the air in the presence of sunlight to produce ozone (O_3) and the other noxious substances contributing to photochemical smog.

The slopes and hills around the TDL site as described in Chapter B.5, are rich in human settlements engaged in extremely productive agricultural plantations and horticulture through multiple cropping systems. The natural vegetation is also plentiful in this area and this together with plantation agriculture influences the micro-climate of the region favourably by enhancing the precipitation which in turn improves the bio-productivity of the region. The possible air emissions due to the power plant and the ensuing chemical processes described above will adversely influence human life as well as vegetation canopy, specifically, in the immediate vicinity of the plant and generally, in the Ponda Taluka. Such a damage may occur either due to the direct toxic effects of the emissions or their indirect effects such as acidic precipitation.

In the particulate matter discharged from power plants there are such substances as oil mist, carbon, metal oxides and acids. These materials are all discharged into the atmosphere and ultimately descend to the land surface in a short period. Most of the particulate matter is composed of Vanadium (V) with a formula of V_2O_5 and this compound is to be found in concentrations of not less than 50 ppm. Other heavy metals produced from the power plant are Fe found in 10 ppm concentrations and Ni, Ca, Al, Si, Mg, Cu, Co, Cr, Zn, Pb and K all in concentrations of about O.1 to 0.01 ppm (F.21)

Unless the wind speed is higher than 4 to 5 metres per second, pollutants discharged from the power plant and other chimneys may not disperse into the atmosphere but rather accumulate in a given zone and continue to concentrate in the air.

Thermal pollution: When hot cooling waters are discharged into recipient waters (the Madei-Mandovi river or a basin within the premises of the factory), thermal pollution could be the result. This can lower the dissolved oxygen level in the river waters by lowering the solubility. Aquatic organisms are then affected due to low oxygen content and consequently because of their reduced tolerance to diseases and toxic chemicals.

B.11.5- Concerns about transportation.

The TDL transportation plan raises several questions. The transport of a highly corrosive, highly soluble and highly alkaline chemical like HMD by barges through Mandovi river/Zuari-Cumbarjua route will endanger marine, estuarine and human life. State Govt. is yet to frame any rules for regulation of such transport through rivers. The iron-ore transport has already congested the inland waterways.

The Mandovi river and its tributaries are navigable for a length of 90 km and barges of about 300 tons DWT can go upto Usgao 41 km. from the mouth of the river. The Zuari river is navigable upto 64km. and barges upto 300 tons DWT can go upto Savordem bridge. There are about 46 loading points on the Mandovi river and 26 loading points on the Zuari river where the barges are loaded. According to the Bhagwati Commission report, transport of material by road would be two to three times costlier than the transport by barges. *Irrespective of the cost, the road system of Goa is already under pressure* and therefore even to move a part of the total ore material by road would be a stupendous task creating immense pressure on the road ways (F.3)

The plans of TDL to transport the raw materials through inland waterways has to be seen with concern against the above background.

The two raw materials, Hexamethylene diamine and Adipic Acid will be forming the bulk of the chemical raw materials for the Nylon 6,6 project and will have to be imported. Adipic Acid will be obtained from Singapore and Hexamethylene diamine from the U.S. Both are supposed to be brought to Goa by sea and offloaded at Marmagoa Port. From there the company intends to transport the HMDA by barges to the site and Adipic Acid by road.

HMDA and Adipic Acid, because of their chemical properties, require careful handling during transportation. It should be noted here that both the substances require *extreme precaution* according to the United States Deptt. of Transportation. Both, Adipic Acid and HMDA, if ignited are capable of producing 'toxic/poisonous' gases. HMDA is extremely corrosive and corrodes metals and tissues.

On human contact, Adipic Acid is known to cause extreme eye irritation. Similarly, HMDA on skin or eye contact could cause severe burns with possible permanent damage. HMDA vapours irritate the eyes, nose, throat and lungs, and could cause difficulty in breathing. Higher exposures to HMDA could cause pulmonary oedema leading to severe shortness of breath (D.4.1).

In case of transportation of such hazardous and dangerous chemicals by road, it is not clear what measures the company would take to ensure that no accidents of any kind occurs during transit. The recent accident involving a BILT (of Thapar group) Chlorine tanker at Cortalim and consequent damage to life and property is a case in point. So also, it is not clear what emergency provisions will be provided for, in case of such accidents. The Company's Protocol in this regard has not been clarified.

The roads in and around Ponda in particular and all over the State in general, are narrow and already crowded due to heavy vehicular traffic and, as such, the present rate of road accidents is also quite high. In the course of its proposed establishment as well as subsequently during its routine working, the Nylon 6,6 industrial complex is bound to multiply the traffic density (specially consisting of heavy vehicles carrying machinery, raw materials, finished products, 'labour/staff' etc.), significantly. It is obvious that in its present condition, the available road system in the region is totally inadequate to serve the anticipated additional traffic due to the project. Serious traffic accidents involving hazardous materials are probable specially along the winding narrow road pathway leading to the proposed site. Such accidents could cause heavy damage to human life, property and vegetation. Besides, the noise generated by the plant machinery, power generation facility, traffic of heavy vehicles, etc., could disturb the tranquillity and serenity of this region, known for its agricultural and religious uniqueness, that is valued by tourists from all over the world.

The relevant questions are:

Is there a provision for immediate rescue operations? What are the compensation programmes? Will the victims be embroiled in endless (and perhaps useless) litigation?

Even in the case of transportation by barges, it is not at all clear what kind of provisions the TDL has made to handle emergency arising from accidents. Given the above background and the fact that tonnes and tonnes of the raw materials need to be transported every day, projects of the 'type/ magnitude' of Nylon 6,6 should not even be considered unless safe transportation is guaranteed.

Of significant relevance here are the (anti) liability clauses included in the Technical Financial Collaboration Agreement detailed in Chapter B.10. Du Pont has made it absolutely safe for itself that it be absolved from any major liability (and responsibility therefore) should any 'damage/loss' to life and property occur as a result of any accident in relation to the plant.

On the question of accidents, Shri Vijay Malik of BILT remarked that, "whenever the material is in our custody and there are certain rules that we have to follow, TDL will see to it that all transport, storage is done safely and in an environmental manner. We have said this right through the meeting on 9.10.90 and probably will be ending the meeting by saying this, and nobody has run away from the responsibility" (E.48). In addition to the unreliability of such verbal claims, the question that remains is the fate of materials that are not yet in TDL's custody but enroute or at the port. Who would be held responsible if an accident occurs at that stage?

Also, it is not clear what would happen to the raw materials transportation by barges when the inland river navigation is suspended during the monsoon (every year) due to the closure of the Aguada sandbar.

During their appearance before the House-Committee on 9.10.90, the TDL officials appeared to be uncertain of the exact mode of raw materials transportation. (E.48)

B.11.6- Socio-Cultural Consequences.

As described in details in Chapter B.6, the area adjoining the proposed plant site at Kerim in particular and the Ponda Taluka in general, is noted for its ecological assets, temples and historical relics. This quiet, peaceful, productive and largely agricultural society of Ponda with a rich cultural heritage is a much sought after touristic attraction. The proposed establishment of Nylon 6,6 project is very likely to transform a quiet nature, peaceful and culturally rich society into aggressive and hostile industrial society involving deleterious social implications.

The agro-ecosystem of the region will be threatened not only by the probable pollution impact of the proposed Nylon 6,6 plant but also due to the diversion of young agricultural 'entrepreneur/labour'towards the pseudo-security and short-term lucrative nature of 'construction/industrial' jobs. There is also the possibility of additional rich 'agricultural/plantation' land being converted for 'real estate/construction' purposes, as is presently happening in our coastal tract. Thus, by allowing this plant we may be knowingly commencing the slow degradation of a highly sustainable and resilient agro-ecosystem.

Other multiplier effects such as traffic congestion, population migration and pollution has the potential of disturbing the serene environment and typical social ethos prevalent in the region.

Although the TDL claims that over 1000 job opportunities would be created and the major beneficiaries would be the local people, our past experience clearly shows the opposite. Mostly, the 'managerial/technical' posts coupled with the unskilled labour force (which may together amount to about 70% of the total number of jobs created), will 'mostly/entirely' comprise of people from outside the State. A majority of the job opportunities for the locals will be created within the remaining 30% of the clerical and skilled work force required (see B.11.7).

As is apparent around Zuari Nagar and Vasco areas, it is not likely that the anticipated influx of migrant labour will lead to the formation of slum colonies in the vicinity of the industrial site and thus lead to the problems of unhygienic settlements, increase in crime rate and degradation of cultural ethos around the region. The slum population may subsequently grow substantially causing significant deforestation (firewood collection) and encroachments upon the privileges of the local population. The latter may very well lead to social conflicts presently visible in places like Vasco, Sancoale, Porvorim etc. This type of degradation should not be allowed to occur at least in Ponda region due to reasons cited earlier. In this context, it is pertinent to note that the existing problem of 'garbage/pollution' generated due to the present 'resident/tourist' population already appears to be beyond the control of our city Municipal Councils. It is therefore questionable if our authorities would be able to accommodate more migrant population around the Kerim site and, yet, take proper care of the ensuing problems of sanitation, health and crime, in the region.

B.11.7- The exploitative side of the Nylon 6,6 project's economy.

The Nylon 6,6 project will benefit from all sorts of subsidies since it is being located in 'industrially backward area', category 'A'. It has been pumping out unlimited ground water without any costs. It has to contribute almost nothing for power infrastructure as 220 KV high tension power lines cross the site. It proposes to draw 2500 cubic metre of water/day from Khandepar river, probably free of charge. It will continue to exploit groundwater for normal operations as till this day the Government does not have the necessary 'infrastructure/facility/ supervision' to ensure 'judicious/regulated' use of precious groundwater of the locality. It will get cheap unskilled and semi-skilled labour mostly from outside Goa.

The TDL has not been able to furnish detailed information about the manpower which will be employed in the proposed project. Inflated figures have been cited in the media creating an impression that the Nylon 6,6 project will be indeed a solution to the unemployment problem, specially in Ponda Taluka. We have compared the statistics available to us, based on two sources: The first is EDC's letter of intent application dated 19.11.83 and the second is the BILT project report of January 1989. (E.28)

We get the following information from the first-source about manpower (staff and labour) employment (vide from I.L.19) (E.1)

Staff & Labour proposed to be employed in the implementation of the project:-	Existing	Proposed	Total
(a) Managerial	-	10	10
(b) Supervisory	-	25	25
(i) Technical	-	150	150
(ii) Non-technical	-	50	50
(c) Clerical	-	75	75
(d) Labour, skilled, semi-skilled, unskilled	-	310	310
(e) Other categories, if any	-	-	-
Total	-	750	750

(Notice the wrong total. We have quoted the exact typed figures).

No explanation is given about the 130 people, included in the total of 750. *The total in fact should have been 620* instead of 750. But this 'error' was overlooked. Even if we consider the 'true' manpower i.e. 620 as provided in the application form, there is no noticeable increase in manpower when the licenced capacity of the project was doubled and the project cost was quadrupled. Before doubling the project capacity the project cost was Rs.44.3 crores, which assured 620 jobs (see E.1 & E.28).

If we compare the above figures with the information in BILT report, no breakdown is available about the total number of managerial, supervisory and clerical jobs. The report says, under "No organisation and manpower" that .... "The total number of workforce for the proposed plant is foreseen at 1032 out of which, the total skilled, semi-skilled and unskilled labour is 366, 48 and 422, respectively ....". This means that the category 'd' in the letter of intent application is inflated from 310 to 836. Thus 196 jobs are found to be grouped together under managerial, supervisory and clerical categories (19.a, b & c of the I.L. form). Earlier this figure was quoted as 310, but doubling the capacity brought down the figure to 196 indicating that there is a substantial scope for reduction of jobs in this highly automated and capital intensive project.

To sum up the above, we could conclude that:-

(1) The total staff and labour proposed to be employed in the project as per the first source (19.11.83) is a wrong figure.

(2) The true figure should be 620 instead of 750.

(3) Out of 620 jobs, managerial, supervisory, technical, non-technical and clerical posts constituted 310.

(4) As per 2nd source (BILT report), skilled, semiskilled and unskilled labour went up from 310 to 836, but no. of higher posts came down from 310 to 196.

(5) Quadrupling of project-cost, i.e. from Rs.44.3 crores in 1983 to Rs.167 crores in January 1989 did *not* result in creation of substantial additional job opportunities.

(6) Number of higher posts were reduced after doubling the licenced capacity and quadrupling the project costs.

(7) The project report assures that ..... "it is proposed to hire most of the skilled workers from Goa ....". That means most of 346 skilled workers, only.

(8) Considering the nature of technology and management skills required, there is very little opportunity for Goans to get high-level jobs i.e. any of the 196 proposed.

(9) The investment for creation of one job works out to be a staggering Rs.16 lakhs. Hence, at a juncture when we may be badly in need of labour intensive small-scale industries, a highly subsidized mega-industry may set up the dubious example of employment generation by investing an average of 16 lakhs/job.

It is significant to note that the pseudo-economics of this mega-industry was perceived by the then Director of Industries, Mr. Denghnuna, who wrote to the Secretary, Industries, Govt. of Goa, on 2.4.1987 that ... "The area asked by the party is 500 acres which is equivalent to 20 lakh sq.mts. which is unreasonably on the higher side. Infact, 20 lakh sq.mts. can easily accommodate more than 10 industrial estates, can encourage more than 500 small industries and can create employment to 4500 people approximately and give boost to our economy by opening various other avenues for other trades and small activities"...

Mr. Denghnuna had given alternative for sustainable employment generation by encouraging labour-intensive industries. (E.12)

The profit-making machine:

TDL and Du Pont have done some cold-blooded calculations to ensure that after they have a strong foothold in Goa the project will virtually turn into a profit making machine. This motive can easily be derived from an analysis of the BILT report, as listed below:

(1) In the 2nd year, the profit before dividend will be Rs.352 lakhs.

(2) In the 3rd year of plant operation, TDL profit before dividend will jump to Rs.982 lakhs, in the 8th year to Rs.3464 lakhs and in the 10th year to Rs.4262 lakhs.

(3) The total cumulative profit for TDL after 5 years of operation will be Rs.3607 lakhs and after 10 years Rs.17780 lakhs.

(4) The entire project cost would be recovered within 7-8 years.

(5) The cost of production shows that to achieve this magnitude of profit TDL will be paying only Rs.255 lakhs in the 1st year of operation and Rs.395 lakhs in the 10th of operation as total labour charges.

(6) TDL will be able to declare a 15% dividend on the equity capital in the 4th and 5th year of operation and thereafter 20% every year.

(7) The dividend will be distributed as:-

EDC	11%
BILT	40%
Du Pont	40%
Public issue	9%

(8) From (7), it is clear that by ensuring low EDC and public participation in equity, the major share-holders BILT and Du Pont plan to deprive the Goa Govt. and the people of their 'realistic/rightful' share of profit.

(9) Considering (6), at 15% dividend for the 4th and 5th year and 20% dividend for 6-10th year, at present level of equity participation, the respective parties will gain an amount (Annexure S.7 of BILT report) indicated in the following table:-

Year of operation	Profit before dividend Rs. Lakhs	Rate of dividend	Total dividend distributed (Rs.Lakhs).			
			EDC 11%	BILT 40%	DUPONT 40%	PUBLIC 9%
4th	1697	15%	28.00	101.82	101.82	22.91
5th	976	15%	16.10	58.56	58.56	13.18
6th	1106	20%	24.33	88.48	88.48	19.91
7th	1494	20%	32.87	119.52	119.52	26.89
8th	3464	20%	76.21	277.12	277.12	62.35
9th	3847	20%	84.63	307.76	307.76	69.25
10th	4262	20%	93.76	340.96	340.96	76.72
		Total	355.90	1294.22	1294.22	219.19

From this table, we see the net benefit to the EDC and Public as a negligibly small amount compared to BILT and Du Pont figures. Thus, the project seems to be a clear strategy to churn out profits solely in the interest of BILT and Du Pont.

To sum up the above, we could conclude that:-

(1) Each job in Nylon 6,6 project needs an investment of Rs.16 lakhs.

(2) The entire project cost will be recovered by TDL within 7-9 years.

(3) The total labour cost is a very small contribution to the economy. And there is no guarantee that Rs. 2.5 -3.0 crores will be disbursed only to local unemployed.

(4) The State Govt. represented through EDC and the Public have been strategically kept out of major equity contribution, employing clever deceiving strategy.

(5) Lowering of EDC's equity from 26% to 11% *will result in a dividend loss of about Rs. 5-6 crores for a period of 7 years* (i.e. 4th year - 10th year)

(6) M/s. BILT and Du Pont will get a lion's share of dividend i.e. Rs. 26 crores between them, from 4th to 10th years of operation.

(7) Hence, the claims of economic benefits to Goa, employment to locals, economic prosperity etc. made by TDL do not stand the test of scrutiny.

As for the National benefits, through import duties, excise etc. all these will go the the Central Govt. and unless a large quantum is statutorily reinvested or refuelled in Goan economy, it will not make any difference to this State, or any other State if the plant is located elsewhere. However, the net savings to the company due to proximity of Marmagao Port, reduced transport cost, no demurrage costs, subsidies on 'water/power/land' price far outweigh the perceived 'national benefits'. The social costs of location of such a mega-industry have not been considered either.

It is therefore naive to assume that an exploitative and expansion-ambitious project such as Nylon 6,6 will make any worthwhile contribution to Goan economy. The inflated manpower figures also establish the real nature of this capital intensive project. And as rightly pointed out by Mr. Denghnuna, alternatives do exist. We must honestly look for them.

PART C

C. RECOMMENDATIONS

We have studied and discussed various aspects of the proposed Nylon 6,6 project. We have noticed a number of discrepancies in the claims of the promoters and several other irregularities have been identified. The possible adverse impacts of the proposed plant on the environment, socio-cultural life and economic parameters of the State have been explained.

Decision making about the proposed Nylon 6,6 project is not an ordinary exercise. It is a question of Goa's industrial, ecological and social destiny. The self-proclaimed 'secretive nature' of the Nylon 6,6 manufacturing technology adds a new and complex dimension to the decision making exercise.

It need not be emphasized that apart from pollution/environment impacts, huge capital intensive chemical industry can totally change the lifestyle of any locality adversely due to its logistical, social, economic and other multiplier effects.

Despite the claims of effective pollution control through effluent treatment plants, facts indicate that large chemical industries in developing countries and many even in the developed world, have not been able to keep their word. Rampant and disastrous pollution of atmosphere and rivers in developing world (eg. river Ganga in India) and in developed world (eg. rivers Seine, Rhine, Thames etc.) that has occurred till very recent times, is indicative of the above. In fact, to reverse the pollution effects, many developed countries and developing countries including India have now undertaken extremely expensive river Clean-Up projects.

Against the above background, it would be ill advised to allow large chemical industries discharging even their "treated" effluents in our so far eco-rich and virgin rivers. Zuari and Mandovi rivers linked by the Cumbarjua canal are the lifelines of our tiny State. They support most of our land based `human/wildlife', `marine/estuarine' life(fisheries) including rich mangrove ecosystems, our agro-ecosystem and river navigation facility. Additionally, these riverine systems are directly linked to the well being of our coastal beach ecology and green landscape, making our State a world famous tourist spot. As such, we have to safeguard our rivers against any conceivable `environmental/pollution' threat.

While deciding on the establishment of large chemical industries in a small, relatively densely populated and socio-ecologically, rich State such as, ours, we should consider, not only statistical probability of a possible industrial accident but *also* the disastrous danger to human and ecology that may result from such an accident.

It is also imperative to realize that in a tiny State like Goa, any large capital intensive industry is bound to 'consume/utilise' a very significant percentage of available natural resources and infra-structural facilities, but in turn contribute negligibly to local economy

After having satisfied ourselves about the real nature of the Nylon 6,6 project, its capability of influencing the decision making process and on 'careful/detailed' consideration of various connected issues, this Committee recommends the following:-

C.1.1 - The EDC should dissolve its agreement with M/s. BILT immediately. This should also be applicable to any revised agreement after 1986.

C.1.2 - The EDC should immediately apply for cancellation of the respective letters of intent LI-173(85) of 28-2-1985 and LI-1052 (85) of 30-9-1985.

C.1.3 - TDL and TDSL should be asked to wind up their activities in Goa.

C.1.4 - GDDIDC should withdraw its earlier letter permitting TDL to carry on developmental work at Kerim site.

C.1.5 - No further development work on the Kerim site should be permitted.

C.1.6 - GDDIDC, after fulfilling the normal procedures for land acquisition should take the possession of the said Kerim site.

C.1.7 - GDDIDC should develop the 88.63 ha. site for its own industrial estate.

C.1.8 - Besides the 88.63 ha.land already fenced by TDL, to be developed by GDDIDC for its own industrial estate, no extra land notified earlier should be acquired. Steps should be taken by appropriate authorities to suspend the land acquisition procedure for the rest of the 170 ha. of land.

C.1.9 - GDDIDC should prepare a model plan for making plots and optimal utilisation of Kerim site as Industrial Estate incorporating non-polluting small-scale industries.

C.1.10 - The Govt. of Goa should introduce necessary legislation for changing the parameters of EDC's work.

C.1.11 - The EDC's powers for promoting Joint-Sector industrial projects should be restricted as per its investment capacities and technical expertise.

C.1.12 - Criteria for procuring letters of intent for indigenous/imported technology should be drafted through the concerned authority by giving due consideration to the under mentioned points:-

(1) The nature of the technology.

(2) Availability of all informational aspects of the technology.

(3) Environmental compatibility of the technology.

(4) Socio-cultural compatibility of the technology/project.

(5) Magnitude of the project.

(6) Developmental priorities of the State.

(7) Availability of suitably skilled local manpower.

(8) Regional Plan: 2001 A.D. proposal.

(9) Govt. of India circular, dtd. 17-2-1987 declaring Goa as 'protected district'.

(10) Guidelines of Deptt. of Environment, Govt. of India, for siting of the industries.

(11) Scope and nature of possible ancilliarisation/SSI unit formation downstream.

(12) Quantum of stress on utility infrastructure and natural resources of the State vis-a-vis its small size.

(13) Investment/equity participation potential of EDC and State Govt.

(14) Net cost: benefit analysis statement showing real benefit to State of Goa.

(15) Geographic limitations of Goa.

(16) Relatively high population density.

(17) Projected impact on State's rich bio-diversity.

(18) Scope for full utilisation of industrial area/estate already earmarked.

(19) Availability of baseline studies, land capability studies etc. for any new site.

(20) Availability of a full proof and regular monitoring and supervision infrastructure for ascertaining the normal functioning of any effluent treatment plant and emission control systems.

The indiscriminate application procedure for procuring letters of intent presently in vogue should be discontinued.

C.1.13 - The applications for letters of intent should be 'notified/published'in the official gazette for public information.

C.1.14 - Necessary legislation should be introduced to regulate the transport of hazardous/toxic/polluting/obnoxious chemicals, gases etc. by road and through inland waterways and other rivers. Legislation existing in other States in this regard should be examined.

C.1.15 - NRSA-Hyderabad and GSI should be consulted for identifying precious water catchment areas and groundwater reserves. These areas should be notified and conserved. Regulations for 'commercial/industrial' use of groundwater should be drafted in consultation with experts.

C.1.16 - Land evaluation should be entirely based on scientific land capability studies and not on superficial visual observations.

C.1.17 - The irregularities noticed at various levels in the context of Nylon 6,6 project i.e. casual/questionable applications for letters of intent for a complex foreign technology, the issue of EDC's equity participation, the objectionable indemnity clause/s in TDL-Du Pont agreement, the apparent favoritism of top authorities, the land acquisition and allotment issues etc. should be investigated, through a competent agency like C.B.I., to uncover the possible malpractices.

C.1.18 - The State Pollution Control Board should be revamped. The Technical Committee should be reconstituted. At least three non-government ecological experts should be appointed on the Technical Committee.

C.1.19 - The procedure for examining the industrial proposals from environmental angle should be suitably laid down on the basis of up-to-date 'ecological/environmental' baseline studies in Goa. A system of cross-checking/counterchecking the technical information provided in the proposal should be evolved. Independent information/database sources should be identified and consulted. A statutory format specifying the nature of technical documentation should be prepared and all the industrial proposals should be submitted as per the said format. Copy of such a proposal to be included in the agenda of Goa State Pollution Control Board should be available for public perusal.

All proposals based on patented foreign technology should be published in the official gazette. Public comments should be invited on the same before the Technical Committee gives its verdict.

C.1.20 - People's participation and co-operation in decision making is vital for development. Before selecting any site for any industry having an investment of above Rs. 100 lakhs, the clearance of the Gramsabha/s of the respective Village Panchayat/s should be obtained. All necessary details of the project should be supplied to the Panchayat in advance. The Government should consider necessary amendments to Panchayat act or any other relevant act in order to implement this recommendation.

C.1.21 - The Government of Goa should constitute a working group of experts including economists, managements experts, scientists, technologists, ecologists, environmentalists, industrialists, representatives of SSI, progressive farmers and horticulturists, representatives of EDC, IDC, KVIC, etc. to prepare a 'Master Plan for balanced and sustainable industrial development of Goa'.

C.1.22 - On the basis of the Master Plan, a draft statutory industrial policy should be formulated and debated in the Legislative Assembly.

C.1.23 - The future course of industrial development of Goa will be guided by the outcome of recommendations C.1.21 and C.1.22 above.

Considering the issues raised by the Nylon 6,6 project, the Committee is of the opinion that in future, a rigorous scrutinisation setup, with legislative control and public accountability will be necessary. The interests of the people of Goa, its ecology, society and culture should be paramount and the decision making should not be dictated, influenced or modulated by industrial lobbies.

PART D

ANNEXURES

Questionnaires & Correspondence

D.5.1   General questionnaire on pollution and
               other aspects referred to in 9.10.90
               meeting of the House-Committee

D.5.2   Questionnaire to the Industries Deptt.

D.5.3   Questionnaire to the Revenue Deptt.

D.5.4   Response of Industries Deptt. dated
               30.10.90 .

D.5.5   Response of Deptt. of Science, Technology
               & Environment dtd. 29.10.90

Agreement

D.6   Beginning and end page of the Technical
               & Financial Collaboration Agreement between
               Du Pont and TDL (18.12.1988).

ANNEXURES

D.1 - D.6

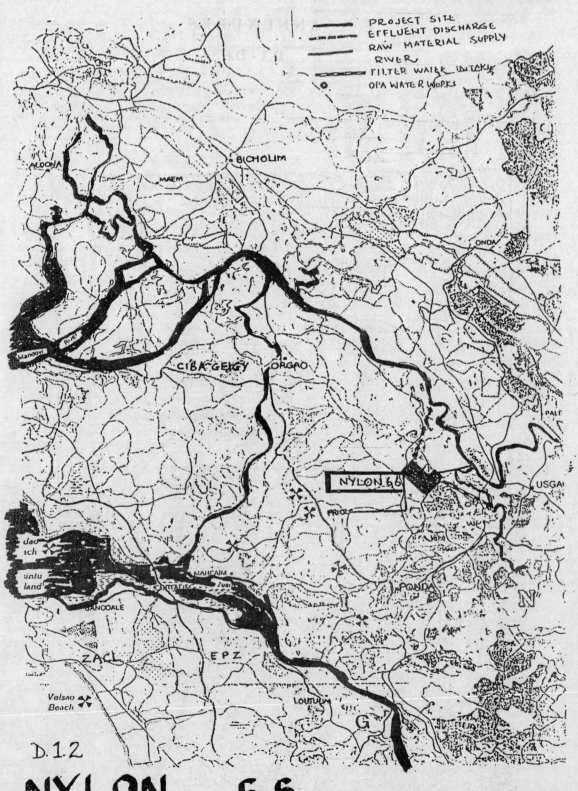

PROJECT SITE
EFFLUENT DISCHARGE
RAW MATERIAL SUPPLY
RIVER
FILTER WATER INTAKE
OPA WATER WORKS

D.1.2

NYLON 6,6.

MAP: IMPACT ON RIVER DRAINAGE BASINS
MAP: EXISTING MINING CONCESSIONS AND PROJECT-SITE
MAP: PROJECT SITE IN RELATION TO TOURISM PLACES

MAP SHOWING THE POSITION OF NYLON 6,6 PROJECT IN RELATION TO HYDROGRAPHY

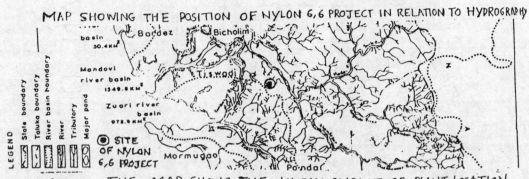

D.1.2.1   THE MAP SHOWS THE LIKELY IMPACT OF PLANT LOCATION
          IF EFFLUENTS, TREATED AS PER THE CLAIMS ARE
          DISCHARGED DOWNSTREAM.

THE PROJECT SITE IN RELATION TO EXISTING MINING CONCESSIONS

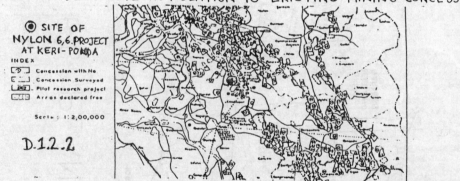

D.1.2.2

THE DENSITY OF MINING CONCESSIONS IN THE VICINITY OF NYLON 6,6 PROJECT

TOURIST PLACES IN RELATION TO THE NYLON 6,6 PROJECT

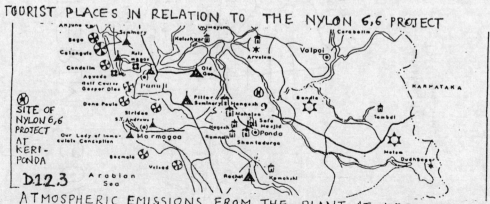

D.1.2.3

ATMOSPHERIC EMISSIONS FROM THE PLANT AT KERIM, INCREASE
IN TRAFFIC DENSITY ETC. WILL AFFECT TOURIST PLACES.

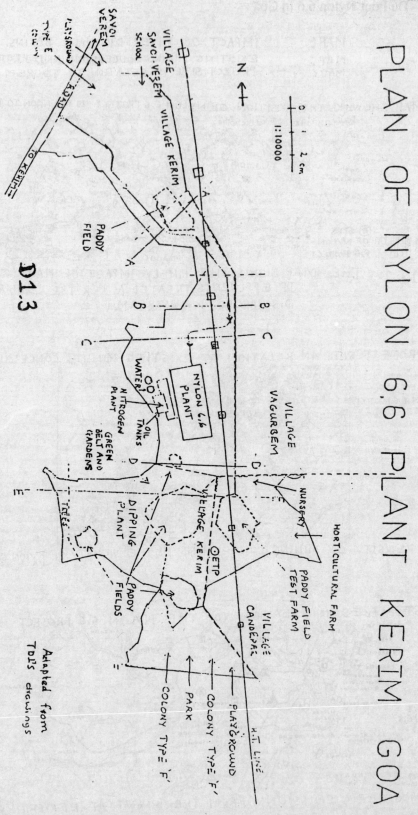

PLAN OF NYLON 6,6 PLANT KERIM GOA

D1.3

N ↑

1:10000
0   1   2 cm

Adapted from
TDI's drawings

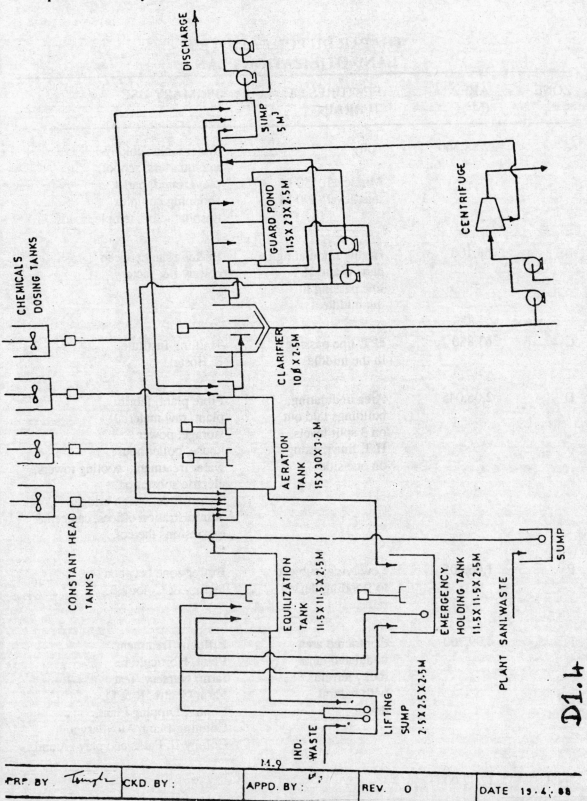

THAPAR DU PONT LIMITED
LAND UTILIZATION PLAN

ZONE	AREA (M²)	FEATURES OF TERRAIN	PRIMARY USE
A	2,88,300	Hilly Min.level: 150 M max.level: 190 M	Water tanks, colony-I viz. quarters, school, playground, parks, shopping complex, hospital, club, temple, roads.
B	68,100	Highly undulating narrow and H.T. line passing in the middle.	Buffer zone between colony I & factory.
C	63,850	H.T. line passing in the middle.	Training Institute & Hostel.
D	2,06,045	Area undulating, buildings laid out on 3 split levels, H.T. line passing on one side.	Fibre plant, fabric plant, raw material storage, power house, boiler house, water treatment, cooling towers, electric substation, Time office, weigh bridge, administration offices, canteen & expansions thereof.
E	1,06,005	Low lying, subject to flooding during rains.	Buffer zone between factory & Colony II.
F	4,99,700	Contoured area undulated land rocky terrain with natural drain	Effluent Treatment Plant, Horticulture farm, Nursery, Test Farm Centre, R & D Centre, Dipping Plant, Conning Plant, Auxillary unit, Colony II, Parks and play ground.

Total: 12,32,000

ZONE : A

Structure	Size (Meters)	Area (M²)
Play ground	140 x 70	9800
Colony Quarter (A)	1 x 288	288
Colony Quarter (B)	5 x 240	1200
Colony Quarter (C)	10 x 144	1440
Colony Quarter (D)	20 x 120	2400
Colony Quarter (E)	25 x 90	1800
Temple	30 x 20	600
School	50 x 60	3000
Shopping centre	40 x 60	2400
Hospital	50 x 20	1000
Social Activity Centre (Club)	25 x 20	500
Water & fire tank	60 x 25	1500
Exhibition Hall	60 x 60	3600
Garden	110 x 40	4400
Total covered area		33928
(a) Plot area (140% of covered area)		47500
(b) Area required (60% extra for open space, land scaping, gardening etc.)		28500
(c) Effective area (a + b)		76000

ZONE : B
Buffer zone		68100

ZONE : C

Structure	Size (Meters)	Area (M²)
Training Institute and Hostel	50 x 40	2000
Swimming pool	15 x 7.5	115
Total covered area		2115
(a) Plot area (140% of covered area)		2960
(b) Area required (60% extra for open space, land scaping, gardening etc.)		1775
(c) Effective area (a + b)		4735

ZONE : D

Structure	Size (Meters)	Area (M²)
Administrative block	40 x 20	800
Car shed, cycle stand	80 x 15	1200
Security and Time Office		70
Canteen, change room locker	40 x 33	1320
Weigh bridge		75
Raw material handling	30 x 12	360
Raw material platform	40 x 42	2520
Fibre plant	114 x 78	8890
Fabric plant	128 x 73.7	9440

Polymerisation	75 x 65	4875
Workshop	40 x 12	360
Air compressor room	25 x 13	325
Nitrogen plant	22 x 13	286
Boiler house	25 x 45	465
Cooling tower	30 x 15	450
DG Set room	25 x 32	880
Control room + HT room	(7x32 + 15x32)	704
Filtration plant and pump room		220
Refrigeration room (Fibre + Fabric)		300
Electrical sub-station	80 x 40	3200
Oil storage and handling	50 x 25	1250
DM/Water tank		280
Transformer room	6 x 25	150
Demineralised plant	30 x 10	300
MCC room	10 x 13	130
Pipe racks		600
Total covered area		39450
Circulation area (Foot path, process requirement & open etc. space 100%)		39450
(A) Effective area		78900
Ist Expansion:		
Fibre plant	114 x 50	5700
Fabric plant	33.5 x 128	4288
Cooling tower	18 x 15	270
Utilities (Nitrogen plant, Compressure room, MCC, Cooling tower etc.)	77 x 13	1000
Total covered area		11258
Circulation area (100%)		11258
(B) Effective area		22516
Effective area utilisation for Zone "D" (A + B)		101416

ZONE : E
Buffer zone		106005

ZONE : F
R&D Centre	100 x 80	8000
Dipping plant	128 x 80	10240
Conning Department	128 x 80	10240
Auxillary units	60 x 40	2400
Colony Quarter Type 'F'	270 x 80	21600
Children park and play ground	60 x 75	4500
Effluent treatment plant	40 x 30	1200
Total covered area		58180

Circulation area (Foot path, roads, land scaping, open area etc. 100%)   58180

(A) Effective area		116360
ETP Test Farm centre		31100
Horticulture farm		75225
Nursery	80 x 60	4800
(B) Effective area		111125

Total area utilisation
in Zone 'F' (A + B)   227485

Zone : G

In addition to this, other land uses are as follows:

1. Boundary buffer zone (Tree plantation)   9500 x 10   95000
2. Roads & roadside
   plantation, foot path and drains   2000 x 25
   + 2500 x 15   87500
3. H.T. Line affected area   1600 x 30   48000
4. Land scaping, tree plantation on Zone "A"
   hillock (steep gradient area)   38800
5. Green Belt in "F" Zone valley and low lying
   area   45000
6. Ditches, natural drains etc.   55000

Total area utilisation 'G'   369300

NYLON 6,6 PROJECT

Details of various sites visited

ANNEXURE 'A'

Sr No	Name of Place and Location	Ava-ilable Land in acres	Type of land	Distance in Km. from				Water Availability	Power Availability	Effluent Disposal	Other Features	Remark
				Main Road	Barge Point	Port by Road	Port by Barge					
(1)	(2)	(3)	(4)	(5)	(6)	(7)	(8)	(9)	(10)	(11)	(12)	(13)
1.	Marcaim 30KM South east of Panjim. In Ponda Taluka 12-13KM from Ponda in between River Zuari and canal Cumbarjua.	200	Rocky and highly undulating	6-7 from N.H. 4 A	3	20	20	No proper water supply. Tubewell to be investigated. Pipe for Ponda via Mardol 3-4KM from site. Ponda supply from 18 M.C.D. (W.T.P) by making dam on river Khandepar	From Ponda sub-station. Natural drain/make open drain to road. Also right in the centre of the site there is a highly undulating.	Look for site is through a very narrow road to discharge in the nearby rivers. Maharashtra & Karnataka rivers.	Approach to the considered suitable due to land being rocky & highly undulating.	Not considered
2.	USGAO 40KM south east of Panjim. In Ponda Taluka 8-10 KM from Ponda.	300	Bunger flat land	2 from N.H. 4 A	2	40-45 30-35		Water will have to be pumped from upstream of river Khandepar. Location of pumping point will be decided after checking salinity of water & may be more than 2 KM. Underground water availability to be investigated.	From Ponda as in case of Marcaim.	To be discharged in rivers at a distance of 0.5 to 1 KM.	There are a number of factories in the vicinity. MRF factory is also close by. There is a meat processing factory nearby which could be considered as pollution hazard. Also mining activities close to Usgao is undesirable.	Partly suitable.

(1)	(2)	(3)	(4)	(5)	(6)	(7)	(8)	(9)	(10)	(11)	(12)	(13)
3.	Navilim Cudnaem This area consists of two locations i.e. Surla and Amona in Bicholim Taluka about 60KM from Panjim via Usgao by road & 30KM via Amona crossing a ferry.	400+	Almost flat land (Commu-nidade land)	On Main Road	2-3	55	35	Underground water to be investigated.	No problem. Already other factories are nearby.	Can be put in downstream of river Mandovi.	This area has dust problem due to iron/muck handling & transportation.	Not considered suitable due to dust problem and also distance from the port is relatively more.
4.	Betul/Kanakini 60 KM south of Panjim & about 30 KM south of Madgao. In Quepem Taluka.	400	Almost flat Bunger Land.	7-10 from N.H. 17	Very near the site but at about 100m below	50	30-35 but high sea anchor-age pos-sible	Tubewell water to be investigated. Pipeline water may be available at 2-3KM from down slope.	From substation at Cuncolim about 3-4KM from site.	To be disposed directly in the sea.	100 Mt. above sea level, overlooking Mabor beach, very scenic site. Distance from Madgao will reduce to 15KM once the bridge near Vetem is made.	Suitable, but distance from port is relatively more. Also the infrastructure such as power, & water may not be available at this site for next 5 years.
5.	Cuncolim about 55 KM south of Panjim in Salcete Taluka.	150	Flat, partly agricul-tural	3	15	35	Not appli-cable	Could be drawn from irrigation canal 2-3 km away provided allowed by Irrigation Deptt. Or else, underground water shall have to be investigated.	No Problem as sub-station is located in this area itself.	Natural drain shall have to be looked for or open drain shall have to be made. May be a bit problematic.		Land availability not adequate. distance from port also relatively more.

(1)	(2)	(3)	(4)	(5)	(6)	(7)	(8)	(9)	(10)	(11)	(12)	(13)
6.	Xeldem - Cur-chorem In Quepem Taluka. About 55 KM south east of Panjim. 25 KM from Margao.	200+	Generally flat, partly agricul-tural	1	3	60	60	Possibility of drawing water from Salaoli irrigation project would have to be confirmed. Or else, underground water to be investigated.	Substation under construction in Xeldem & through natural drain or by making an open drain upto the river.	Could be disposed of in the river Zuari Material could be transported through Barges.	Railway station is close by. Raw suitable if water and power are made available at this site in the near future. Also as per the Town Planning Dept. the area of 200 acres can be suitably increased to 450 acres but land hold is with private owners and acquisition may take years.	Can be considered
7.	Loliem in Cancona Taluka. About 90KM south of Panjim, 55KM south of Margao. On sea shore.	400-	Almost flat, Bunger land	Along side NH 17	On Sea Shore	12-15	12-15 From Karwar Port	Underground water to be investigated.	HT Lines shall have to be extended upto this point.	Could be easily disposed of into the sea.	20 KM north of BILT's chemical complex at Karwar	Suitable site. But Power Dept. & PWD Dept. could not confirm availability of power & water to this site.

Sr No	Name of Place and Location	Ava--ilable land acres	Type of Land	Distance in Km. from					Water Availability	Power Availability	Effluent Disposal	Other Features	Remark
				Main Road	Barge Point	Port by Road	Port by Barge						
(1)	(2)	(3)	(4)	(5)	(6)	(7)	(8)	(9)	(10)	(11)	(12)	(13)
8.	Colvale in Bardez Taluka. About 20KM north of Panjim. Nearest town Mapusa 7-8 KM away.	400+	Almost flat land	Along side NH 17				Underground water to be investigated.	HT Lines proposed till Tivim, 5 KM from site.	Could be easily disposed of.	This land has not been declared industrially backward.	Suitable site.
9.	Querrim in Ponda Taluka. About 34KM south east of Panjim via Ponda. 8 KM from Ponda town. Located at uninhibited plateau.	500+	Bunger land with no vegetatio	Along side NH 4A	5	45	35	Underground water to be investigated. Water may be available from Opa water works. Main water line 5KM from site.	220 KV HT line passing through site which will be terminated at Ponda and power will be made available.	Could be easily disposed of.	This is the only site where power & water can be made available. Bunger land and no trees are to be cut for setting up the factory. Since there are no inhabitants in this cummunidade land, no shifting will have to be done. Though approach to the site is little difficult it could be set right.	Most suitable.

PROCESS EMISSION

SOURCE	ABATEMENT DEVICE	POUNDS PER HOUR EMISSIONS	
		PROJECTED	PERMITTED USA
Evaporator	Reflux Column	2.0	10
Reactor	Reflux Column	1.0	8.5
Separator	Vent condensor	0.2	7.0
Finisher	None	0.02	6.0
Spin room exhaust.	None	None	
Monomer	None	0.75	6.0
Hot tube	catalytic oxidation	0.2	6.0
Miscellaneous	Cat. ox. & scrubber	0.02	-
TOTAL LINE		4.2	10

Note: ALL EMISSIONS ARE "PARTICULATE"
- Diamine carbonate
- Low molecular weight nylon

PROCESS EMISSIONS CONTAIN NO:
- Sulfur dioxide
- Carbon monoxide
- Volatile organic compounds.
- Nitrogen Oxides.

Source:
BILT P & D DIVN.

CHARACTERISTICS OF THE EFFLUENT

S.NO.	CHARACTERISTIC	INFLUENT	TREATED EFFLUENT	POLLUTION BOARD STANDARD
1.0	pH	8.3	6.5-8.0	6.5-8.0
2.0	TSS, mgl	120	Less than 50	Not to exceed 100
3.0	BOD5 20 Deg.C,mgl	450	Less than 20	Not to exceed 30
4.0	COD, mgl	650	Less than 250	Not to exceed 250
5.0	TKN, mgl	80		Not to exceed 100 (IS: 2490-pt. 1981)
6.0	Ammonical Nitrogen, mgl	20		Not to exceed 50
7.0	Phenol, mgl	0.1		Not to exceed 1
8.0	No3-N, mgl	15		

Source:
BILT P & D DIVN.

10th October, 1990
Ref: TDL/HC/90-91/2
The Chairman
House Committee
Nylon 6,6 Project,
Panaji-Goa.

Dear Sir,

Yesterday in our presentation, we believe that the aspect of 'Additives' in Nylon 6,6 Yarn was not fully understood. Herebelow is an explanation as to how these additives are fully captured by Nylon yarn during the process of manufacture and not released to either air or liquid effluent.

In the process of polymerization of Nylon 6,6, 99.7% ingredients are an equimolar mixture of Adipic Acid and 1,6 Hexamethylene Diamine (HMD). For controlling the polymerization, 0.3% salts (Potassium Iodide, Potassium Bromide, Aqueous solution of Cupric Bromide, Potassium Bicarbonate and Organophosphorous Acid) are added. As an alternative to Cupric Bromide, we add Cupric Acetate as a backup to complete the desired degree of polymerization. These additives are quantitatively utilized in the process of polymerization, and nothing detectable of any of these salts appears in the effluent before the treatment, leave alone after. Also, there is no detectable copper and potassium impurities in the air emissions. That these salts are quantitatively utilized is estimated by Atomic Absorption Spectrophotometry (AAS). Using this technique we have reproducibly observed that Nylon 6,6 Yarn contains all the Ionic additives as listed above. This is also confirmed independently by other methods like ASH Test.

We hope that the above clarifies the issue.

Thanking you.

Yours faithfully,

For THAPAR DU PONT LTD

K S PAL

Encl: 1. Process emissions

        2. Plant discharges

PROCESS EMISSIONS

| SOURCE | ABATEMENT DEVICE | POUNDS PER HOUR EMISSIONS | | |
		PROJECTED @ GOA	RICHMOND ACTUAL	PERMITTED
Evaporator	Reflux Column, Vent Condenser	0.0	0.0	10
Reactor	Reflux Column, Vent Condenser	0.0	0.0	8.5
Separator	Vent Condenser	0.0	0.0	7.0
Finisher	None	0.02	0.02	6.0
Spin Room	None	none	none	none
Monomer	Scrubber	0.0	0.0	6.0
Miscellaneous	Catalytic Oxidation & scrubber	0.2	0.2	6.0
TOTAL LINE		0.22	0.22	10

PLANT DISCHARGES

	BEFORE TREATMENT	AFTER TREATMENT	TOLERANCE LIMITS (INDIA & U.S.)
Flow, gpm	169	169	not limited
pH	8.3	6.5-8.0	6.0-9.0
Temperature, degrees C	25-35	25-35	<40
Total Suspended Solids	96	46	92
COD	560	120	230
BOD-5	380	23	28
Dissolved Oxygen	<2	>2	-
Oil & Grease	-	<9	9.2
Nitrogen			
TKN	66	26	91
Ammoniacal	-	5	46
Free Ammonia	-	3	46

EXHIBIT 1
INDIAN NYLON VENTURE
WASTEWATER TREATMENT SCOPE
MAJOR EQUIPMENT
(See Figure 1)

Vessels (all vessels carbon steel, coated, with cathodic protection)

Emergency retention tank - 52 M gallon liquid capacity

- eg, 22 ft deep plus 3 ft freeboard x 20 ft diameter.

Equilization tank - 52 M gallon liquid capacity

- eg, 22 ft deep plus 3 ft freeboard x 20 ft diameter.

Aeration tank - 128 M gallon liquid capacity

- eg, 20 ft deep plus 5 ft freeboard x 33 ft diameter.

Clarifier - circular vessel, center feed, peripheral overflow,   Rexnord "Tow Bro" type sludge withdrawal (see Deer Park Project 1661 except substitute steel for concrete)

- 30 ft diameter, 10 ft SWD.

Equipment

Air blowers - 2 units (no spare) at 800 scfm at 25 ft head.

Air headers and 2" laterals in each tank for air distribution.   Drilled with 2 orifices per "station" (34 stations on 5 ft centers in aeration tank, 13 stations at 5 ft centers in both the equilization and emergency tanks).

Lift station pumps - three (incl. one installed spare) 150 gpm water pumps.

Sludge recycle pumps - two (incl. one installed spare) 150 gpm pumps.

Drum metering pump for maximum 1 gph 35: H_3PO_4 (phosphoric   acid) addition to lift station.

Polymer feed facilities - two (clarifier and filter) - Stranco   Polyblend Model PB200-1.

Belt filter press - eg, Arus Andritz (phone 817/465-5611)

- 1 meter wide belt (Note: This unit has sufficient excess capacity to filter water treatment plant sludge as well).

*** OR ***

Sand drying beds (see Figure 2) - Four units, 18 ft x 44 ft, with sludge distribution pipes and valving to isolate flow to any single unit.

Buildings

Belt filter/polymer building - at minimum, provide roof over 30 ft x 30 ft concrete pad with drain: smaller if filter not provided.

ECR/ICR - probably attached to belt filter building.

Small lab room with sink, cabinet space, electricity, and ventilation. Probably attached to belt filter building.

Instruments

Two level indicators and alarms - equilization and emergency tanks.

Dissolved oxygen probe and readout in aeration tank.

Four flow meters - feed to equilization, clarifier overflow, waste sludge, recycle sludge.

Clarifier torque switch and alarm.

Belt filter common alarm (individual control panel is provided with the unit) if filter provided.

RAR: ams/15.16

9/23/87.

FIGURE 1
INDIAN NYLON VENTURE
WASTEWATER TREATMENT FACILITIES

TANK ALTERNATIVE

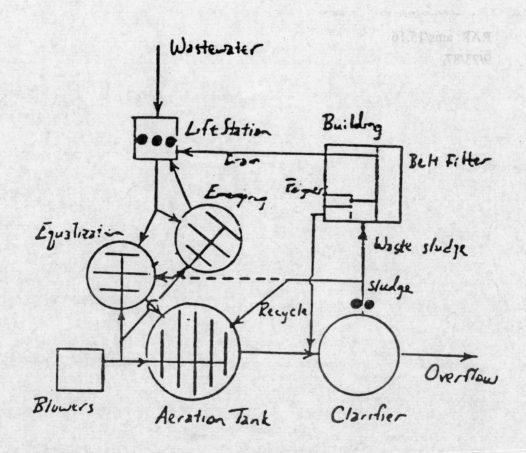

Note : Pumps indicated by ●
       "Contingency recycle"

New Jersey Department of Health
HAZARDOUS SUBSTANCE FACT SHEET

Groups A, B, C, and D   **April 1988**

The following Hazardous Substance Fact Sheets are available for distribution. The code *new* between the substance number and the common name indicates that the Fact Sheet was never distributed before. The code *rev* between the substance number and the common name indicates that the Fact Sheet has been revised and should replace any other Fact Sheet with the same name.

Substance number		Common name	Substance number		Common name
___0001		ACETALDEHYDE	___0054		ALUMINUM
___0003		ACETALDEHYDE OXIME	___0057		ALUMINUM CHLORIDE
___0004		ACETIC ACID	___0061		ALUMINUM NITRATE
___0005		ACETIC ANHYDRIDE	___0062		ALUMINUM PHOSPHATE
___0006		ACETONE	___0063		ALUMINUM PHOSPHIDE
___0008		ACETONITRILE	___0068		ALUMINUM SULFATE
___0010		2-ACETYLAMINOFLUORENE	___0070		2-AMINO-4-CHLOROPHENOL
___0011	new	ACETYL BENZOYL PEROXIDE	___0071	new	2-AMINO-5-DIETHYLAMINOPENTANE
___0012		ACETYL BROMIDE	___0072		4-AMINODIPHENYL
___0013		ACETYL CHLORIDE	___0078		AMINOPHENOLS
___0014	new	ACETYL CYCLOHEXANE SULFONYL PEROXIDE	___0081		2-AMINOPYRIDINE
___0015		ACETYLENE	___0083		AMITROL
___0016		ACETYLENE TETRABROMIDE	___0084		AMMONIA
___0017		ACETYL IODIDE	___0085		AMMONIUM ACETATE
___0020		ACETYLSALICYLIC ACID	___0088		AMMONIUM BICARBONATE
___0021		ACROLEIN	___0089		AMMONIUM BIFLUORIDE
___0022		ACRYLAMIDE	___0091		AMMONIUM CARBAMATE
___0023		ACRYLIC ACID	___0092		AMMONIUM CARBONATE
___0024		ACRYLONITRILE	___0093		AMMONIUM CHLORIDE
___0026		ADIPIC ACID	___0094		AMMONIUM CHLOROPLATINATE
___0028		ADRIAMYCIN	___0095		AMMONIUM CHROMATE
___0031		ALDICARB	___0096		AMMONIUM CITRATE
		Aliphatic Naphtha see BENZINE	___0097		AMMONIUM DICHROMATE
___0036		ALLYL ALCOHOL			Ammonium Ferric Citrate see FERRIC AMMONIUM CITRATE
___0039		ALLYL CHLORIDE			Ammonium Ferric Oxalate see FERRIC AMMONIUM OXALATE
___0043		ALLYL GLYCIDYL ETHER			
___0044		ALLYL IODIDE			
___0045		ALLYL ISOTHIOCYANATE			Ammonium Ferrous Sulfate see FERROUS AMMONIUM SULFATE
___0046		ALLYL PROPYL DISULFIDE			
___0047		ALLYL TRICHLOROSILANE			

NEW JERSEY DEPARTMENT OF HEALTH
RIGHT TO KNOW PROGRAM
CN 368
TRENTON, NJ 08625-0368

___0307		CADMIUM BROMIDE
___0309		CALCIUM
___0312		CALCIUM CARBIDE
___0313		CALCIUM CHLORATE
___0315		CALCIUM CHROMATE
___0316		CALCIUM CYANAMIDE
___0319		CALCIUM FLUORIDE
___0320	new	CALCIUM HYDRIDE
___0322		CALCIUM HYDROXIDE
___0323		CALCIUM HYPOCHLORITE
___0324		CALCIUM NITRATE
___0325		CALCIUM OXIDE
___0329		CALCIUM PHOSPHIDE
___0334		CAMPHOR
___0337		CAPROLACTAM
___0338		CAPTAFOL
___0339		CAPTAN
___0340		CARBARYL
___0341		CARBOFURAN
___0342		CARBON BLACK
___0343		CARBON DIOXIDE
___0344		CARBON DISULFIDE
___0345		CARBON MONOXIDE
___0346		CARBON TETRABROMIDE
___0347		CARBON TETRACHLORIDE
		Cellosolve Acetate see
		2-ETHOXYETHYL ACETATE
___0354		CESIUM HYDROXIDE
___0360	new	CHLORAMPHENICOL
___0361		CHLORDANE
___0366		CHLORINATED DIPHENYL OXIDE
___0367		CHLORINE
___0368		CHLORINE DIOXIDE
___0370		CHLORINE TRIFLUORIDE
___0372		CHLOROACETALDEHYDE
___0377		CHLOROACETYL CHLORIDE
___0378	new	CHLOROANILINE
___0379		CHLOROBENZENE
___0381		CHLOROBROMOMETHANE
___0385		CHLORODIFLUOROETHANE
___0386		CHLORODIFLUOROMETHANE
___0388		CHLOROFORM
___0391		CHLOROMETHYL METHYL ETHER
___0392		3-CHLORO-4-METHYL PHENYL ISOCYANATE
___0395		1-CHLORO-1-NITROPROPANE
___0397		4-CHLORO-o-TOLUIDINE HYDROCHLORIDE
___0398		CHLOROPENTAFLUOROETHANE
		Chlorophenate see CHLOROPHENOL
___0401		4-CHLOROPHENOL
___0402		3-CHLOROPHENOL
___0403		2-CHLOROPHENOL
___0404		CHLOROPHENYL TRICHLOROSILANE
___0405		CHLOROPICRIN
___0406	new	CHLOROPLATINIC ACID
___0407		CHLOROPRENE
		Chlorotoluidine see
		CHLORO METHYL ANILINE
___0417		2-CHLORO-4-METHYL ANILINE
___0418		3-CHLORO-4-METHYL ANILINE

___0419		3-CHLORO-2-METHYL ANILINE
___0420		2-CHLORO-5-METHYL ANILINE
___0421		5-CHLORO-2-METHYL ANILINE
___0422		2-CHLORO-3-METHYL ANILINE
___0423		6-CHLORO-2-METHYL ANILINE
___0424		4-CHLORO-3-METHYL ANILINE
___1424		o-CHLOROSTYRENE
___1425		o-CHLOROTOLUENE
___0426		CHLORPYRIFOS
___0428		CHROMIC ACETATE
___0429		CHROMIC ACID
___0431		CHROMIC SULFATE
___0432		CHROMIUM
___0434		CHROMIUM(III) OXIDE(2:3)
___0435	new	CHROMIUM NITRATE
___0437	new	CHROMIUM(VI) OXIDE(1:3)
___0438		NEOCHROMIUM
___0439		CHROMOSULFURIC ACID
___0441		CHRYSENE
___0510		CISPLATIN
___0514		CLOPIDOL
___0517		COAL TAR CREOSOTE
___0518		COAL TAR NAPHTHA
___0520		COBALT
___0523		COBALT NAPHTHENATE
___0528		COPPER
___0533		COPPER CYANIDE
___0535		COTTON FIBER AS RAW COTTON
___0536		COUMAPHOS
___0537		CRESYLIC ACID
___0538	new	CROTONALDEHYDE
___0541		CRUFOMATE
___0542		CUMENE
___0546		CUPRIC ACETATE
___0547		CUPRIC NITRATE
___0549		CUPRIC SULFATE
___0552		CYANAMIDE
___0554		CYANOGEN
___0555		see Cyanogen #0554
___0565		CYCLOHEXANE
___0569		CYCLOHEXANOL
___0570		CYCLOHEXANONE
___0572		CYCLOHEXENE
___0573		CYCLOHEXENYL TRICHLOROSILANE
___0576		CYCLOHEXYLAMINE
___0577		CYCLOHEXYL ISOCYANATE
___0578		CYCLOHEXYL TRICHLOROSILANE
___0579		CYCLONITE
___0582		CYCLOPENTADIENE
___0583		CYCLOPENTANE
___0588		CYCLOPROPANE
___0597		DECABORANE
___0604		DEMETON
___0606		DIACETONE ALCOHOL
___0616		DIATOMACEOUS EARTH
___0617		DIAZEPAM
___0618		DIAZINON
___0620		DIAZOMETHANE
___0627		DIBENZYLDICHLOROSILANE

___1501		PHENYL ISOCYANATE
___1502		PHENYLMERCURIC ACETATE
___1418		n-PHENYL-beta-NAPHTHYLAMINE
___1505		PHENYLPHOSPHINE
___1506		PHENYL TRICHLOROSILANE
___1508		PHORATE
___1510		PHOSGENE
___1514	new	PHOSPHINE
___1516		PHOSPHORIC ACID
___1518		PHOSPHOROUS ACID, ortho
___1520		PHOSPHORUS, AMORPHOUS, RED
___1535		PHTHALIC ANHYDRIDE
___1536		PICLORAM
___1540		PIPERAZINE
___1541		PIPERAZINE DIHYDROCHLORIDE
___1547		PLATINUM
___1548	new	p-NITROANILINE
___1554		POLYCHLORINATED BIPHENYLS
___1555		POTASSIUM
___1556		POTASSIUM ARSENATE
___1559		POTASSIUM BROMATE
___1560		POTASSIUM CHLORATE
___1561		POTASSIUM CHROMATE
___1562		POTASSIUM CYANIDE
___1563		POTASSIUM DICHLORO-ISOCYANURATE
___1564		POTASSIUM DICHROMATE
___1565		POTASSIUM FLUORIDE
___1567		POTASSIUM HEXACHLOROPLATINATE
___1571		POTASSIUM HYDROXIDE
___1575		POTASSIUM NITRITE
___1578		POTASSIUM PERMANGANATE
___1580		POTASSIUM PERSULFATE
___1583		POTASSIUM SULFIDE
___1585		POTASSIUM TETRACHLOROPLATINATE
___1588		PREDNISOLONE
___1589		PREDNISONE
___1593		PROPADIENE
___1594		PROPANE
___1597		PROPARGYL ALCOHOL
___1599		PROPIONIC ACID
___1604		PROPOXUR
___1419		n-PROPYL ACETATE
___1605		PROPYL ALCOHOL
___1609		PROPYLENE
___1610	new	PROPYLENE CHLOROHYDRIN
___1612		PROPYLENE GLYCOL DINITRATE
___1613		PROPYLENE GLYCOL MONOMETHYL ETHER
___1614		PROPYLENE IMINE
___1617		PROPYL ISOCYANATE
___1623		PYRETHRUM
___1624		PYRIDINE
___1634		RESORCINOL
___1641		SACCHARIN
___1643		sec-AMYL ACETATE
___1644		sec-BUTYL ACETATE
___1645		sec-BUTYL ALCOHOL
___1648		SELENIUM
___1656		SILICA, AMORPHOUS (FUSED)
___1659		SILICA, MICA

___1660		SILICA, QUARTZ
___1664		SILICA, TRIPOLI
___1668		SILICON TETRAHYDRIDE
___1669		SILVER
___1671		SILVER CYANIDE
___1672		SILVER NITRATE
___1673		SILVER PICRATE
___1674		SODIUM
___1675		SODIUM ALUMINATE
___1676	new	SODIUM ALUMINUM FLUORIDE
___1677		SODIUM ALUMINUM HYDRIDE
___1682		SODIUM ARSENATE
___1683		SODIUM ARSENITE
___1684		SODIUM AZIDE
___1685		SODIUM BISULFITE
___0241		SODIUM BORATES
___1688		SODIUM CHLORATE
___1691		SODIUM CHLOROPLATINATE
___1692		SODIUM CHROMATE
___1693		SODIUM CYANIDE
___1694		SODIUM DICHLORO-ISOCYANATE
___1695		SODIUM DICHROMATE
___1698		SODIUM DODECYLBENZENE SULFONATE
___1699		SODIUM FLUORIDES
___1704		SODIUM HYDROGEN SULFATE
___1706		SODIUM HYDROXIDE
___1707		SODIUM HYPOCHLORITE
___1708		SODIUM METABISULFITE
___1718		SODIUM PEROXIDE
___1723		SODIUM PHOSPHATE, DIBASIC
___1724		SODIUM PHOSPHATE, TRIBASIC
___1731		STANNIC CHLORIDE, HYDRATED
___1733		STANNOUS CHLORIDE
___1734		STANNOUS FLUORIDE
___1735		STIBINE
___1736		STODDARD SOLVENT
___1742		STRONTIUM CHROMATE
___1743		STRONTIUM NITRATE
___1748		STYRENE MONOMER
___1750		SUBTILISINS
___1756	new	SULFOTEPP
___1757		SULFUR
___1761		SULFURIC ACID
___1766		SULFUR TETRAFLUORIDE
___1770		SULPHAMIC ACID
___1771		SULPROFOS
___1773		TALC
___1780		TEMEPHOS
___1781		TEPP
___1787		tert-BUTYL ALCOHOL
___1788		tert-BUTYL CHROMATE
___1804		TESTOSTERONE
___1807		1,1,1,2-TETRACHLORO-2,2-DIFLUOROETHANE
___1808		1,1,2,2-TETRACHLORO-1,2-DIFLUOROETHANE
___1809		1,1,2,2-TETRACHLOROETHANE
___1810		TETRACHLOROETHYLENE
___1811		TETRACHLORONAPHTHALENE
___1814		TETRACYCLINE
___1817		TETRAETHYL LEAD

___1821		TETRAFLUOROMETHANE
___1823		TETRAHYDROFURAN
___1831		TETRAMETHYL LEAD
___1833		TETRAMETHYL SILANE
___1837		TETRASODIUM PYROPHOSPHATE
___1846		4,4'-THIOBIS(6-tert-BUTYL-m-CRESOL)
___1848		THIOGLYCOLIC ACID
___1853		THIOUREA
___1857	new	THORIUM NITRATE
___1858		TIN
___1859		TIN TETRACHLORIDE
___1860	new	TITANIUM
___1861		TITANIUM DIOXIDE
___1866		TOLUENE
___1869		TOLUENE-2,4-DIISOCYANATE
___1318		m-TOLUIDINE
___1442		o-TOLUIDINE
		TREMOLITE see ASBESTOS
___1878		TRIBUTYL ALUMINUM
___1883		TRICHLOROACETIC ACID
___1887		1,2,4-TRICHLOROBENZENE
___1889		1,1,2-TRICHLOROETHANE
___1890		TRICHLOROETHYLENE
___1891		TRICHLOROFLUOROMETHANE
___1892		TRICHLOROISOCYANURIC ACID
___1904		1,1,2-TRICHLORO-1,2,2-TRIFLUOROETHANE
___1906		TRIETHYL ALUMINIUM
___1907		TRIETHYLAMINE
___1912	new	TRIFLUOROBROMOMETHANE
___1914		TRIFLUOROETHANE
___1919		TRIISOBUTYL ALUMINIUM
___1922		TRIMELLITIC ANHYDRIDE
___1926		TRIMETHYL ALUMINUM
___1927		TRIMETHYLAMINE
___1929		TRIMETHYL BENZENE
___1931		TRIMETHYLCHLOROSILANE
___1935		TRIMETHYL PHOSPHITE
___1950		TRIPHENYL AMINE
___1954		TRIPROPYL ALUMINUM
___1959		TUNGSTEN
___1960		TUNGSTEN CARBIDE
___1961		TUNGSTEN HEXAFLUORIDE
___1962		TURPENTINE
___1986		URETHANE
___1987		VALERALDEHYDE
___1990		VANADIUM
___1993		VANADIUM PENTOXIDE
___1994	new	VANADIUM TETRACHLORIDE
___1996	new	VANADIUM TRIOXIDE
___1997	new	VANADYL SULFATE
___1998		VINYL ACETATE
___1999		VINYL BROMIDE
___2001		VINYL CHLORIDE
___2003		VINYL CYCLOHEXENE DIOXIDE
___2006		VINYLIDENE CHLORIDE
___2014		XYLENES
___1320		m-XYLENE-a,a'-DIAMINE
___2015		XYLENOL
___2017		XYLIDINE

___2021		ZINC
___2022		ZINC ACETATE
___2026		ZINC BORATE
___2027		ZINC BROMIDE
___2028		ZINC CARBONATE
___2029		ZINC CHLORATE
___2030		ZINC CHLORIDE
___2031		ZINC CHROMATE
___2032		ZINC CYANIDE
___2033		ZINC DITHIONITE
___2034		ZINC FLUORIDE
___2036		ZINC NITRATE
___2037		ZINC OXIDE FUMES
___2038		ZINC PERMANGANATE
___2039		ZINC PEROXIDE
___2042	new	ZINC POTASSIUM CHROMATE
___2044		ZINC SULFATE
___2047		ZIRCONIUM
___2055		ZINC OXIDE

New Jersey Department of Health
Hazardous Substance Fact Sheet

August 1988

Group E

Substance Number	Common name	Substance Number	Common name
___ 0015 Rev.	Acetylene	___ 1098	Lead Arsenate
___ 0110	Ammonium Permanganate	___ 1154	Maneb
___ 0116	Ammonium Sulphite	___ 1200	Methallyl Alcohol
___ 0162	Arsenic Trisulfide	___ 1265	Methyl Hydrazine
___ 0172	Avitrol	___ 1266	Methyl Iodide
___ 0197 Rev.	Benzene	___ 1275	Methyl Mercaptan
___ 0255	Briomine Trifluoride	___ 1317	m-phthalodinitrille
___ 0283	Butyl Bromide	___ 1325	1-Napthylamine
___ 0284	Butyl Ether	___ 1349	Nicotine
___ 0328	Calcium Peroxide	___ 1392	2-Nitropropane
___ 0333	Camphene	___ 1432	Octafluorocyclobutane
___ 0351	Castrix	___ 1455	Paraldehyde
___ 0373	Chloroacetic acid	___ 1530	Phosphorus Trichloride
___ 0436	Chromium Oxychloride	___ 1587	Prazepam
___ 0543	Cumene Hydroperoxide	___ 1606	Propylamine
___ 0564	Cycloheptene	___ 1615	Propylene Oxide
___ 0630	Diuromobenzene	___ 1657	Silica, Cristobalite
___ 0693	Diethyl Aniline	___ 1689	Sodium Chlorite
___ 0688	Diethoxypropene	___ 1702	Sodium Hydride
___ 0718	Diglycidyl Ether....	___ 1716	Sodium perchlorate
___ 0734	3,3,Dimethoxybenzidine	___ 1767	Sulphuric acid, fuming
___ 0736	Dimethyl Acetamide	___ 1806	2,3,2,8, Tetrachlorodibenzo-p-dioxin
___ 0759 Rev.	Dimethyl Formamide	___ 1816	Tetra Ethylenepentamine
___ 0795	Diphenyl		Tetra Ethylsilicate
___ 0850	Ethyl Aniline		see Ethyl silicate No.0909
___ 0862	Ethyl Butyrate	___ 1819	Tetra Fluoro Ethylene
___ 0866	Ethyl 2,Chloropropionate	___ 1840	Thallium
___ 0895	Ethyl Mercuric Chloride	___ 1870	Toluene Sulfonic Acid
___ 0909	Ethyl Silicate	___ 1889	Tributyl Phosphate
___ 0917	Ferbam...	___ 1896	2,4,5, (Trichlorophenoxy) Acetic Acid
___ 0939	Fluoro Benzene	___ 2010	Vinyl Toluene
___ 0956	Gallium	___ 2020	Zeolite

Revised Hazardous Substance Fact Sheet.

NEW JERSEY DEPARTMENT OF HEALTH
RIGHT TO KNOW PROGRAM
CN 368
TRENTON, NJ 08625-0368
609-984-2202

>>>>>>>>>>>>>>>>>> E M E R G E N C Y I N F O R M A T I O N <<<<<<<<<<<<<<

Common Name: **HEXAMETHYLENE DIAMINE**
DOT Number: UN 2280 Solid
               UN 1783 Solution
DOT Emergency Guide code: 60
CAS Number: 124-09-4

DRAFT

Hazard rating	NJ DOH	NFPA
FLAMMABILITY	Not Found	Not Rated
REACTIVITY	Not Found	Not Rated
CORROSIVE SOLID OR SOLUTION		
POISONOUS GASES ARE PRODUCED IN FIRE		
MAY CAUSE ALLERGIC REACTION		

*Hazard Rating Key: 0-minimal; 1-slight;
2-moderate; 3-serious; 4-severe*

FIRE HAZARDS
* Hexamethylene Diamine may burn, but does not readily ignite.
* Hexamethylene Diamine in solution is combustible.
* Hexamethylene Diamine may ignite combustible materials on contact.
* Use dry chemical, CO_2, water spray, or foam extinguishers.
* POISONOUS GASES ARE PRODUCED IN FIRE, including *Nitrogen Oxides*.
* Use water spray to keep fire-exposed containers cool.
* If employees are expected to fight fires, they must be trained and equipped as stated in OSHA 1910.156.

SPILLS AND EMERGENCIES
If Hexamethylene Diamine is spilled take the following steps:
* Restrict persons not wearing protective equipment from area of spill until clean-up is complete.

If Hexamethylene Diamine in solution is spilled or leaked, take the following steps:
* Restrict persons not wearing protective equipment from area of spill or leak until clean-up is complete.
* Remove all ignition sources.
* Ventilate area of spill or leak.
* Absorb liquids in vermiculite, dry sand, earth, or a similar material and deposit in sealed containers.
* Collect powdered material in the most convenient and safe manner and deposit in sealed containers.
* It may be necessary to contain and dispose of Hexamethylene Diamine as a HAZARDOUS WASTE. Contact your Department of Environmental Protection (DEP)

or your regional office of the federal Environmental Protection Agency (EPA) for specific recommendations.

FOR LARGE SPILLS AND FIRES immediately call your fire department. You can request emergency information from the following:
CHEMTREC: (800) 424-9300
NJDEP HOTLINE: (609) 292-7172

HANDLING AND STORAGE (See page 4)

FIRST AID
In NJ, POISON INFORMATION 1-800-962-1253

Eye Contact
* Immediately flush with large amounts of water for at least 15 minutes, occasionally lifting upper and lower lids. Seek medical attention immediately.

Skin Contact
* Quickly remove contaminated clothing. Immediately wash contaminated skin with large amounts of water.

Breathing

DRAFT

* Remove the person from exposure.
* Begin rescue breathing if breathing has stopped and CPR if heart action has stopped.
* Transfer promptly to a medical facility.
* Medical observation is recommended for 24 to 48 hours after breathing overexposure, as pulmonary edema may be delayed.

PHYSICAL DATA
Flash Point: 178°F (81.1°C)
(Hexamethylene Diamine solution)
Water Solubility: Highly soluble

DRAFT

OTHER COMMONLY USED NAMES
Chemical Name:
1,6-Hexanedeamine
Other Names and Formulations:
HMDA; 1,6-Diaminohexane;
1,6-Hexamethylenediamine   DS
Not intended to be copied and sold for commercial purposes.
NEW JERSEY DEPARTMENT OF HEALTH
Right to Know Program
CN 368, Trenton, NJ 08625-0368
(609) 984-2202

DRAFT

NATIONAL TOXIC CAMPAIGN FUND - U.S.A.

The National Toxic Campaign Fund (NTCF) with the citizen's environmental Laboratory at Massachussets, U.S.A., is an organisational set up that works to highlight and counteract the environmental/human harm caused by the industrial complex in U.S.A. through the release of hazardous/toxic emissions and effluents.

The NTCF has its National office at Boston, Massachussets and several regional offices throughout the U.S.A.

D.4.2

General Questionnaire on Pollution and Other Aspects

(1)   The Ministry of Environment and Forests, Government of India, stipulates that all development projects require an Environmental Impact Assessment (EIA) study prior to site selection and investment decisions. The EIA is a procedure for bringing out the potential effects of human activities identifying the possible positive and negative impacts on the environment, resulting from a proposed project. EIA is meant for inter-comparison of the development options and screening of alternate sites for locating the projects. This is followed by Environment Impact Statement (EIS) preparation, which is a final analysis to an EIA. Finally, an Environment Management Plan (EMP) is prepared which is an implementation plan for mitigation, protection 'and/or' enhancement measures recommended in the EIS. The EMP presents in details how these measures should be operated, the resources required, and the schedule for implementation. It is intended that in the EMP, the implementation status of protection measures will be elevated to a level suitable for incorporation in the design phase of the proposed project.

How many sites were considered for the establishment of Nylon 6,6 project and whether Environmental Impact Assessment reports were prepared before site selection?

(2)   If so, why this was not done?

(3)   All the developed countries are now conscious of environmental degradation due to 'chemical/allied' industries and go out of their way to 'protect/conserve' their remaining Nature Spots against the rigours of an industrial culture. They have realised that despite stringent pollution control measures, many water bodies in Europe and North America are polluted till this day, either due to inadequate effluent treatment or occasional accidents. Their environmental protection laws are becoming very stringent. Specifically, Du Pont, USA, claims that it ranks high among the safest and environmentally most conscious Multi-national Companies.

Against the above background, it is not odd that the proposed site for the Nylon 6,6 project is chosen in one of the few remaining socio-ecologically rich, clean and virgin regions of the world.

(4)   Do you agree that the fact that a large chemical industry such as the Nylon 6,6 plant, apart from its possible chemical pollution hazards, can be detrimental to the present environment of the proposed site in the following manner?

   (i)   Influx of labour from neighbouring States into the already crowded township of Ponda.

   (ii)   Proliferation of slums in the vicinity of the plant as has happened in the case of Zuari Agro-Chemicals.

   (iii)   Deterioration of the serene, peaceful and 'agriculturally/culturally/religiously' rich lifestyle of Ponda taluka, having a large collection of 'temples/churches', through the advent of a vicious industrial culture.

   (iv)   Spurt in traffic of heavy vehicles due to the 'industrial/commercial' operations, of the Nylon 6,6 plant.

    (v)   Possible diversification of vitally needed local agricultural labour towards the industrial sector.

    (vi) Increase in criminal offences, etc.

    (vii) Indirect environmental degradation impacts due to the installation of new 'power lines/pipelines', 'expansion/widening' of road network, illegal firewood cutting for meeting the needs of the slum dwellers etc.

    (viii)Considerable pressure on surface water (fresh) supply and depletion of ground water resources.

    (ix) Likely seepage and running of 'toxic/other' wastes from the factory site (specially, during monsoon), leading to the pollution of ground water and plantation lands all around slopes of the Kerim plateau.

    (x)   Possibility of disastrous human and ecological damage in the event of an industrial accident.

(5) Considering the high cost: benefit ratio of this project to the local economy, do you think that the Company is justified in asking the Goa Govt. to provide road access, water supply and power at the door step of the plant?

(6) Please react to the following:

    (i)   The present 'machinery/technology' of Nylon 6,6 manufacture is likely to be shifted outside the United States as it does not specify the emission specifications under "Clean Air Act" of USA 1990.

    (ii) The Nylon 6,6 based tyre technology is being exported to the third world, because the developed world is now opting for the modern "HYTEN" and `steel/kevlar' - based Radial tyre technology.

    (iii) If Du Pont, USA, is proud of its safety record in industrial operations, why is the firm shy of accepting liabilities for in-plant accidents, and possible pollution due to faulty operation that may affect the plant workers, the public and the environment?

    (iv) As per the Warranty and Liability Clauses of the Agreement between Thapar and Du Pont, Du Pont has decided to have the arbitration proceedings in London. What is the reason for this?

         Is Du Pont prepared to conduct the arbitration proceedings in USA?

    (v)   Kindly substantiate the statement: "Any worker at a Du Pont Factory is 19 times safer at work than at his residence"?

    (vi) Kindly give the detailed Accident Management Protocol of your Company applicable to the proposed project in Goa?

    (vii) Can Du Pont, USA, guarantee the safe operation of its factories in India?

    (viii)What are the Contingency Plans of the Company to combat probable accidents during the transportation of hazardous 'raw materials/chemicals/finished products' by river, road and rail? Who will be held liable in case of such accidents?

    (ix) Kindly give the details of catalysts, anti-oxidents and other additives to be used in the process of Nylon 6,6 manufacture, as under:

(a) Quantity to be used.

(b) Probable pollution hazards and their control due to the same.

(c) Facilities for the safe storage of these materials at the site.

(d) Possible effect of these chemicals on human health and environment.

(x) What type of bio-assays are to be adopted for the treatment of factory wastes? What proportion of the water employed for effluent treatment will be reused and for what purpose?

(xi) Please clarify the following giving the necessary details:

(a) The exact mode of discharging of effluents in the river (eg. length of pipeline, discharge point etc.).

(b) The qualitative and quantitative composition of various effluents generated.

(c) Qualitative and quantitative compositions of 'domestic/human' 'wastes/effluents' and mode of their disposal.

(d) Composition and quality of gaseous and particulate emissions in the area.

(e) Quality and quantity of solid wastes produced and mode of their 'disposal/treatment'.

(f) Quantity of scrap materials produced per annum and their composition alongwith the method of 'treatment/disposal'.

(g) Please submit a complete sketch of the total manufacturing process, pollution control plan alongwith the outlets of products and emissions. An exact site plan may please be included in the above.

(7) Have you conducted any hydrogeomorphological survey of ground water and other land parameters at the project site?

(8) Will Mecury or its compounds be used in the manufacture of Nylon 6,6 or its intermediates? If so, what will be the method of 'disposal/treatment' of the effluents produced by the above? Can you rule out the possibility of the repeat of Minimata Bay tragedy in Japan?

(9) It is learnt that the release of particulate matter and aerosols during the manufacture of Nylon 6,6 gives rise to a Blue Haze in the surrounding atmosphere. Have you studied this phenomena in the United States, and if so, could you please give us the relevant information with the necessary references?

(10) Does the manufacturing process involve the use or production of Cyanides, Disocyanates or Nitroso amines?

(11) Regarding the captive power plant that is being proposed at the site, we would like to know the following:

(a) The fuel that is proposed to be used. (LSHSD)

(b) Sulphur contents of this fuel.

(c) Quantity of the fuel burnt per year.

(d) Mode of transportation of this fuel.

(c) Various emissions such as Sulphur Dioxide, Nitrogen Oxides etc. in the power production process.

(f) Quality and quantity of the above mentioned emissions.

(g) Pollution control measures proposed to mitigate the above.

(12) (a) "Du Pont, USA, is one of the major sources of industrial pollution in the United States".

(b) "According to the Environmental Protection Agency, USA, Du Pont is one of the largest producer of hazardous substances."

Please comment on the above statements.

(13) It is learnt that Fuel Oil for the plant will be transported by barges from the Port to the site. What percentage of this oil is likely to be washed into the river during the barge cleaning operations? Have you considered the effects of the above possibility on the aquatic ecology and environment in general?

(14) What do you think is the probability of the proposed Nylon 6,6 establishment, diversifying and expanding for the manufacture of raw materials and other allied products?

(15) Most of the chemical industries functioning in the country, either have faulty Effluent Treatment Plants or such plants may be deliberately shut off for economic reasons. Similarly, due to high cost of operation and complex nature, there is no incentive to repair such plants promptly if a genuine fault occurs.

Considering the above, what guarantee can you give that the Effluent Treatment Plant installed by the Nylon 6,6 project will run as per specifications?

(16) What proportion of the total plant 'establishment/operation' budget in proposed to be earmarked for pollution control in this project?

(17) Please give the following details:

(a) The total cost of the proposed project at the present prices?

(b) Please give the exact number of employment opportunities opened up due to the Nylon 6,6 plant in the following categories:

(i) Managerial post

(ii) Technical post

(iii) Supervisory post

(iv) 'Administrative/clerical' post

(v) Skilled workers

(vi) Unskilled labourers.

(18) What is the planned area covered under

a) Buildings of all types

b) Structures like tanks (both overhead + underground)

c) Roads, parking lots, loading and unloading yards.

d) Playgrounds.

(19) What is the arrangement for site water drainage which will be carrying pollutants?

(20) Which department has given permission to let the effluents in the river?

(21) Is land acquired for laying the pipeline?

(22) What are the chemical compositions of the effluents?

(23) How are they analysed? Specify the method of analysis.

(24) Do you have any standard chromatographor mass spectra of the analysis of the effluents?

(25) Do you have any toxicity data of hexamethylene diamine or adipic acid?

(26) What would be the possible side products, in case of excess release of hexamethylene diamine into the reactor?

(27) What are the primary precautions being incorporated in order to face the eventuality of an accident?

(28) Is there any possibility of the formation of any toxic heterocylcic compound in the event of excess release of hexamethylene diamine?

(29) Do you have any data in regard to the effect of the effluents on the aquatic life or agricultural crop?

(30) Do you have any data about the human tolerance limit of consuming hexamethylene diamine?

(31) What ratio of adipic acid to hexamethylene diamine will be used in the proposed process of the manufacture of Nylon-66?

(32) Do you have any information on the bio-degradation of hexamethylene diamine (HMDA)? If available, the party may be requested to furnish the information in writing.

(33) How do you remove HMDA present in the effluent? What concentration of HMDA in ppm would be present after the proper treatment of effluents?

(34) How do you estimate quantitatively the percentage of HMDA in the effluent? What is the extent of accuracy?

(35) If the desired quota of the water is not available from the potable water reservoirs, how do you plan to meet the situation?

(36) Whether the company proposes to tap the ground water resources? If yes, whether the total ground water resources have been estimated? What is the safe yield of the ground water? What measures are visualised to recouperate the ground water?

(37) Whether a geological study of the potential sinks of the effluents has been carried out and what is the effect of effluents on aquatic life?

(38) What facilities have been provided at port and the contingency plans in case of accident in dealing with hazardous chemicals used in the manufacturing process?

(39) Will the Bilge washings be dumped into the Nadi-Mandovi River? And what will be its impact on aquatic fauna and flora?

(40) Has Thapar and Du Pont got approval for a Spandex Fibre Plant in Goa?

(41) What is the mode of storage and transportation of hexamethylene diamine?

(42) Is the company prepared for self management of water resources and power generation? If so, how?

(43) If there are plans for future expansion, the promoters may be requested to submit the detailed plans alongwith requirements in writing.

(44) What type of ancillary units are expected to come up around the complex? Details may be furnished in writing.

(45) Has the company prepared a report on the study of eco-system of area including soil system, vegetation, river basin structure, sedimentation etc., where the treated effluents are supposed to be disposed.

(46) What safety management system you have in mind for the workers and the residents of nearby areas in case of accidents/emergencies?

(47) If furnace oil is used as a fuel, what will be its sulfur content? What the promoters plan to do about the fuel residues? What is the waste management programme?

(48) Since the Nylon 6,6 plant is already functioning in USA, has the company submitted the safety values of the composition of the effluents on the basis of up-to-date approval from the United States Environment Protection Agency, Washington D.C. (U.S.E.P.A.)?

INDUSTRIES DEPARTMENT

1. Is there a State Industrial policy promulgated in State of Goa? If yes from which date and if no then what is the current status?

2. Which areas in Goa have been declared as protected areas, where only schedule Non-Polluting Industries can be instated.

3. Is the department committed to the guidelines prescribed for Industries in the Regional Plan 2001 A.D.; If so have they been examined vis-a-vis T.D.L. Nylon 6,6 Project?

4. What is the procedure for indentification and selection oi sites for setting up chemical plants or Industrial Estates in Goa? What is the criteria used?

5. Is there any Master Plan for Industrial Development of Goa and if not what were the constraints in preparing the same.

6. Has the Department identified the type of Industries which could be considered as Environmentally friendly Industries? If yes, whether Nylon 6,6 manufacture is one of those?

7. Is there any Co-ordination between Industries Department the Town and Country Planning Department, E.D.C., the State Pollution Control Board, Department of Science Technology and Environment, I.D.C. for processing proposals from Industries based on imported technology?

8. Whether the Directorate of Industries could make an appropriate provision for incorporating the need of Environmental Impact Assessment studies for big projects before any site selection and land acquisition proceedings start? Could there be an Environmental Impact Evaluation Cell in the Department?

9. Was the Department consulted on any of the aspect of T.D.L, Nylon 6,6 Project? If yes at what stages? What were the comments of the Department on the aspects consulted?

10. How employment potential is linked with the permission to start Industries in Goa?

11. How it is ensured that Goans are preferred for jobs in the Industries permitted in Goa?

12. What is the criteria used for appointing of Goa State Pollution Control Board and in nominating of members of Technical Committee? Please give details. How many non-officials/ environmentalists are there on the Committee?

13. Is same criteria applied by other States "Pollution Control Board"?

14. What are the rules laid down for routine working of the Board and please define the mandate given with the specific term of reference to the technical Committee for examining proposals of Industries? Please supply the references of the respective gazette notifications, office orders/circulars.

15. In case of highly complex technological proposals, assessment or scrutiny of which may not be possible by the members of the technical Committee, what options or methodology is followed? For example Nylon 6,6 technology is new to India and is a proprietary of Du Pont. The technical Committee members will have to entirely depend on the submissions of the people who monopolise the technology and they may be groping in the dark for various technical aspects of the proposals?

16. Who/which is the final authority in the State for clearing any Industrial Project from environmental angle? What is the statutory position of this authority?

17. What is the mode of coordination between the Town & Country Planning Department, the State Pollution Control Board, its technical committee and the Directorate of Industries?

18. What is the legal status of the conditional NOCs as granted by Goa State Pollution Control Board for production of Nylon 6,6 Plant? Is it good in law?

19. In case a multi-crored project is installed on the basis of provisional NOC and then fails to comply with the environmental standards what would happen then? What actions will be initiated by the Board?

20. Have any studies been carried out by the Government for the Mandovi and Zuari basins and the Cumbarjua Canal for examining the hydrological characteristic, the sediment load, etc as recommended by Central Water and Power Research Institute, Pune? Kindly supply a copy.

21. If not, is there any plan to carry out such studies?

22. Whether the Govt. has any regulations which defines the constitution of survey teams for selecting sites for industry or sending the representatives of the Govt. Department, as member of any survey team?

23. Whether the projected needs of the people in the area in particular and State in General vis-a-vis, the huge needs of such industry has been looked out? (i.e. water, electricity, transport, etc.)

REVENUE DEPARTMENT

1. What is the criteria used for denotification of non-Industrial area?

2. Were any such criteria taken into account for Querim site selected by T.D.L. The categorisation of the land as traditional grazing ground/orchard area etc. and what norms are used to evaluate its existing potential economic productivity if non Industrial alternatives are employed?

3. Whether the recommendations of Dr. M.S. Swaminathan task force 1982 and those in Regional Plan 2001 A.D. 1986 regarding surface utilisation Policy are scrutinised by the department before commenting on any proposal, were looked into?

4. What are the priorities of the Revenue Department as regards conversion of protected and notified areas into Industrial areas?

5. Presently which managing Communidade is in charge of Querim Communidade? Whether old or new?

6. Why the books of Communidades were confiscated by the Administrator of Communidades? And under whose orders?

7. How the work of the Communidades is carried out in the absence of the books? What is the category of staff posted at the Communidade?

MOST IMMEDIATE

No.3/8/90-IND
Government of Goa,
Industries Department,
Secretariat, Panaji.
Dated:- 30th Sept. 1990

To,
The Under Secretary (Legislature),
Legislature Department,
Secretariat, Panaji.

Sub: House Committee to inquire
into the irregularities as
regards to possession of land
from Querim Communidade and
Pollution aspect of Nylon 6,6
Project in Ponda.

Sir,

I am directed to state that the House Committee in its meeting held on 24.10.1990 has handed over to the Secretary (Industries) a Questionaire and had desired information in respect of Questions at Sr. Nos. 1,2,4,6,7,8,9,10,11,20,21,22 and 23 latest by 29.10.1990.

In this connection, I am forwarding herewith replies to the above Questions for perusal of the House Committee.

Yours faithfully,

Sd/-

(S.S. Keshkamat)
Under Secy. (Industries)

Encl: as above
(2 copies)

Q.1   Is there a State Industrial policy promulgated in State of Goa? If yes from which date and if no then what is the current status?

Ans: There is no codified State industrial policy as such, in the State of Goa. Policy decision on various aspects of industry/industrialisation in the State have been taken from time to time.

Q.2   Which areas in Goa have been declared as protected areas, where only schedule non-polluting industries can be installed?

Ans: Vide Government of India's letter No.10/157/85-LP dated the 17th Feb., 1987, East and South belt of Goa along the Western Ghats have been declared as protected areas (copy of G.O.I's letter is enclosed).

Q.4   What is the procedure for identification and selection of sites for setting up chemical plants or Industrial Estates in Goa? What is the criteria used?

Ans: As intimated by the IDC normally suggestions/requests come from the local people and also the representatives of the people for establishment of Industrial Estate in a particular locality. Thereafter various sites are inspected to ascertain whether the Industrial Estate could be established in one of the sites. Once it is decided that the Industrial Estate has to be established in a particular place considering the availability of power, water, accessible road etc. to the site then the decision in the Board meeting is taken for acquisition of that sites for establishment of Industrial Estates. Normally uncultivable barren waste lands are selected for establishment of Industrial Estates. Thereafter administrative approval is obtained. Before final selection of the site, necessary clarifications from the PWD, Electricity Department, Town Planning Department are obtained. The sites of the Industrial Estates are acquired through the Land Acquisition Proceedings.

Q.6   Has the Department identified the type of industries could be considered as Environmentally friendly Industries? If yes whether Nylon 6,6 manufactured is one of those?

Ans: The Government has taken note of the guidelines given by the Government of India identifying XX industries as highly polluting industries. Other than these, all other industries are treated as friendly industries. (List is enclosed).

Q.7   Is there any co-ordination between Industries Department and the Town & Country Planning Department, E.D.C., the State Pollution Control Board, Department of Science, Technology and Environment, I.D.C. for processing proposals from Industries based on imported technology?

Ans: Proposal for setting up of industries requiring huge infrastructural requirements are placed before the High Powered Co-ordination Committee, headed by the Chief Secretary of which the members are:-

1. The Secretary, Industries - Vice-Chairman
2. The Secy. to Chief Minister - Member
3. The Collector of Goa - Member
4. The Chief Electrical Engineer - Member
5. The Chief Engineer, P.W.D. - Member
6. The Director of Health Services - Member
7. The Commissioner, Lab. & Employment - Member

8. Chief Town Planner - Member

9. The Managing Director, EDC - Member

10. The Chief Executive Officer, GDDIDC - Member

11. The Regional Manager, MSFC, Panaji - Member

12. The Director of Industries & Mines - Member Secy.

13. The Member Secy., Goa State Pollution Control Board.

Q.8   Whether the Director of Industries could make appropriate provision for incorporating the need of Environmental Impact Assessment studies for big project before any site selection and land acquisition proceedings start? Could there be an Environmental impact Evaluation Cell in the Department?

Ans: Some of the preconditions for setting up of large industries are incorporated in the licence issued by the G.O.I. itself. These are:

1)   The State Director of Industries confirms that the site of the project has been approved from the Environmental angle by the competent State Authority.

2)   The entrepreneur commits both to the State and Central Government that he will install the appropriate equipments and implement the prescribed measures for the prevention and control of pollution.

3)   The concerned State Pollution Control Board has to certify that the proposal meets with the environmental requirement and that the equipments installed or proposed to be installed are adequate and appropriate to the requirement.

The above certificates are issued only after getting the clearance from Pollution Control Board.

Q.9   Was the Department consulted on any of the aspect of T.D.L.'s Nylon 6,6 Project? If yes at what stages? What were the comments of the Department on the aspects consulted?

Ans: The Directorate of Industries had given its comments vide letter No. 2/72/MST/DIM/3942 dated 2.4.1987 (copy enclosed).

Q.10   How employment potential is linked with the permission to start Industries in Goa?

Ans: By Law or Rules of Industrial Development Act, there is no linkage between Employment and Industries. However, that is generally one of the considerations for permitting such large industries to be set up in Goa.

Q.11   How it is endured that Goans are preferred for jobs in the Industries permitted in Goa?

Ans: When the High Powered Co-ordination Committee meets to deliberate on the issue of granting permission to the large scale industries, the entrepreneurs are requested to absorb preferably locally available personnel.

Q.20
& 21   Have any studies being carried out by the Government for the Mandovi and Zuari basins and the Cumbarjua Canal for examining the hydrological characteristic, the sediment load, etc. as recommended by Central Water and Power Research Institute, Pune. Kindly supply a copy.

If not, is there any plan to carry out such studies?

Ans.20

& 21   Following studies have been carried out by the Central Water and Power Research Institute, Pune as detailed:

Title	No.	Date
1. Hydraulic Model studies pertaining to improvement of navigability in the Cumbarjua Canal, Goa.	Specific Note:2024	17.2.82
2. Prototype studies for evaluating mixing characteristics at the mouth of the Mandovi River, Goa.	Specific Note: 2098	31.12.1982
3. Hydraulic Model studies pertaining to improvement of navigation conditions in Aguada Bay, Goa.	Specific Note:2148	11.10.1983

Q.22   Whether the Government has any regulations which defines the constitution of survey teams for selecting sites for industry or sending the representatives of the Govt. Department as member of any survey team?

Ans: There are no such regulations defining the constitution of survey teams for selecting sites for industries.

Q.23   Whether the projected needs of the people in the area in particular and State in General vis-a-vis, the huge needs of such industry has been looked out? (i.e. water, electricity, transport, etc.)

Ans: While clearing any large projects of this nature, matters connected with water, power, transport, etc. are discussed in the meeting of High Powered Co-ordination Committee.

ANNEXURE - I

INDUSTRIES OF HIGH POLLUTING NATURE AS DECLARED BY THE CENTRAL GOVT. AS WELL AS STATE GOVT.

(i)   Primary Metallurgical producing Industries viz:- Zinc, Lead, Copper, Aluminium and Steel.

(ii)   Paper, Pulp and Newsprints.

(iii)   Pesticides/Insecticides.

(iv)   Refineries.

(v)   Fertilizers.

(vi)   Paints.

(vii)   Dyes.

(viii) Leather Tanning.

(ix)   Rayon.

(x)   Sodium/Potassium Cyanide.

(xi)   Foundry.

(xii)   Basic Drug.

(xiii) Storage Batteries (Lead acid type)

(xiv)   Acids/Alkalis

(xv)   Plastics

(xvi)   Rubber Synthetics

(xvii) Cement

(xviii) Asbestos

(xix)   Fermentation Industry and

(xx)   Electroplating.

Government of India

Ministry of Industry

Department of Industrial Development

New Delhi, the 17th Feb. 1987.

To,

The Secretary.

Industries Department

Govt. of: Jammu & Kashmir, Himachal Pradesh

Uttar Pradesh, Bihar, West Bengal, Sikkim, Assam,

Gujarat, Madhya Pradesh, Orissa, Kerala, Meghalaya,

Manipur, Nagaland, Tripura, Arunachal Pradesh,

Mizoram and the

Union Territories of: Andaman & Nicobar Islands,

Lakshdweep, Goa Daman & Diu and Pondicherry.

Subject: Identification of protected districts, non polluting industry districts and the industries that can be considered for setting up in these districts.

Sir,

With a view to ensuring that ecologically fragile regions in the country are protected from adverse effects of industries which emit harmful effluents, the Deptt. of Environment in the Ministry of Environment and Forest have identified a list of districts which they consider as totally protected and also those districts where non-polluting industries could be located. They have also identified a list of industries which could be set up in these districts in the various States/Union Territories. A list of protected districts and non-polluting industry districts (List-I) and industries which could be set up in these districts so identified is enclosed. (List-II and List-III). Together with these lists, are sent guidelines which have been prescribed in the case of protected districts.

State Governments/Union Territories concerned are requested kindly to keep in view the districts and the list of industries attached herewith while considering applications for setting up industrial capacities in the respective States/Union Territories.

Yours faithfully,

(Sd/-)

(P.K.S. IYER)

COPY TO: 1. Ministry of Environment and Forests, Deptt. of Environment.

2. P.M.'s Office w.r.t. their D.O. No. 2(242)/86-PMS dated 19th August, 1986

3. SIA (DS-SS)

List-I

LIST OF PROTECTED DISTRICTS AND
NON-POLLUTING INDUSTRY DISTRICTS
IN CATEGORY 'A'

	Protected Districts	Non-polluting Industry Districts
BIHAR	Aurangabad	
GUJARAT	Dangs	
KARNATAKA	-	
M.P.	Balaghat	
	Mandla	
	Panna (except middle portion)	
	South & East Seoni	
	Sidhi	
	Suguja	
MAHARASHTRA	-	-
ORISSA	Boudh Khondmals	
RAJASTHAN	-	
U.P.	Chamoli	Fatehpur
	Pauri Carhwal	Pithoragarh
	Tehri Garhwal	Dehradun
	Uttar Kashi	
	Nainital	
	Almora	
W. BENGAL	Darjeeling	Jalpaiguri
KERALA	Wynad	-
	Idukki	
ASSAM	-	North Cacher Hills
		Lakhimpur
H.P.	Champa	Kangra
	Kulu	Solan
	Kinnaur	Sirmur
	Lahaul & Spiti	Bilaspur
	Mandi	Hamirpur
		Simla
J & K	Kupwara	Hoda, Ladhakh, Poonch,

	Pulwama	Rajori, Srinagar,
	Anantnag	Udhampur, Baramula
	Kargil	Jammu, Katjua Badgam
MEGHALAYA	East Garo Hills	West Garo Hills
	Jaintia Hills	East Khasi Hills
	West Khasi Hills	
MANIPUR	Manipur East	Manipur Central
	Manipur South	Manipur North
	Manipur West	
	Tengnowpal	
NAGALAND	Mon	Kohima
	Wokha West	Mekokchung
	N. East Zunhebote	Tuensang
		Phok
SIKKIM	Gyalshing	Gangtok
	Mangan	
	Namchi	
TRIPURA	Tripura North	Tripura West
	Tripura South	
A & N	Nicobar Islands	-
	Andaman Islands	
ARUNACHAL	Kameng	
PRADESH	Siang	
	Subansiri	
	Tirap	
	Dibang Valley	
	Lohit	
DADRA &		
NAGAR HAVELI	-	
LAKSHDWEEP	Lakshdweep	-
MIZORAM	Aizwal	Dunglex
GOA DAMAN &	East & South	Daman & Diu
DIU	belt of Goa	
	along W. Ghats	
PONDICHERRY	-	Pondicherry

List-II

LIST OF INDUSTRIES THAT CAN BE CONSIDERED

IN PROTECTED DISTRICTS

Subject to the fulfilment of the four conditions listed below, the following industries can be considered:

1. Assembly of
    - Musical instruments
    - Scientific and surgical instruments
    - Domestic electrical appliances
    - Electronic equipment
    - Photographic and optical equipment

2. Cottage level units of
    - Handloom weaving
    - Cotton and Woollen hosiery and garments
    - Handicrafts.

CONDITION

1. Should be non-obnoxious and non-hazardous.
2. Setting up of the unit, appurtenant structures and other infrastructural facilities including approach roads do not involve:
    (a) Forest and agriculture land
    (b) Butting of hill features; and
    (c) Removal of orchards, trees or mangroves.
3. Do not discharge any effluents of a polluting nature.
4. Do not use fossil fuel in their manufacturing process.

LIST-III

LIST OF INDUSTRIES THAT CAN BE CONSIDERED

IN NONPOLLUTION DISTRICTS

The following industries can be considered with adoption of suitable pollution control measures and fulfilment of the conditions as stated in List-II.

1. Rubber Processing Industries
    1. Repair of tyres and tubes
    2. Footwear (rubber)
    3. Rubber goods involving cold process only.
2. Solid Waste disposal
    4. Composting
    5. Refuse incineration (controlled)
3. Food Processing Industries
    6. Flour Mills
    7. Bakery products and confectioneries
    8. Malted Food
    9. Vegetable oils including solvent extracted oils
    10. Milk processing
    11. Chilling
    12. Pasteurisation
    13. Canned food including fruits and vegetables
    14. Fragrance: flowers and food additives
    15. Aerated water/soft drink
4. Assembly Units:
    16. Musical Instrument
    17. Scientific and surgical instruments
    18. Domestic Electrical Appliance
    19. Electronic equipment
    20. Photographic and technical equipment

		PLOT AREA (M²)
1.	ADMINISTRATIVE BLOCK & OFFICES	10000
2.	TIME OFFICE	200
3.	SECURITY MAIN/CHECK POSTS	200
4.	WORKERS SHELTER/REST ROOM/CYCLE STAND	400
5.	POLYMERISATION)	
	SPINNING)	
	STORAGE & TWISTING)	60000
	WEAVING)	
	PACKING)	
6.	FINISH GOODS GODOWN)	
7.	AIR CONDITIONING)	
8.	STORES RAW MATERIAL)	
9.	CANTEEN	2500
10.	COOLING TOWERS	1500
11.	GARDEN/FOUNTAIN	30000
12.	WORKERS EDUCATION/TRAINING CENTRE	2500
13.	WORK SHOP	
14.	BOILER HOSE	2500
15.	HOSPITAL	10000
16.	HIGHER SECONDARY SCHOOL	24000
17.	COLONY PLAY GROUND/GARDEN	115000
18.	SHOPS	8000
19.	COMMUNITY CENTRE	8000
20.	EFFLUENT TREATMENT PLANT	60000
21.	POWER HOUSE	10000
22.	TANK FARM	6000
23.	WATER SUPPLY & TREATMENT	8000
24.	COMPRESSOR REFRIGERATION	1500
25.	FIRE FIGHTING STATION	1500
26.	TRANSPORT VEHICLES/GARAGES/SERVICE STATION	8000
27.	LAB	2500
28.	R & D BUILDING	2500
29.	TEACH OFFICE	2500
30.	CAR PARK/PARKING	
31.	N2 PLANT	1500

32. GUEST HOUSE JR. STAFF 20 ROOMS	10000
33. GUEST HOUSE MANAGEMENT STAFF 20 ROOMS	10000
34. BACHELORS HOSTEL 45 ROOMS	20000
35. QUARTERS 550	7000
36. BUNGALOWS 25	12500
37. STAFF 70	21000
38. STAFF 150	15000
39. OFFICERS CLUB	10000
40. WORKERS COMMUNITY CENTRE	10000
41. DIVERSIFICATION	
i) CORD. FIBRE	40000
ii) ENGG. PLASTIC	40000
iii) A.H. PLANT	400000
iv) DIPPING PLANT	60000
42. FUTURE EXPANSION MAIN. PLANT	60000
43. FUTURE EXPANSION UTILITIES	6000
44. FUTURE EXPANSION HOUSING	40000
45. ROADS, PARKING, ENVIRONMENTAL AREAS, PARKS, DRAINS, ELECTRIC LINES, TREES WALKWAYS AND INCIDENTAL SPACES	839700
GRAND TOTAL	2000000

(Say 200 H.A.)

(Say approx. 500 acres)

No.2/72/MSY/DIM/
Govt. of Goa, Daman & Diu,
Directorate of Industries & Mines,
Udyog Bhavan,
Panaji - Goa.

Date: 3/1987

To,
The Secretary,
Industries,
Secretariat,
Panaji - Goa.

Sub:- Nylon 6,6 Tyre Cord Project.

Sir,

I am returning herewith the letter dated 9.3.87 of M/s. Ballarpur Industries Ltd. on the subject mentioned above.

As desired, the comments of all the concerned departments are obtained and sent herewith for kind perusal. The departments whose comments are enclosed herewith are:-

1. Chief Engineer, P.W.D.
2. Chief Town Planner, Town & Country Planning Department.
3. Managing Director, E.D.C.
4. Chief Electrical Engineer, Electricity Department.
5. Directorate of Health Services.

After careful examination of various aspects involved in the implementation of this project of M/s. Ballarpur Industries Ltd. for the manufacture of Nylon 6,6 Tyre Cord Unit, we have to offer our comments as follows:

M/s Economic Development Corporation of Goa, Daman & Diu agreed to participate in a joint venture with BILT of New Delhi and M/s E.I. Du Pont de Nemours & Co. of U.S.A.. Accordingly E.D.C.'s application for an industrial licence was approved by the Govt. of India in the year 1983. This licence has been further renewed from time to time and is valid upto 30th Sept. 1987.

Though E.D.C. has obtained the Industrial Licence and their equity participation is only to the extent of Rs. 5 lakhs, the major share holders are BILT & Du Pont. Hence BILT being a major shareholder in India, they have been pursuing this matter since the issue of the licence.

The project is proposed to be located at Querim in Ponda taluka & M/s BILT has requested the Govt. to make available the following infrastructure facilities at the selected site at Querim.

1. Land - 500 acres equivalent to 20 lakh sq. mtrs.
2. Power - 75 MVA
3. Water - 1500 m³/day.

The above are the facilities demanded at site. In addition to this they have asked for other facilities and incentives in respect of cost of land, subsidy, power tariff, tax concessions, access roads, etc. which are specified in their letter dated 9.3.87.

Before giving final approval on the site location for this project, it may be worthwhile examining it from the point of view of ecology, pollution and loss of huge area of 20 lakh sq. mtrs..

This industry has been categorised by the Govt. of India as an Industry of a highly polluting nature. According to the Govt. of India entire territory of Goa, Daman & Diu has been identified as Protected District and non-polluting industry District vide their letter No. 10/157/85-LP dated 17-2-87 (copy enclosed) & hence encouraging such an industry needs careful examination.

We already have in this territory quite a large area which is occupied by highly polluting industries. Should we bring in within the grip of pollution, still larger areas by encouraging this industry is a matter for greater study particularly, in the light of the comments of the Chief Town Planner, who has not agreed to support the location of the project at Querim.

The area asked by the party is 500 acres which is equivalent to 20 lakh sq. mtrs. which is unreasonably on the higher side. In fact 20 lakh sq. mtrs. can easily accomodate more than 10 Industrial Estates, can encourage more than 500 small industries and can create employment to about 4500 people approximately and give a bigger boost to our economy by opening various other avenues for other trades and small activities.

In any case, the project is yet to be cleared by the Central Pollution Board and their expert opinion is still awaited.

The E.D.C. who are participating in this joint sector, have expressed their clear opinion that Govt. should not acquire the land and should be left to M/s. BILT only.

In the earlier meetings of the High Powered Co-ordination Committee, members have expressed their view that the land asked for by M/s. BILT is unreasonably on the higher side which is established by their own statements showing area utilisation details (copy enclosed). The Town & Country Planning Dept. had suggested an alternative site at Xeldem/Xelvona in Quepem taluka where other infrastructure facilities was readily available. They had also cleared this site from the point of view of Planning. This alternate possibility may have to be explored.

Regarding other incentives like investment subsidy, sales tax loan etc. could be considered in the light of the proposals under consideration.

And finally, before clearance is given for its location at an alternative site, it may be prevailed upon the BILT to expose the functioning of their similar unit elsewhere by means of a video cassette particularly in respect of pollution, treatment and disposal.

Yours faithfully,

Sd/-

(Denghnuna)

Director of Industries & Mines

Encl: as above

No. 17-8-90-STE
Government of Goa,
Department of Science,
Technology & Environment,
Secretariat, Panaji-Goa.

Dated: 29th October, 1990.

To,
The Joint Secretary (Legislature),
Legislature Department,
Secretariat,
Panaji-Goa.

Sir,

I am directed to refer to your letter No.LA/S/2082/1990 dated 21.10.1990 and to furnish the requisite information as below:-

1. The criteria followed for appointing the Goa State Pollution Control Board are the same as prescribed in the Water (Prevention and Control of Pollution) Act, 1974 - Chapter 2 under the heading, "the Central and State Board for prevention and control of pollution". A copy of the Act is enclosed for favour of reference.

    As per Section 9 of the above Act, the Board may constitute as many Committees consisting wholly of members or wholly of other persons or partly of members and partly of other persons, and for such purpose or purposes as it may think fit. Further under Section 11 of the Air (Prevention and Control of Pollution) Act, 1981, the Board may constitute as many Committees constituting wholly of members or partly of members and partly of other persons for such purposes as it may think fit. As many other State Pollution Control Boards and the Central Pollution Control Board have constituted various Committees to advise the Board on technical matters as per the different fields involved, it was decided to constitute a Technical Committee consisting mainly of technical people to serve the Board. Besides its specialised function the formation of a technical committee is essential for the following reasons:-

    (a) It has to meet very frequently and this is not possible if all the members of the Board are involved;

    (b) It is not practical to expect all the members of the Board to devote their time to study in depth all the proposals placed before them;

    (c) To arrange a meeting of the Technical Committee is much easier as it does not require other formalities required to call the meeting of a statutory body.

    The constitution of the present Technical Committee is as follows:-

    1) Dr. R. Sen Gupta, Dy. Director, ...Chairman
        National Institute of Oceanography.
    2) Dr. R. Nagendran, Assistant Professor,
        (Environmental Sciences)
        Goa Engineering College.   ....Member

3) Shri Vincente Estibeiro,
    Ex-Director of Agriculture.   ....Member

4) Shri V.S. Hede,
    Chief Development Officer,
    Chemical Engineer (E.D.C.)   ....Member

5) Dr. A.A. Bokade,
    Chief Medical Officer,
    Directorate of Health Services.   ....Member Convenor

6) Shri A.A. Parulekar
    Member Secretary, Goa State
    Pollution Control Board.   ....Member Convenor

2. The criteria followed by other State Pollution Control Boards in the Country, are generally the same.

3. For its routine work the Board follows the provisions made as under:

    i) Provisions of Chapter IV of the Water (Prevention and Control of Pollution) Act, 1974 and Chapter III of the Air (Prevention and Control of Pollution) Act, 1981.

    ii) Provisions of Water (Prevention and Control of Pollution) Rules, 1988 and the Goa Air (Prevention and Control of Pollution) Rules 1989.

Copies of the above mentioned acts/rules are enclosed.

The terms of reference given to the Technical Committee are as follows:-

1. To analyse consent and N.O.C. applications placed before it and give its specific recommendations.

2. To analyse quotations called for purchase of laboratory equipments and make recommendations thereon.

3. To recommend reference books for the Board Library.

For processing applications for consent and N.O.Cs the Technical Committee follows the following steps:-

Step 1:- The Member Secretary of the Board arranges to make the enquiries to collect all the informations relevant to the applications.

Step 2:- The application and information collected thereof are placed before the 'Technical Committee' for scrutiny.

Step 3:- The 'Technical Committee' analyses the application placed before it and gives its specific recommendations thereon.

Step 4:- The Member Secretary places the abstract of the applications and recommendations of the 'Technical Committee' before the Chairman, who will withhold only those applications requiring further study and allow the Member Secretary to dispose off the rest of the applications as per the recommendations of the Committee.

Step 5:- A brief summary of each case and recommendations made thereon by the 'Technical Committee' would be circulated alongwith agenda of the Board Meeting.

The applications withheld as per step 4 will be placed before the Board for deliberation.

A copy of the resolution No.2 and 3 from the minutes of the Second Meeting of the Goa State Pollution Control Board held on 8th December, 1988 are enclosed for kind perusal.

4. In case of highly complex technological proposals, wherein the Board feels that it does not have the requisite competence to decide on certain proposals, the Board is empowered to constitute as many committees as needed as per the provisions of the Water (Prevention and Control of Pollution) Act, 1974 and Air (Prevention and Control of Pollution) Act, 1981.

    These may constitute wholly of members or wholly of other persons or partly of members and partly of other persons and for such purpose or purposes as it may think fit;

    The Board may also associate with itself in such manner and for such purposes as may be prescribed any person whose assistance or advice it may desire to obtain for performing any of its functions under the Act.

5. The authority to give consent under the Water (Prevention and Control of Pollution) Act, 1974 and Air (Prevention and Control of Pollution) Act, 1981 is the Goa State Pollution Control Board. Every State Board shall be a body corporate with the name specified by the State Government in the notification under Sub-Section(1) of Section 4 of the Water (Prevention and Control of Pollution), Act, 1974, having perpetual succession and a common seal with power, subject to the provisions of this Act, to acquire, hold and dispose of property and to contract, and may, by the said name, sue or be sued.

6. Generally, the views of Town and Country Planning Department and the Directorate of Industries are obtained before proposals are processed by the Goa State Pollution Control Board. The mode of interaction between the Technical Committee and the State Pollution Control Board has been indicated at Sr. No.3 above.

7. The conditional N.O.C. is issued by the Goa State Pollution Control Board, which is a Statutory Body.

8. Unless the conditions mentioned in the N.O.C. granted by the Board are fulfilled, the Board cannot grant final consent to the industry.

Yours faithfully,

Sd/-

(N.P. GAUNEKAR)

JOINT SECRETARY (S.T.E.)

TECHNICAL AND FINANCIAL COLLABORATION AGREEMENT

THIS AGREEMENT made on this 18th day of September, One Thousand Nine Hundred Eighty-Eight, between

E. I. DU PONT DE NEMOURS AND COMPANY,

> a corporation organised and existing under the laws of the State of Delaware, USA ("DU PONT"), and having its Registered/Principal/Head Office at 1007 Market Street, Wilmington, Delaware 19898, USA (hereinafter referred to as "DU PONT", which expression shall include its successors and assigns) of the one part,

> and

THAPAR DU PONT LIMITED,

> a company registered under the Indian Companies Act, 1956, and having its Registered Office at Trionara Apartments, Panaji, Goa - 403 001, and correspondence office at 124, Janpath, New Delhi - 110 001, India, (hereinafter called "TDL", which expression shall include its successors and assigns) of the other part.

WITNESSETH, THAT:

WHEREAS, DU PONT, together with BALLARPUR INDUSTRIES LIMITED (BILT) and Economic Development Corporation of Goa, Daman and Diu Limited (EDC) have formed a company for the manufacture and sale of Nylon 6,6 industrial yarn and fabric in India, namely THAPAR DU PONT LIMITED (TDL);

WHEREAS, TDL requires technology for the production of Nylon 6,6 industrial yarn and desires to purchase such technology from DU PONT; and

WHEREAS, DU PONT desires to provide such technology for the use of TDL subject to the terms and conditions set forth in this Agreement, and

WHEREAS, DU PONT intends to assign to CHEMTEX FIBERS, INC. of New York (Assignee) its obligations to provide basic ...

Du Pont and both this Agreement and the Equipment AGREEMENT have been approved by the appropriate Indian authorities. TDL shall promptly notify DU PONT of the date of the government approvals.

IN WITNESS WHEREOF, the parties have caused this Agreement to be executed on their behalf by their duly authorised representatives.

THAPAR DU PONT LIMITED

By   Sd/-

Title   DIRECTOR

Date_____

E.I. DU PONT DE NEMOURS AND COMPANY

By   Sd/-

Title   Vice PResident

Date   18th Sept. 1988

By_____

Title_____

Date_____

Part - E

E. DOCUMENTS/CORRESPONDENCE/REFERENCES

E.1.   No. EDC/PRIS dtd. 19.11.83.
       EDC to Sect. for Industrial Approval, Ministry of Industrial Development, New Delhi.
       Annexure: Memorandum of Understanding for a Nylon 6,6 Tyre/Industrial Yarn Plant -
       Goa.
       Sd. EDC and BILT
       Annexure: Memorandum of Understanding ...
       Sd. BILT and Chemtex Fibres Inc.
       Annexure: EDC Application for Licence or Permission.
       (Form I.L.) (dtd. 19.11.83).

E.2.   No. LI: 171 (1985) dtd. 28.2.85
       Central Govt. L.O.I. to EDC for Nylon 6,6 Industrial/Tyre Cord Yarn.

E.3.   No. LI:1052 (1985) dtd. 30.9.85.
       Govt. of India, Secretariat for Industrial Approvals to EDC

E.4.   Ref. No. 3510/85-TCP/4985 dtd. 20.11.85
       Letter of Town & Country Planning Deptt., Govt. of Goa to Joint Director, Directorate of
       Industries & Mines, Panaji.

E.5.   Dtd. 12.12.8
       Agreement signed between EDC & BILT.

E.6.   Dtd. 1986
       Govt. of India, Secretariat for Industrial Approvals to EDC (permission granted to expand
       capacity for manufacture of Nylon 6,6 Tyre Cord from 6000 TPA to 14,000 TPA).

E.7.   Dtd. 5.11.86
       Agenda Note for 92nd Board meeting of EDC Ltd.

E.8.   No. LI: 1052 (85)/86 Amendment, dtd. 21.6.86
       Govt. of India, Secretariat for Industrial Approvals to EDC.

E.9.   Dtd. 11.1.87
       Agreement signed between EDC & BILT.

E.10. No. 11012/55/85 dtd. 19.1.87
       Govt. of India, Ministry of Textiles to EDC (extending LIO upto 31.3.87 - for Tyre Cord
       Fabric).

E.11. Dtd. 9.3.87
       From V.K. Malik, TDL to Chief Secretary, Govt. of Goa, Daman & Diu, Panaji.

E.12. No. 2/72/MSI/DIM/3942 dtd. 2.4.87.
       Directorate of Industries & Mines (Director, Denghnuna), Govt. of Goa, Daman & Diu,
       Panaji to Secretary, Industries, Panaji.

E.13. Dtd. 23.6.87
       Minutes of the meeting of High Powered Co-ordination Committee held in the Chamber
       of Chief Secretary/Chairman

E.14. No.3/32/87/ILD dtd. 6.7.87
       Industries & Labour Deptt., Govt. of Goa, Panaji to the Chief Town Planner, Town &
       Country Planning Dept., Panaji.

E.15. No.12014/46/83-PCI.I dtd. 7.12.87
       Govt. of India, Deptt. of Chemicals & Petro-Chemicals to EDC.

E.16. Dtd. 1.2.88.
L. Ciporin, Director, Technology Transfer, Du Pont, U.S.A. attestation - "To whomsoever it may concern".

E.17. No.TFF/41/EE/GOA/87/7680 dtd. 5.2.88.
NOC from Central Pollution Control Board (Sectional Office, Dhavali, Ponda, Goa) to Directorate of Health Services,Panaji.

E.18. No. LI: 171(85)/88 Amendment dtd. 16.6.88.
Govt. of India, Secretariat for Industrial Approval to EDC

E.19. Dtd. 22.6.88
Minutes of the Meeting held on 22nd June 1988 with Hon'ble Chief Minister.

E.20. Dtd. 6.7.88
Govt. of India, Deptt. of Chemicals & Petro-Chemicals to EDC.

E.21. Dtd. 5.9.88
Minutes of the High-Powered Co-ordination Committee held under the Chairmanship of Chief Secretary.

E.22. Dtd. 18.9.88
Technical & Financial Collaboration Agreement signed between Thapar Du Pont Ltd., and Du Pont de Nemours and Company.

E.23. Dtd. 26.9.88.
TDL to Secretariat for Industrial Approvals, Deptt. of Industrial Devp., New Delhi (for Capital Goods Import Approval).

E.24. Dtd. 26.9.88.
TDL to Secretariat for Industrial Approvals, Deptt. of Industrial Development, New Delhi, (for Technical & Financial Collaboration Approval).

E.25. No. IDC/LND/65/11957 dtd. 26.10.88.
R.S. Vaidya, President of Kerim Communidade's N.O.C. that IDC may start immediately developmental works.

E.26. Dtd. 7.12.88.
TDL application for 1201 and approval of Foreign Collaboration for manufacture of 800 TPA of Spandex Fibre in State of Goa to Secretariat for Industrial Approvals, Deptt., of Industrial Development, New Delhi.

E.27. No.7/369/88-LA/ dtd. 14.12.88.
Dy. Collector, North Goa District to Under Secretary, Govt. of Goa, Revenue Deptt.

E.28. Dtd. January, 1989.
Techno-Economic Project Report for TDL (Preliminary) by BILT.

E.29. No. IDC/LND/65/(III)/1243 dtd. 16.1.1989.
G.D.D.I.D.C. to Secy, Industries, Panaji.

E.30. No. 3/32/87-IID dtd. 9.2.89.
Industries Deptt. Panaji, to Dr. P. Deshpande, Chief Executive Officer, G.D.D.I.D.C.

E.31. No.IDC/LND/65-1/14542 dtd. 9.2.89.
Dy. Chief Executive Officer to Shri V.K. Malik, General Manager, TDL, Delhi.

E.32. Dtd. 3.3.89.
Minutes of the 141st meeting of the IDC held on 3-3-89.

E.33. No.3/32/87-ILD dtd. 9.3.89.
Under Secretary, Industries Deptt., Goa to G.D.D.I.D.C.

E.34. No.IDC/LND/65(II)/14830 dtd. 29.3.89.
Dy. Chief Executive Officer to V.K. Malik,
General Manager (Fibre), TDL, New Delhi.

E.35. No. 3/32/87-ILD Dtd. 17.4.89.
Industries Deptt., Govt. of Goa, Panaji to the Chief Executive Officer, GDDIDC, Panaji.

E.36. Dtd. 8.5.89
TDL to Deputy Chief Executive Officer, IDC.

E.37. No. IDC/LND/65(II) 1567 dtd. 10.5.89.
Dy. Chief Executive Officer to V.K. Malik, TDL, New Delhi.

E.38. Dtd. 16.6.89.
Panchayat of Kerim to TDL (Construction Licence).

E.39. No. 12014 dtd. 19.7.89.
Govt. of India, Deptt. of Chemicals & Petro-Chemicals to EDC.

E.40. Dtd. 10.8.89
Govt. of India to EDC (extending L.O.I. upto 30.3.90 - for Tyre Cord Fabric).

E.41. No. 4/6/89-PCB/859 dtd. 2.2.90.
Goa State Pollution Control Board (*NOC* to TDL for Nylon 6,6 Tyre Cord manufacture).

E.42. No. 12014/46/83-PC dtd. 9.7.90
Ministry of Petroleum & Chemicals, Govt. of India to EDC, Goa.

E.43. Ref. No. TDL/HC/90-91/1 dtd. 10.10.90
TDL to Chairman, House-Committee, Nylon 6,6 project, Panaji.

E.44. TDL/HC/909-91/32 dtd. 5.11.90
TDL to Chairman, House-Committee, Legislature Deptt., Panaji.

E.45. TDL:HC/90-91/33 dtd. 5.11.90
TDL to Chairman, House-Committee, Legislature Deptt., Panaji.

E.46. TDL:HC/90-91/34 dtd. 5.11.90
TDL to Chairman, House-Committee, Legislature Deptt., Panaji.

E.47. TDL/HC/90-95/35 dtd. 5.11.90
TDL to Chairman, House-Committee, Legislature Deptt., Panaji.

E.48. Verbatim transcripts of the meetings of the House Committee on 5.10.90, 8.10.90, 9.10.90, 31.10.90.

178 Unwanted Guest

PART - F

F. SELECTED REFERENCES

F.1 Govt. of Goa, 1988, 'Regional Plan 2001 A.D. proposals' Town and Country Planning Dept.

F.2 Govt. of India, 1982 "Report of the Task Force on Eco-development of Goa, Planning Commission, New Delhi.

F.3 Geological Survey of India, 1985 "Earth Resources for Goa's Development; A Collection of Seminar Papers, Hyderabad".

F.4 Centre for Policy Research, 1985 "Economic Development of Goa Through Applications of Science and Technology - A Report proposed for Govt. of Goa" by P.D. Malganvkar and V.A. Pai Panandikar, New Delhi, Oct., 1988.

F.5 NCAER, 1964, "Techno-economic Survey of Goa, Daman and Diu", Delhi.

F.6 Angle Prabhakar, 1983, "Goa, an Economic Review", Goa Hindu Association.

F.7 Govt. of Goa Daman and Diu, (1961-1981) 1981 "Goa, Then and Now" Govt. Printing Press, Panaji - Goa.

F.8 Almeida Dr. J.C., 1967, "Aspects of the agricultural activity in Goa, Daman and Diu", Govt. Printing Press, Panaji-Goa.

F.9 District Census Handbook, 1983 "Census of India 1981", Series 29, Goa, Daman and Diu.

F.10 Wilkins Glynda 1977 "Plastics and Resins Industry", Radian Corporation, Austin, Texas, United States Environment Protection Agency.

F.11 Radian Corporation, 1986, "Polymer manufacture and Health Effects", Austin, Texas, U.S.A.

F.12 The Hindu, 1989, "A Survey of Indian Industry - 1988", Madras.

F.13 The Hindu, 1990, "A Survey of Indian Industry - 1989", Madras.

F.14 Parulekar A.H., Ansari Z.A. and Ingole B.S. 1985, "Effect of Mining Activities on the clam Fisheries and Bottom Fauna of Goa Estauries". Indian Journal of Marine Sciences, September 1985.

F.15 Anonymous, 1977, "Master Plan for Pollution Control of the Rivers Zuari and Mandovi", (NIO) Technical Report No. 00/79.

F.16 Kamat S.B. and Sankarranarayan V.N., 1974, "Concentration of Particulate Iron in Estuarine and Coastal Water of Goa", Indian J. Mar. Sci. 3.

F.17 Parulekar A.H., Dwivedi S.N. and Dhargalkar V.K., 1973, "Ecology of Clam Beds in Mandovi, Cumbarjua Canal and Zuari Estuarine System of Goa", Indian J.Mar. Sci. 2.

F.18 Government of India (Planning Commission),1982, "Report of the Task Force on ECO-Development Plan for Goa", INSDOC, New Delhi.

F.19 Centre for Science and Environment, 1985, "The State of Indian Environment 1984-85 - The Second Citizens Report", New Delhi.

F.20 R. Sen Gupta, and S.Y.S. Singal NIO Dona Paula Goa, "Water Quality of the Rivers Mandovi and Zuari during 1977-78", reprinted from Earth Resource for Goa's Development, Geological Survey of India 1985.

F.21 KOGAI - Newsletter of polluted Japan, No. 2, Winter 1974, pgs 10-15

F.22 United Nations Environment Programme, 1988, "The Role of Community Action Groups in averting and coping with Industrial Accidents", by Martin Abraham, Industry and Environment, July- Sept., 1988.

Ashwin Tombat, editor of the Gomantak Times, Panaji, wrote the following series of articles exposing Du Pont's corporate and environmental history in the United States of America.

Du Pont in the US

by
Ashwin Tombat

Far from "non-polluting"
(Gomantak Times, 26/7/91)

"Modern science has advanced so much that it is possible to control any kind of pollution." How many times have we heard these words uttered in the context of the Thapar-Du Pont Nylon 6,6 project proposed to come up at Keri, Ponda. From utterances of this sort, we presume that supporters of the project mean that the plants that Du Pont operates in the United States are pollution-free, that they have the very latest in pollution control equipment and that they will install the same machinery in their plant at Keri, so that Nylon 6,6 and Goa may live happily ever after.

This series of articles therefore proposes to examine Du Pont's record in its country of origin, and in other countries around the world. Most of the material relied on for the articles comes from US government agencies:

- Far from being "non-polluting", Du Pont is among the largest releasers of toxic wastes into the air, water and land in the United States of America!

- Whenever confronted with charges of pollution - whether by government or citizen's groups - the company routinely resorts to blanket denials, has often lied to avoid liability.

- Of the 500 most polluting chemical plants in the US, around 25 belong to Du Pont; probably the largest single presence.

- In a number of lawsuits filed by both government bodies and citizen's associations regarding pollution by Du Pont plants, the corporation has been convicted by US courts and ordered to pay huge sums as compensation, or has chosen to settle out of court, so as to avoid embarrassment.

- Du Pont was cited in 1981 for having the "worst safety record" in the decade of the 1970s, of all the eight leading chemical companies in the USA, by the Council on Economic Priorities, which conducted a study based on government data.

Authentic details of all the above points will be brought to you day after day by Gomantak Times, starting tomorrow.

Du Pont is one of the largest chemical companies in the world. But that by no means indicates that its processes and plants are clean, safe and non-polluting. No, not even in the United States of America, where regulations are very tight.

This is nothing new, but a part of the very history of the corporation; that it will not clean up its act unless it is forced to and even then, resist to the last.

What sort of havoc this doublefaced multinational can wreak in a Goa totally unequipped to even monitor pollution properly, we leave to the reader's imagination.

And, we hope, the articles that follow this one will be read carefully by all those politicians who support the project and claim that those who oppose it are "obsessed" with pollution. If Goan scientists do not impress them (the experts who worked on the House Committee report did an excellent job), we hope that American experts, the American government, affected American citizens and the American courts, which have repeatedly indicted and convicted Du Pont for fouling US air, land and water as well as knowingly endangering the lives of its own workers, will.

'Safety' claims are hollow

(Gomantak Times, 29/7/91)

How non-polluting is Du Pont's Nylon 6,6 manufacturing process, which will be set up a Keri in Ponda? To examine this, we will have to see the performance of the Du Pont plant at Richmond, Virginia, in the US.

While critics say that the Richmond Nylon 6,6 plant will be lifted lock stock and barrel, and brought to Keri, the company contends that only certain minor items of machinery will be transplanted from Richmond, but admits that the Keri facility will be modelled on the lines of the Richmond plant.

A Toxic 500 Company!

First, the Du pont Spruance plant at Richmond in Virginia's Chesterfield county is listed at No.220 in The Toxic 500, a list of the 500 largest releasers of toxic substances into the air, water and land in the United States of America, issued by the US National Wildlife Federation in 1987.

Two hundred and twenty might not sound so alarming a ranking in India, but in a country like the US which has lakhs of chemical plants, it is significantly high on the list.

It must be recalled here that around 25 Du Pont plants are "honoured" with ranks in the list of the 500 most polluting plants in the US.

For the record, the Richmond plant produces a total of nearly 6.59 million pounds (nearly 3000 tonnes) of toxic effluents every year.

According to figures supplied by the company, most of this effluent is stored after treatment in special tanks off site, but a good amount is let off in the air as stack emissions and fugitive air emissions.

This is precisely the method proposed by the company to tackle the problem of effluents at Keri. The company claims it is foolproof, and that after treatment the effluent can be evaporated and the residue used as fertiliser!

It all sounds very grand, especially since we Indians have a tendency to be overawed by technological miracles from abroad. But, in real terms, how foolproof is the company's claim that its effluent treatment system is safe and non-polluting?

Contaminated Ground Water

In December 1989, Du Pont admitted that its Spruance plant at Richmond had contaminated the ground water around the plant with four hazardous substances.

The company agreed to voluntarily commence a multi million dollar clean-up under the supervision of the Virginia State Water Control Board.

However, the process of decontaminating the groundwater will take several decades. Just the first phase, costing $ 3.5 million, is likely to take over 20 years!

This phase will involve pumping out the groundwater and treating it. However, what effect this will have on the water table in the area is something that no one has yet calculated for.

The chemicals involved were hexamethylphosphoramide (HMPA), chloroform, trichlorofluoromethane (TCFM) and carbon disulphide. All these are involved in the manufacture of a polymer brand-named Tybeck, which is also produced at the plant.

The contamination was discovered when there was an unexplained loss of TCFM, from a storage facility.

It was later discovered that a concrete walled vessel which held the TCFM had developed hairline cracks, through which the chemical had seeped into the ground.

While the Nylon 6,6 facility was not involved in this case, a leak could easily have occurred there, since similar storage facilities are used, and have been planned for the Keri plant as well.

Imagine what would be the fate of the lush arecanut orchards on the slopes below the proposed site of the Nylon 6,6 plant at Keri, should such a leak occur there. Imagine what could happen if the wells get contaminated and people drink the water.

Du Pont's anti-pollution measures are far from foolproof, and the company is only banking on the lack of knowledge among Indians of its record in the US.

Contaminated rivers

Also on record is the fact that Du Pont contaminated two rivers - the South river and the south fork of the Shenandoah river - with mercury, over a 20-year period.

In 1984, Du Pont finally agreed to pay $ 1.98 million as compensation to the State of Virginia for its part in pollution. The contamination, which occurred between 1929 and 1950, was discovered only in 1977.

The tragedy is, nothing can be done to reverse the process, and nature will have to take its own course.

The contaminated area extended for about 140 km along the rivers, and people continued to eat the contaminated fish till it was banned in 1978. The next year, a safe consumption limit of less than a quarter kilo per head was imposed.

Moral of the story

All those who believe that American technology will save Goa's environment despite the setting up of the Nylon 6,6 plant must once again examine Du Pont's record in the US.

Moral #1: Du Pont cannot be trusted, even in the highly environment-conscious US, to be non-polluting. Imagine what will be the fate of our little riverine state.

Moral #2: Just as technology has no absolute solutions to prevent pollution, it also has no absolute solutions to clean up pollution.

Moral #3: Goa is better-off without Nylon 6,6. There is no point crying over spilt milk later. Heed the House Committee report and bounce the project out of the state while we still can. Remember, once it gets in, there's no getting it out.

Why is Du Pont in a hurry?

(Gomantak Times, 30/7/91)

Why is Du Pont so anxious to set up its Nylon 6,6 plant in India? According to Du Pont Chairman Edgar Woolard Jr. nylon consumption in the Asia-Pacific region is growing at twice the world average rate. The company defines the Asia-Pacific region as "the area from Korea to Indonesia and Australia, and west to India".

In a press conference held in January 1990, the Du Pont chairman said that his company intended to invest more than $ 2 billion (Rs. 6000 crore) in the region in the next ten years (of which $ 1 billion is for nylon facilities alone), to position Du Pont as a major nylon supplier in Asia in the 1990s and to strengthen its leadership of the nylon market internationally into the next century.

As the first part of its Asia offensive, Du Pont is setting up a $ 200 million Adipic Acid plant in Singapore, which is to go into production in 1993. It is the Singapore plant which will supply nearly half the raw material necessary for the Keri Nylon 6,6 plant. That is why Thapar-Du Pont is in such an unholy hurry to set up the Keri Nylon 6,6 plant.

Why is Nylon consumption on the decline in the US? Because the largest single consumer of nylon-tyre manufacture - are now no longer using nylon in tyres. Tyres in the West are now mostly radial, where steel, polyglass, and another Du Pont product - Kevlar - are used, displacing Nylon.

Du Pont is actively developing new technology for these new tyres. It recently launched a new hi-strength polyamide fibre that is 10 per cent stronger than nylon cord, which is to be used in sidewalls of radial tyres.

Consequently, nylon tyrecord technology, which is rapidly getting outdated, is being transferred to the third world countries of the Asia-Pacific region, including India.

Eventually, Du Pont hopes to make Asia the hub of its entire nylon manufacturing activities, while its American plants modernise and go on to more marketable products in the US.

Part of these moves is the Adipic Acid plant in Singapore, which is to supply Nylon 6,6 plants (all, probably, transplanted from the US) in Indonesia; Goa, India; and Izmit, Turkey.

And, the nitric acid facility which Thapar-Du Pont hopes to put up in India (hopefully not at Keri) will be a raw material source for the Singapore Adipic Acid plant.

The final part of Du Pont's Asian strategy in Nylons will be set up "world-scale" plant for producing hexamethylenediamine (HMD), the other basic raw material for Nylon 6,6 production, as also nylon intermediates such as adiponitrile.

With this, the grand masterplan of dumping an obsolete technology off onto the poor countries of the world will be complete.

When Du Pont makes its plans, it looks to its own interest. Not to Goa's. Unfortunately, our leaders seem to be unable to keep the interest of the state and country foremost in their minds. Else, they would have argued vociferously against Nylon 6,6, instead of for it.

Du Pont: Profit at safety's cost

(Gomantak Times, 31/7/91)

E I Du Pont de Nemours and Company has a long line of products whose production processes have been severely damaging to the environment. But the point is not so much that these were marketed by Du Pont. The point, instead, is that the company has, for long, tended to completely (critics say, wilfully and knowingly) ignore and deny any reports on the adverse effects of its business activities.

Indeed, if the entire record is examined, it would not be at all out of place to say that Du Pont has consistently treated the long-term interests of humanity as something largely irrelevant to its business.

Ethyl

Let us examine just two cases here. The first is the case of Ethyl, a lead additive for raising the octane content of petrol, developed and marketed by Du Pont since 1924. The second is the case of chlorofluoro carbons, CFCs, the gases that deplete the ozone layer in the atmosphere.

In 1920, Du Pont gained control of the giant automobile manufacturer General Motors, and Pierre Du Pont became chairman of GM. At that time, GM scientists were perfecting a compound to boost the octane content of petrol, which the company began to market in 1922. In 1924, Du Pont formed the Ethyl Corporation, which would market the chemical.

The only problem with Ethyl was that its main constituent was lead, which is poisonous, especially for children. In 1924 itself, Ethyl drew criticism. A chemistry professor called William Clark warned the US Assistant Surgeon general that Ethyl was "a serious menace to public health".

The defence

Executives of a Du Pont-controlled GM replied that in no way was the chemical hazardous. Lead levels, they said "on the average street will be so free of lead that it will be impossible to detect it". In typical Du Pont fashion, the problem was ignored.

Du Pont, however, was forced to address the question when, in late 1924, reports broke that 80 per cent of the workers making Ethyl at Du Pont and Standard Oil plants had been severely poisoned, and several killed by lead. There was such extensive nerve damage among workers that one refinery became known as the House of Butterflies, because its employees were suffering from such severe hallucinations.

The US Surgeon General ordered Ethyl withdrawn from the market and appointed a high-power panel of scientists to study it. What would have been the reaction of an environmentally-aware company (which Du Pont claims it is) to such a disaster? Withdraw the product and go in for research to make it safer. But what did Du Pont Do? Exactly the opposite!

Despite a growing outcry from scientists, Du Pont launched a massive campaign to defend Ethyl, running full-page advertisements in Life magazine. It secretly hired a top consultant, and praised the chemical in hearings before the Surgeon General as "an apparent gift of God".

Calling lead "a certain means of saving petroleum", Du Pont representatives asked: "Because some animals die and some do not die in some experiments, shall we give up this thing entirely?" And this, when workers handling Ethyl in Du Pont's factories were suffering crippling damage to their nerves!

In the face of this severe assault by Du Pont's formidable team of scientists, the Surgeon General's panel determined that "there are at present no good grounds for prohibiting the use of Ethyl gasoline". However, the experts urged that long-term research be conducted and regulations be established because "longer experience may show (that even low levels of lead) may lead eventually in susceptible individuals to recognisable or to chronic degenerative diseases of less obvious character".

This neither-here-nor-there conclusion had little effect. Ethyl was back on the market, and the caution sounded by the scientists was forgotten, the studies recommended never conducted. It was not until half a century later that the chemical was banned after scientists established conclusively that lead was very harmful to humans, though its workers were continuously suffering the effects all along.

It was not as if Du Pont did not realise the effects, but it chose to keep its eyes shut in the face of the facts, banking on the absence of hard scientific evidence. In the intervening 50 years, people suffered. But Du Pont continued to rake in the big bucks.

Had it been that there was no alternative to Ethyl, Du Pont's obstinancy might have been condonable. But this is by no means the case. Because of the controversy, certain refiners refused to use lead in their gasoline. Instead, they produced higher octane petrol using more sophisticated refineries. One of these lead-free hi-octane fuels was Sun Oil's Blue Sunoco which not only did not contain lead, but sold a few cents cheaper than Du Pont's leaded petrol.

But Du Pont fought savagely against this safer alternative. It even went to the extent of getting General Motors - one of the largest producers of cars in America - to design an engine that ran only on leaded petrol. This was done to drive a safer petrol out of the market. And, eventually, with the majority of cars having engines that ran only on leaded petrol. Blue Sunoco disappeared from the US market by the end of the '50s, leaving the field open for Du Pont to unnecessarily fill cities throughout the world with smog. Du Pont's marketing of Ethyl, used for making leaded petrol (93 octane), poisoned two generations of city dwellers around the world for decades, when safer alternatives were available.

That is the Du Pont which is now going to set up Nylon 6,6 - a plant which they say will be non-polluting and environmentally sound - in Goa. Would you believe them?

No change

Ah, you may say, that was all a long time ago. At that time not much was known about pollution. Now, things have changed. For those who feel this way, we are afraid we will have to disappoint you.

In 1988, the US government filed a $ 8.23 million suit against Du Pont and three other companies which put too much lead in petrol at a New Jersey refinery. This was after an administrative complaint was filed in 1986, to which the company absolutely refused to admit any liability.

Du Pont said it only supplied the lead additive, but the Environment Protection Agency (EPA) contended that the company decided how much lead was to be used, injected the compound at the blending plant, determined that the final product was suitable for sale as leaded petrol, and advised the other three participants in the venture about EPA regulations.

The suit says that 2200 extra tonnes of lead were cumulatively added to petrol sold between 1983 and 1986. According to US regulations, leaded petrol has to be steadily phased out; eventually no vehicles running on leaded petrol will be allowed to operate on US roads.

Now, of course, Du Pont has to comply. But it does even that reluctantly, as the above example demonstrates. Had Du Pont cared enough for its workers 64 years ago, US cities might have had significantly less smog problems, as leaded petrol could easily have been withdrawn from the market at that stage. But then, it could not have made millions of dollars of profit selling Ethyl to refiners.

And it chose to drive safer, unleaded petrol out of the market to keep the millions rolling in - to the detriment of humanity. Now, ironically, the Blue Sunoco that Du Pont drove out of the market in the '50s is to become the only kind of petrol allowed in America!

This leopard does not change its spots...

The double danger of CFCs

(Gomantak Times, 2/8/91)

Both Chlorofluorocarbons (CFCs) and the petrol additive based on lead, Ethyl, were developed by the same team of scientists in the same laboratory, at about the same time.

CFCs were principally used for refrigeration and air conditioning, as a cleaning solution in the electronics industry and as a foamblowing agent by makers of synthetic insulation and styrofoam.

The problem with CFCs is that they destroy the ozone layer surrounding the earth, which prevents dangerous ultraviolet rays from reaching the earth's surface.

CFCs

Since the late 70s, CFCs have been known to persist in the lower atmosphere and slowly rise to the upper atmosphere, where they react with and destroy the naturally occuring blanket of ozone molecules.

The consequences of exposure to ultraviolet radiation from outer space include greater incidence of skin cancer as well as environmental damage. CFCs are doubly dangerous since they both destroy the ozone layer and contribute to global warming.

Du Pont is the inventor and the largest manufacturer of CFCs in the world.

Denials

In 1974, after doctors F Sherwood Rowland and Mario Molina warned that Freon (the CFC made by Du Pont) destroyed ozone, Du Pont vice president Raymond L McCarthy told the US Congress that the doctor's statement was "purely speculative, with no concrete evidence having been developed to support it". Half a century earlier, a similar statement had been made about Ethyl, the lead-based additive for petrol.

In 1975, Du Pont paid for full page advertisements in The New York Times to support its views and counter the campaign of the environmentalists. Fifty years earlier, a similar exercise had been conducted with Ethyl in Life magazine.

Nevertheless, the truth cannot hide itself forever, no matter the enormity of the disinformation campaign launched to obscure it. In 1927, Du Pont's campaign succeeded in keeping leaded petrol flowing in the petrol pumps for half a century. With CFCs, however, this could be kept up for just over a decade, as evidence mounted fast and furiously.

But the fact remains that by doggedly refusing to accept the evidence offered, DuPont put the interests of its business firmly before those of the long-term interests of humanity.

The tragedy is, the single largest use for CFCs in the US is - believe it or not - air conditioning cars and trucks! This use accounted for 33 million kilograms of these synthetic chemicals in 1985. The use of these chemicals that threaten the future of the earth for what can only be termed an idle luxury, is nothing short of criminal. The largest CFC release comes when air conditioners are serviced, during which process all the gas in the device is let off into the atmosphere, and a new supply of gas introduced when refitting the A/C.

Not a single manufacturer of CFCs has to date bothered to develop even a simple device for trapping CFCs when servicing air conditioners and later recycling the chemical. Why? Because the present methods of use increase the consumption of CFCs, resulting in greater profits for the manufacturers. That this could be highly dangerous for mankind has been known since the late 70s, but in the intervening 10 years, no move has been voluntarily made towards this.

Opportunism

Du Pont's blanket refusal to accept scientific evidence and recognise that the CFCs were harmful to the ozone layer lasted till early 1988! Senators Max Baucus and Dave Durenburger, the chairman and ranking Republican on the Senate Hazardous Wastes and Toxic Substances Subcommittee, appealed to Du Pont in February 1988 to end the production and sale of CFCs. They were told in a reply on 4 March that such a move would be both unwarranted and counterproductive."

An then suddenly, 20 days later, Du Pont President R.E. Heckert declared that "important new information" had led Du Pont to believe that CFCs were damaging to the ozone layer.

Of course, by then, it had already prepared itself with a "CFC substitute", which manufacturers of appliances dependent on CFC grabbed with both hands, besieged as they were by environmentalists concerned about humanity and its future. But more about this tomorrow.

Illusion and reality Du Pont style

(Gomantak Times, 3/8/91)

Du Pont scientists who want to demonstrate how "safe" their product is, might well pull off an impressive trick to prove their point. Very likely, a scientist may eat a handful of adipic acid, one of the principal raw materials for Nylon 6,6 to show that it is harmless.

Don't be taken in.

This is an old Du Pont trick. In 1924, when scientists raised doubts about the safety of Du Pont's lead additive for petrol, Ethyl, it was first used. Thomas Midgely, an inventor and later a vice president of the Du Pont-controlled General Motors, washed his hands in pure tetraethyl and dried them on his handkerchief, according to one historian. The reporters were impressed. Du Pont had "convincingly" made its point. But it was a mere trick: Du Pont's lead additive was far from safe and caused neurological damage to hundreds of workers, besides smogging up America's cities.

Another 'trick'

Six years later, to demonstrate dramatically the "safety" of the CFCs which he had invented, Midgely took a deep breath of one of the chemicals and then exhaled, to blow out a candle.

But neither lead additive nor CFCs were "safe", it was established later. And this is despite the fact that Du Pont had so convincingly and "conclusively", "proved" their safety earlier.

That's the dichotomy between illusion and reality as far as Du Pont is concerned. Take the CFC substitute it has developed - HCFC-22. For half a century, HCFC-22 was known as CFC-22. It was only when it became imperative that CFCs be phased out that Du Pont picked the least harmful of the CFCs and decided to rename it so that it would go down better with the public: Du Pont claims that HCFC-22 depletes up to 95 per cent less ozone than its more potent relatives. CFC-11 and CFC-12.

CFC-22

CFC-22 contains an atom of hydrogen, so it forms weaker chemical bonds than the chlorine-fluorine bonds in the other CFCs. Because it takes less solar radiation to break down the 22 bond than the other, purer, CFCs, HCFC-22 breaks down closer to earth, and less of it reaches stratospheric levels.

However, the point is that HCFC-22 is a CFC. It does deplete ozone. In that sense, it cannot be considered a substitute. More important, it is not some new chemical developed by Du Pont but has existed for around 50 years. All that HCFC-22 represents is some creative renaming of an old chemical and a keen sense of business; getting a "CFC substitute" out first in the market means millions in the kitty.

Even Du Pont agrees to this. Du Pont spokesperson Kathy Forte says: "22 HCFC and 22 CFC are the same." The term HCFC was brought into use on 5 January 1988. This was more or less the same time that Du Pont decided to admit that CFCs destroyed the ozone layer. In fact, the announcement was made later pledging that it would end the use of CFCs. And, by this simple sleight of nomenclature, Du Pont actually managed to come out with a "CFC substitute" even before it admitted that there was something wrong with CFCs in the first place!

That is the bottomline. Fine words and lofty commitments are something which comes easily to Du Pont, as are dramatic demonstrations of the "safety" of their products and processes. It is up to us to distinguish illusion from reality.

The following statement regarding Du Pont's (proposed) Nylon 6,6 plant was issued by a Sabha (assembly) of environment groups, unions, organizations, associations and citizens in Ponda, Goa, India.

THE PONDA DECLARATION

WHEREAS the environment and its continued degradation have become pressing issues on the planet's global agenda, demanding urgent intervention of all possible kinds from citizens everywhere.

WHEREAS the expansion and growth of multinational corporations and large firms, at the expense of local communities and often involving their destruction, continues to be stimulated and supported in relentless fashion, chiefly by governments fatally susceptible to bribes and political contributions.

NOW THEREFORE THIS SABHA TAKES NOTE that one of the world's largest chemical corporations, Du Pont, in association with the Indian business house of the Thapars, have proposed to set up a plant to produce Nylon 6,6 at Kerim plateau, Ponda, Goa, India which demands the takeover of common lands belonging to several village communities, will generate new pollution and undermine agriculture, horticulture and the development people have raised over several decades;

THAT IN ADDITION the proposed unit is nothing more than a refurbished plant involving equipment first installed in 1938 at Richmond, U.S.A., but now archaic in the US context.

THAT the location of the project in Goa has been decided by Du Pont as part of its worldwide business strategy and has nothing to do with the welfare of Goa, its economy, environment or people.

THAT the interests of Goa in the project are allegedly represented by the Economic Development Corporation (EDC), a financial-cum-development institution owned by the Goa Government. THAT however the EDC has misused its quasi-government status to procure first the letter of intent from the Government of India and has then sought to hand it over to Thapar-Du Pont, thus confirming suspicions that it has been set up for the deal. THAT because of this nominal association, Thapar-Du Pont have been able to procure vast public resources, particularly land, readily and cheaply which they would not have got by fair bidding in the open market.

THAT the project has been rejected by the Government of India on several occasions during the past seven years because of doubtful technology import, severe drain on the country's foreign exchange reserves demanded by constant import of raw materials, and equity participation.

THIS SABHA NOW FURTHER ANNOUNCES:

THAT HAVING CONSIDERED in detail the Report of the House Committee set up by the Goa State Assembly, which has recommended that the project be shelved;

THAT HAVING CONSIDERED in detail the opinions of other experts including learned scientists from the University of Goa, the National Institute of Oceanography, and other Indian experts in polymer technology, that the pollution hazards of the proposed plant are unknown and undisclosed in their entirety; and in addition Du Pont's own abysmal environmental record, documented in detail in the local media including *Goa Today, Gomantak, Herald, Gomantak Times* and *Sunaparant*;

THAT HAVING CONSIDERED the equally atrocious environmental record of Ballarpur Industries and others of the Thapar group including the two callous chlorine accidents in Goa within the space of just two years in which people and plants suffered grossly;

THAT HAVING CONSIDERED the general incompetence and impotence of the State Pollution Control Board and having come to discover that the Board is basically interested in promoting the interests of polluters rather than the integrity of the environment or the health of people;

THAT HAVING CONSIDERED that, accepting the Thapar-Du Pont's own estimates, investment per workplace is Rs.30 lakh, which is incongruous, outrageous and unacceptable in a labour-oriented economy;

THAT HAVING CONSIDERED in addition that even these jobs will not be available to Goans due to lack of skills and will therefore go to people imported to the site;

THAT HAVING CONSIDERED that succeeding governments and politicians of different parties in Goa including the Congress (I) and the Maharashtrawadi Gomantak Party have been successfully neutralized through outright bribery and corruption to support the project and that their patronage of the project is now based on a hideous sabotage of the public interest for outright personal profit and lucre;

THAT HAVING CONSIDERED all this, and HAVING CONSIDERED the fact that the people of Ponda and Goa generally do not wish to have this monstrous unit imposed on them and on their environment, that they have protested peacefully thus far, petitioned their representatives, organized meetings and demonstrations in keeping with the norms of a civil society;

THAT HAVING COME TO THE CONCLUSION that the government, which they have elected, is not inclined to desist from continuing to endorse the Thapar-Du Pont project, a decision that is so openly contrary to public sentiment, desire, need and interest;

NOW THEREFORE WE DECLARE ON THIS THE 31ST DAY OF AUGUST 1991 THAT WE SHALL OPPOSE THE THAPAR-DU PONT NYLON 6,6 PLANT IRREVOCABLY, FIRMLY, PEACEFULLY, AT ALL COSTS, AND TAKE ALL POSSIBLE MEASURES TO PREVENT ITS INSTALLATION NOT JUST HERE IN PONDA BUT IN ANY OTHER PART OF INDIA.

August 31, 1991 at Ponda, Goa.

True copy of Resolution No. 4 (3) of Executive Committee meeting of the Goa Bagayatdar Society held on 3.8.1991.

Subject: Nylon 6,6 Factory

An American company Du Pont is trying to set up a Nylon 6,6 Factory at Kerim, Ponda. The pollution from this factory is going to cause immense damage to the horticulture in Kerim, Karmale and Savoi-Verem. The effluents from the factory if let into the Mandovi river are going to cause further pollution. If this factory is set up the horticulture in this area will vanish and will affect seriously the activities of this Society because there are about 800 horticulturist members of the Society in this area. The horticulture in this area yields mainly arecanuts. Therefore we request the government that in the interests of ecological balance in this area, protection to the horticulturists and eventually in the interests of this society, the Nylon 6,6 factory may not be permitted.

Proposed by: S.P. Savarkar.   *Seconded by: B.A. Sahakari.*